A WOODLAND GARDEN

RHODODENDRON LODER'S WHITE
'. . . the Great White Queen of all white rhododendrons' (p. 176)

A WOODLAND GARDEN

A. T. JOHNSON

Introduction by Charles Elliott

With a Foreword by

THE RIGHT HONOURABLE LORD ABERCONWAY, C.B.E., V.M.H.
President of the Royal Horticultural Society

A *HORTICULTURE* MAGAZINE GARDEN CLASSIC

THE LYONS PRESS

First published in 1937 by Country Life Limited, London, and Charles Scribner's Sons, New York

First Lyons Press edition, 1999

Printed in the United States of America

10 9 8 7 6 5 4 3 2 1

The Library of Congress cataloging-in-publication data has been applied for.

INTRODUCTION

In spite of having written a book called *A Garden in Wales* (which ought to have caught the eye of this gardener in Wales), Arthur Tysilio Johnson was unfamiliar to me as an author until a friend mentioned his delight in *A Woodland Garden*. I'd heard of that splendid geranium 'Johnson's Blue', but of Johnson himself my ignorance was complete. I'm pleased to say that this condition has now been corrected. *A Woodland Garden* is indeed a delight, and an amazing source of information on a range of plants from the familiar to the exceedingly little known—with a bias toward the latter.

A. T. Johnson was (as might be guessed from his middle name) Welsh. For most of his life he lived in North Wales, not far from the great gardens at Bodnant Castle—now a National Trust jewel—or from his friend E. C. Buxton, himself immortalized by two plants: *Anthemis tinctoria*, E. C. Buxton', and *Geranium wallichianum*, 'Buxton's Variety'. First a schoolmaster, Johnson attained non-horticultural fame when in 1910 he published, under a pseudonym, a diatribe entitled *The Perfidious Welshman*. His identity leaked, but sales of the bad-tempered book were substantial enough to allow him and his wife to beat a strategic retreat to California until the fuss died down. Graham Stuart Thomas (to whose short memoir of Johnson I am indebted for biographical details) remarks that "it is difficult to know why he devoted his energies to so vituperative a work except that he was, by nature, a journalist."

In any case, Johnson's subsequent books were of a much less aggressive sort. Most of them—and by the time he died in 1956 he could take credit for a dozen—concerned plants and horticulture, and were based largely on the experiences of himself and his wife (usually referred to as the Lady of the Garden) in the garden they created near the Tal-y-Cafn Bridge in the Vale of Conwy. Begun in a small way "from the raw" around 1907, on an oak-shaded slope running down to a millrace below their bungalow, it gradually grew over the years to incorporate a meadow, a grassy glade, and eventually a narrow stream valley or "dingle," all planted with an eye toward maintaining and enhancing the natural beauty of the setting.

As Johnson remarks in this book, "our main objective here was not a woodland garden, but a garden in a woodland." Graham Thomas praises what they achieved: "Their garden was, I feel, what many of us have aimed at in this century: the growing of plants in positions most suited for them, or if you prefer it, gardening with nature instead of against her." Whether or not Johnson was wholly aware of the originality of this approach, it is clear from everything he wrote that he was absolutely committed to it.

In practical terms, this meant planting as many trees, shrubs, and plants as possible, always concentrating on those comfortable in local conditions. Not that the Johnsons could tell ahead of time what would thrive: Much of *A Woodland Garden* is devoted to intimate discussions of the needs of different varieties and reports on their success or failure, often in happy opposition to received wisdom. Each new addition of space is the occasion for trying out still more new plants, though—markedly—not the latest fancies from plant breeders; Johnson's taste, catholic as it was, ran to species and the less grandiose cultivars. Even so, it is surprising how many plants he introduced, or that bear his name. Simply leafing through *The Plant Finder* I came on at least a half dozen, ranging from *Calluna vulgaris* 'Johnson's Variety' to *Erica xdarleyensis*

'Arthur Johnson', and including *Rhododendron hunni-wellianum* 'Johnson's Impeditum', *Ceanothus* 'A. T. Johnson', and *Mimulus* 'A. T. Johnson'.

And then there is the geranium called 'Johnson's Blue'. Johnson was only indirectly responsible for it. It seems that he grew a particularly attractive pale lilac-white strain of *G. pratense* called 'Silver Queen' in the southern part of the garden. This caught the eye of a Dutch nurseryman who asked for some seeds, and who subsequently bred a lucky cross with *G. himalayense*. The cross, blue with pale violet tones and distinctive red venation, is now the famous 'Johnson's Blue'.

A Woodland Garden covers a wide range of plants, but tends to concentrate on species that take care of themselves ("inviting the garden to do its own gardening, so to speak"). For Johnson and his wife, this was a matter of necessity. They did almost all of the work single-handedly, except for the two-mornings-a-week help of the local factotum Johnson refers to as Promethus. Thus the attention paid to heaths ("the greatest labour-savers that ever came into a garden") and rhododendrons. He is brilliant on ground covers ("those good friends, our ornamental weed-killers"), and manages to inspire interest, if not more, in such unlikely species as wintergreen: "A craze for rhododendron one can understand. The persuasion of the heaths is also comprehensible. But endeavor to fathom the depths of the gaul-theria's bewitching influence and your efforts will be like trying to catch a flicker of marsh gas in a butterfly net."

Graham Stuart Thomas has left a pleasant account of what it was like to take a walk with Johnson through his garden near the end of his life. "There would be sorties up and along the bank," he writes, "down to the glade, up to the mill and round about elsewhere, discussing this and that, peering into a wood-mouse's or robin's nest; throwing dead twigs and the odd weed under rhododendrons ('rhodos can take anything'); securing a rooted offset of this or seed of that." The picture is that of a man thoroughly at ease with his garden, and the garden at ease in its setting. "It has been our constant pleasure to foster the natural in every possible way," Johnson wrote. *A Woodland Garden* beautifully—and infectiously—conveys that pleasure to us.

—Charles Elliott
London, 1999

FOREWORD

ALL GARDEN-LOVERS, and many who would perhaps hardly venture to describe themselves as
such, will welcome Mr. A. T. Johnson's new
book on gardening.

A garden book has two essential qualifications: The
first is that it should be written with an accurate knowledge of its subject. Now the accuracy of a man's knowledge of gardening is essentially founded on his own
garden—even though that knowledge may be broad-
ened and polished by reading of other gardens or by
visits to them.

Those who know Mr. A. T. Johnson's garden can
bear witness that he has no possible excuse for any in-
accuracy on the matter of which he deals in his book,
for within that garden nearly all the plants which he
describes both grow and thrive. Moreover, his is a
garden not run by a skilled professional under the
owner's instructions—it has been laid out and planted
by the owner and his wife themselves, so that he cannot
help but know, and know intimately, the plants of
which he writes.

The garden too is not one of those favoured ones
where plants seem to grow of themselves without
cultivation or garden skill, for neither do the soil or the
climate conduce to this. The success, therefore, that
Mr. A. T. Johnson attains with difficult plants shows
his successful methods of cultivation, methods which
he so clearly describes in his writings.

The second essential qualification for a gardening

book, which is not merely a work of reference, is that it should be readable. Now Mr. A. T. Johnson is a writer who is always readable—his books are not catalogues of plants and of their virtues and vices; they tell the stories of the plants; and to read his books is a pleasure and not a task.

The present volume will, I know, have the same wide appeal and will give the same help to other gardeners as has always been the case with the volumes and articles previously written by him.

ABERCONWAY

BODNANT

January 4, 1937

PREFACE

SINCE *A Garden in Wales* was published ten years ago an appreciative public has shown an increasing appetite for another helping. Indeed, I have been assured for some time by friends in America as well as here, that a second volume has long been over-due. Such approbation is comforting and re-assuring, and in taking this opportunity of thanking all those people—Press reviewers as well as garden readers—for the very generous reception given to the earlier book—a reception at times almost embarrassing in its warmth—let me say at once that my most devout prayer at the moment is that they will not find its successor wanting.

I must, however, say this, though it may sound more selfish than polite, that I write more for my own pleasure than anything else. To my wife ('poor wretch!'), without whose loyal co-operation this volume would never have been carried through, writing is of course a disease. But being a harmless disease and, incidentally, it may be, a means of keeping one out of worse things, it enjoys her approval as well as her loyalty.

It might, therefore, have been nearer the truth had I said just now that this book has been written to please ourselves, for that, in any event, has been its fundamental purpose. To have by us a compact record of our garden doings, a record of failures as well as of successes, something that would give us at least an outline of our little story that is more abiding than memory, is not, in our view, an illaudable objective. And if, in attempting this, we are able to give entertainment to others, to add one more pebble to that great cairn which crowns the horticultural Parnassus, well, so much the greater is our reward.

Had our garden been anything else but a creation that is entirely our own, such observations might be less easily justified. But the fact that it, as many of my readers know, has been made by us from the raw, that everything in it save its singing waters, its contour, its ancestral trees and other natural features, has been put in by our own horny hands, marks it as a garden for which, I think, can be demanded a certain measure of uniqueness. It can at least claim the personal touch.

That earlier volume having related something of our initial efforts this one takes up the tale of fuller years and a wider field. But no attempt has been made to cover the entire round of our garden activities. Samuel Butler once said that the lilies of the field were so busy being lilies that they had no time for anything else. And so, if disappointment should come to some who discover that this or that plant has been omitted from these pages, if my chapters should here and there show a certain lack of continuity, which points to their having been done at odd moments, one can but beg the reader to realise that there are only twenty-four hours in a gardener's day and that an author-gardener has to do with that day cut in half.

Omissions are inevitable in such works as this. They stare at me in bitter reproach from every page. But one can not bind Leviathan with a hook, and rather than make an effort to deal with the garden in its entirety—a plan foredoomed to failure—I have treated a few genera fairly fully, others less fully, and with that, let us hope, the reader will be tolerably satisfied.

Although this bairn of ours is, as I have said, of our own making, it would be ungenerous to allow the occasion to pass without saying how much it owes to our garden friends. That freemasonry which gardening promotes is one of the kindliest fruits of the spade, and but for that mutual goodwill which welds together all good gardeners in a common weal the gardens of England and other countries would not be what they are. Nor would our own garden ever have been what it is but for the liberality of friends, many of whom we have never seen, who have enriched it with treasures often otherwise unobtainable, and, what is more, sustained our sometimes flagging zeal with that spirit of good comradeship which is the very bread of one's garden life. To Lord Aberconway in particular does this garden owe much. His own garden at Bodnant, which to know is an inestimable privilege, has for many years been not merely a light to lighten our darkness but a mine of inspiration, while his own sympathetic interest and practical understanding of our efforts here have been an unfaltering encouragement.

With one exception all the photographs in these pages have

been taken in our own garden, and for them I alone am responsible. For the right of reproducing a few of them my thanks are due to the Editor of *Country Life* and to Mr. Theo. A. Stephens, the Proprietor of *My Garden*. Bibliographical references and extracts are acknowledged in the text, and while the nomenclature is based on the Kew *Hand Lists* my plea for any lapses there may be from the path of accuracy is that this is a book for the everyday gardener rather than the botanist.

A. T. J.

CONTENTS

ILLUSTRATIONS

A WOODLAND GARDEN

CHAPTER I

Autumn Crocus and Hardy Cyclamen

YESTERDAY, BEING Martinmas Day, I was planting crocuses under an old elm whose dipping boughs made a golden tent over the plot reserved for these little bulbous things. The autumn crocuses were already in flower, rising out of the sinking grass hard-by in a mosaic of blues, lavenders and kindred colours. And I suddenly thought of a story I had once read somewhere of a slip of a girl who came into a garden. She had blue eyes and a mischievous smile, but the smile hovered on the brink of tears for she was alone, very young and a little afraid. She carried, if I can trust a defective memory, a little bag of brown bees and a few simple flowers. At her waist some cowslips hung like a bunch of golden keys. What else she had I have forgotten, but I do remember how, when a tulip opened his petals wide and kissed her, the whole earth began to throb with the pulse of green and tender things which all at once had become vital with new life.

Planting crocuses under the yellowing trees we always regard as a solemn rite. Like the gathering of fallen leaves it marks an epoch in our garden year. It is one of those things which one never does hastily. Indeed, some of autumn's most gracious hours are consecrated to the ceremony, and this may be because the putting-in of a crocus corm seems to give one a closer, more intimate touch with spring than the planting of anything else.

However, whether it was a vision of those dry corms, all rollicking with colour and laughter as they raced over the sward in the April sunshine, or some momentary quiver in the ranks of the autumn crocuses, which gave rise to the thought I do not know. But I found myself wondering what the purple and lavender fairies over there would say if that little blue-eyed girl in the story, with her brown bees and her cowslips and her unkissed lips, happened to appear among them at that moment.

But if the thought vanished as quickly as it had come—for I knew they would not say anything unkind at any rate—why did it come at all? I suppose one can only explain it by having to admit with grovelling humility that there still lurks somewhere in the dark dregs of one's mind lingering relics of the notion that crocuses belong only to spring. But if I ever did nurse such an illusion I have done my utmost 'to shatter it to bits' by planting autumn crocuses every year. Tell it not in the streets of the field-mice, but these happy, confiding little things are dibbled-in in ever-increasing numbers, and this attention to their claims does help to make amends for an unpardonable if unintentional slight.

However, there are people who still will tell you that a crocus in an autumn garden is all wrong. How, they will ask, is it possible to get the 'crocus feeling' when leaves are drifting and when the only proper adornment for a lawn is a besom and a wheelbarrow? But the fact that there were no crocuses of any kind in our gardens a few generations ago should be enough to deprive spring of any claim on traditional grounds in respect to them. We do not always realise that Bacon never saw 'the ground flame of the crocus break the mould', which means that the common yellow Dutch was once as rare as the choicest species is to-day. It is time and custom which are here the deciding factors. We are wont to forget that old and new are but comparative terms and that the most familiar of our flowers, even those like the snowdrop, to which the lichen of long association most tenaciously clings, were not less strangely exotic to our forebears than the most sensational novelty is to us.

As for the matter of colour, autumn crocuses, and colchicums too, are essentially in tune with the season. The poet who

> *Heard the beechnut rustle down,*
> *And saw the purple crocus pale*
> *Flower about the autumn dale*

strikes precisely the right key. For instead of these flowers breaking-in with a false note upon the symphony of autumn they harmonise so well with the spirit of the season that one comes to regard them as much a part of October as the daffodil is of March. The mallow-purples, harebell-blues, ivory, amber and orange which one finds among these crocuses and colchicums are the dominant tones of flower and leaf in every garden, field and hedgerow throughout the later months.

So let me show you the violet and orange with which *Crocus speciosus* is dappling the turf beneath the gathering gold of that ancient elm. Or, *C. zonatus*, very chaste and elegant, a dainty rosy-mauve embracing her golden heart. Here, also, is *C. pulchellus*, whose lilac-blue is as fresh as a may-flower's frock. With her is the fragrant *C. longiflorus* flaunting with daring courage a wine-red bouquet in a vase of pavlova-blue. And then there is *C. sativus* whose warm lilac is feathered with violet rays as if the better to show-off the glistening orange-scarlet with which, one supposes, she beckons the passing bee.

Now come to where the leaning alders fringe the stream, and among the dull umbers of their crisping leaves we shall find *Colchicum autumnale* in a soft shell-pink. Sometimes this pretty lady will appear in wine-red or lilac. And again we may find her dressed in a white of so deathly a pallor that she looks like the pale wraith of some flower which died unloved long ages ago. Yet when this marble vision appears in what the lists call her *album plenum* dress, there is a generous milk-like warmth in her white ribbons, and so full and ample is the flower that one would think the autumn sod had given birth to a magnolia.

C. speciosum, large and handsome and early in the field, adopts some shade of rosy-carmine as everyday wear. But she also raises chalices of white which gleam with a crystal finish, and these are never quite so striking as when they have for bedfellow that most gorgeous of the household, the wine-crimson, Ruby Queen. And so I could go on to where the splendid *C. Bornmuelleri* is challenging the leaf-fall with a flush of rose to be followed by the dainty *byzantinum*, on to that sunny corner among the heaths where dwells a little and beautiful lady of the East in a shimmery rose-silk whom only the unimaginative and base could label, *C. giganteum*.

With autumn crocuses some of us may explain their absence from so many gardens on the grounds already suggested. But no such excuse can be made for allowing the appeal of the colchicums to go unheard. As a matter of fact the main reason why both of these are still comparatively rare is due to planting too late. The bulb merchants who insist upon showering their lists upon us by every post from midsummer onwards may tell us that they, at any rate, are not to blame if we find in the treasures we have a reminder of the many others which might have been as easily acquired. And we can attempt to excuse ourselves by retaliating that a bulb list in August is an outrage upon one's sense of propriety, and that few gardeners possess a faith so courageous that they can possibly raise a thrill of anticipation at the sight of a snowdrop bulb packed in sawdust so long as a single red admiral remains to flirt with the sweets of a michaelmas daisy. But they are right, those astute purveyors of bulbs, always right, and we are wrong. If, like the butterflies, we persist in dandling a tender sentiment for the passing summer and forget all about those catalogues until what appears to be a more seasonable occasion we shall find we have missed the boat.

Ask almost any of the anemones, any of the earlier bulbs, when it is that they first hear the call of spring and they will tell you that it comes to them with that patter of early September rain which rouses them from their summer sleep. That, then—or even before they have actually gone to rest if it can be managed—is the moment to plant. Every week subsequently lost places an embargo on one's hopes, every week gained brightens the prospects of a hearty and more permanent reward.

Autumn crocuses and colchicums give one still stronger reasons why they should be put-out before the orthodox bulb-planting season opens. They are so quick in their response, so eager to do their best for us that they will often break into bloom (which is nearly enough to break our hearts) before they are out of their paper bags. We may renew again and again our efforts to win the golden autumn smiles of *Sternbergia lutea*, the Lily of the Field, or those of her equally unresponsive sisters. We may try our patience over the chilling perversity of that southern beauty, *Zephyranthes candida*, the Flower of the West Wind, and others after her kind, and in desperation raise over them a wooden label bearing the encouraging inscription, 'Resurgam'. But no faltering hopes need be associated with the planting of autumn crocuses and colchicums. So spontaneously do they respond that corms put into the ground to-day will next week be gracing the garden with an enchantment of colour and form not less delightful than that of the happy little creatures which herald the news of spring.

Meadow saffrons and autumn leaves are closely associated with cyclamen in our garden round. And this should need no explanation, for is it not during the waning year that the best of all hardy cyclamen, *C. neapolitanum* (*hederaefolium*), comes to brighten the darkening days with its lovely colour and matchless grace? Still more, it is then that this delightful plant puts forth those beautiful leaves which are among the most precious adornments of our winter woodland.

Few, indeed, are the genera which will give you blossoms throughout the year. At the moment I can think only of one—that of our beloved heaths—but these hardy cyclamen will very nearly do so. And this is the more remarkable when one realises that the genus is a small one and that the enjoyment of an almost unbroken sequence of blossoms for twelve months does not involve the growing of more than about half-a-dozen of the easiest kinds.

Let us suppose the cyclamen year to open with the Neapolitan. This charmer's jaunty shuttlecocks in some shade of soft pink which deepens to a crimson base, or in pure white, will spring up in such abundance that their colour will run like a rosy stain through the russet and gold of the woodland carpet. Their delicate cowslip scent will linger in the still, receptive air and then, before the flowers are over, come those fascinating leaves. Roughly heart-shaped these may be, but so variable are they that one can imagine them being described as cordate, hastate, palmate or ovate. Their margins are waved, or goffered, merely nibbled or entirely plain, and, as for their colour, you will rarely find those of two plants quite alike. Yet if those clouded greens, usually in three shades—cucumber, jade and emerald which melts into silver—are laid-on in patterns that are bewildering in their eccentricity a common design governs their pencilling, pervading every lovely leaf as a melody will pervade a sonata.

That cyclamen should still be so uncommon in our gardens fills me with astonishment, for their elfin beauty is not their only claim to recognition. To the fact that some of them will be in bloom at all seasons one may add the ease with which they may be grown and propagated. All they ask is a well-drained loam, preferably in light shade, and they are easily and quickly raised from seed. Then I know of none other plant which will grow so contentedly as these in the dry and arid soil pockets about the roots of trees. They will even flourish under the smothering canopy of pines and other conifers or among rocks. Moreover, when you plant a cyclamen corm you can do so with the confidence that, barring accidents, it will be there for ever. Like the immortals it seems to have been blest with the elixir of everlasting life. The corm goes on steadily growing until it is as big as a bowler hat and, what is still more surprising, it increases in vigour and fecundity with the gathering years.

Canon Ellacombe had cyclamen at Bitton which were over eighty years old, yet they bore all the appearance of youth. And Mr. E. A. Bowles has, I believe, records of some nearly as old. Yet these imperishable little gems which ask nothing of us but the meanest subsistence, which give us so generously increasing dividends of pleasure with each passing season, are, as I have said, still comparatively unknown. And the knowledge that some of them have been appealing in vain to our hospitality for three hundred years, even demonstrating their willing sweetness by naturalising in battalions in some English woods, does not tend to alleviate that prick of conscience which sometimes reminds us that we have left undone the things we ought to have done.

C. graecum and *cyprium*, also autumn bloomers, seem closely allied to the Neapolitan, but there is this difference. Whereas the last-mentioned, having begun life wrong side up, grows its roots out of the top of its head (this often leading the unwary to plant the unfortunate thing upside-down) the other two make basal roots in the orthodox way. I have been told that the big-leaved *C. africanum* (*macrophyllum*) also makes a tap-root and grows reserves in the way of side-whiskers, but I shall never have the courage to dig him up so as to prove it. This Algerian is much like *C. neapolitanum*, but the flowers are larger and the bold, long-stalked leaves rounder and duller in tone. To these three we give a rather warmer, sunnier spot,

CYCLAMEN NEAPOLITANUM

CROCUS SPECIOSUS
A drift of violet and orange under October's yellowing leaves

COLCHICUM
BYZANTINUM

*Finely-wrought vases of
silver-crystal and rose*

COLCHICUM
SPECIOSUM

*'... Large and handsome
and early in the field ...'*

which will ensure a summer baking, and this is shared by the October-blooming *C. cilicium*. This Cilician alpine has almost round deep green leaves indistinctly clouded with emerald. The rather small flowers are a delicious shade of pink, but while the mouth of each is enriched with ruby dots the wee auricles, so conspicuous at the base of *C. neapolitanum*, are absent. *C. alpinum*, which has bright rose, rather short little flowers and distinctly small round leaves, runs the Cilician closely. But as both seem to amuse themselves by imitating one another's peculiarities, even invading the privacy of *C. coum*, perhaps the less said here the better.

With the above cyclamen—the free and adventurous Neapolitan always preponderating—we can make sure of having bloom to near the end of the year, when a few days of genial weather will call up *C. coum*. These chubby little blossoms, an intense crimson-pink, which peep forth with a Puck-like air just when the earlier snowdrops are whitening in the sheath, are inexpressibly charming, especially perhaps when they are white. *C. coum* is like none other in the even leaden green of its changeless leaves. *C. ibericum*, which follows hard upon its heels, may resemble it in flower, but having leaves which are shadow-patterned, not to mention the slight waviness of their edges, it should be at once distinguished. Even so, one too often sees the latter masquerading in the garden as *C. coum*. The fact is, *coum* has for some years been scarce, and one supposes that nurserymen, finding their stocks running low, have sent out *ibericum* instead. They may, of course, defend their integrity by saying that they themselves have been deceived by those who supplied them with such wares, a not improbable event. But I prefer to think that the nurserymen have so tender a regard for the feelings of their patrons that, rather than inflict upon us the disappointing truth that they have no true *coum* left, they heroically perjure their spotless reputations by sending along something else.

Whether *C. pseudo-ibericum* and *C. Atkinsii* are one and the same plant (and I feel fairly convinced that they are, even if one does sometimes see both names in the same list) one has to record the sorry fact that here the bar sinister crosses the honoured escutcheon of the cyclamen household. No nice people will ask how it happened, nor need I say more than that the said *Atkinsii* is the natural daughter of *C. coum* and *ibericum*. However, she's a dear girl and everybody likes her, and she goes about expressing entire approval of her two parents by impersonating their respective characteristics with disarming frankness.

All the above cyclamen[1] consider flowers-first the correct thing, thus following the lead of the autumn crocuses and colchicums whose leafless blossoms our plain-spoken forebears indelicately called 'naked-ladies'. But we have in *C. balearicum* a plant which boldly violates the family code by producing its leaves first. This foliage, narrowly heart-shaped and of a sullen grey-green, tufts the moss beneath our woodland trees in autumn and not until spring is in the air do the pure white flowers come, hastening to fill the place of the departing *coum* lest we should lose a link in the sequence of these sylvan fairies. *C. balearicum* may give blush tinted flowers but the white one is to us a dearer joy, possibly because its whiteness is so very white. But one can not compare where all are so good. *C. balearicum*, with its twirled petals and perfectly proportioned flowers and stems, would stand out in gracious beauty among the choicest of its kind, even if it did not have the field to itself which it generally has.

There are some who are base enough to suggest that *C. balearicum* may be a white form of *repandum* who trips on to the stage of spring as the Majorcan nymph is concluding her turn, but there is half-a-world of difference between the two. The flowers of *C. repandum* are, commonly, a ferocious red-crimson and the leaves are thin in texture and a brighter green. Further, these have scalloped margins and do not appear until just before the flowers. Moreover, instead of sitting in a tight little clump, these leaves run underground before rising to the surface, a trick (also indulged in by *neapolitanum*) which leads the incautious to believe the plant has yielded a family of seedlings. *C. repandum* enjoys a wall crevice as much as anywhere. It lives quite happily among some of our retaining stones, pushing its way through the green lace of helxine and flaunting its ardent red in the pearl-pale faces of the white hepaticas which share its

[1]Coum is an exception, its flowers and leaves coming together.

retreat. But *C. repandum* did not learn to be a wall-plant here. It adopted the practice in its native Italy and, seeing no reason why other cyclamen should not do equally well under similar conditions, we intend to offer them the opportunity.

C. repandum loyally keeps the cyclamen flag flying until full summer is approaching. Then the sweet-scented *C. europaeum* will come along to round-off this cycle of blossom with gleaming rubies which will jewel the woodland floor until the Neapolitans once more take up the endless chain with which the family girdles the year. *C. europaeum* is the only one of its genus which is not altogether content with our conditions. It grows but it does not abound with that abandon which marks its progress in some localities, and I rather think that, being more exacting in its demands for lime or chalk, in which the whole race delights, it may resent our acid soil. The dull green, almost orbicular, faintly mottled leaves of *C. europaeum* are, curiously enough, practically evergreen. The vivid crimson or rose-pink flowers, more deliciously scented than those of any other, are singularly appealing in their daintiness of form and deportment, and in the many places where it does well there is no happier plant for sun or shade.

Whether *C. europaeum* is entitled to a place in our native flora will probably never be decided. If it is not, then it must be one of the most ancient of our naturalised aliens. Old Gerard writes of it as a wild plant, but Johnson, his editor, doubted its claim to being indigenous. Turner (1548) was frankly sceptical about it, and John Parkinson, who never let slip an opportunity of having a dig at Gerard, bluntly states, 'There groweth none in the places where some have reported them to grow.'

The coiling of the seeding stems common to most of these cyclamen has puzzled science for generations. For what useful end can be achieved by the winding-up of the spent flower stems until they gently deposit their seed upon the corky bosom of the maternal corm? Since many of the seedlings that arise must perish of overcrowding, wholesale infanticide and ultimate race-suicide seem inevitable. Then, if some species can get along without this curious and rather tedious operation, why should others have adopted it? Farrer describes the 'tight little corkscrews' as suddenly uncoiling in spring and so dispersing their seed. But while this would certainly appear to be the obvious thing for them to do has anyone ever 'eye-witnessed' the performance? I can find no other authority who is of Farrer's opinion. On the contrary, patient investigators from the great Darwin down to the botanists of to-day have declared themselves unable to fathom the cyclamen's secret.

COLCHICUM
AUTUMNALE
ALBUM PLENUM

*Loveliest and best of
all double colchicums*

CYCLAMEN
REPANDUM

*Enjoys a niche in a
mossy wall*

CYCLAMEN COUM

ANEMONE TRIFOLIA

CHAPTER II

Woodland and other Anemones

WE ONCE nursed aspirations desperately sincere to raise *Anemone blanda* and *apennina* in such battalions that our woodland trees would stand ankle-deep in pools of violet and azure from February to April. But these virtuous daughters of the wind-flowers were not to be so easily won. We hurt their tender modesty by imprudent haste. Our robust precipitancy failed, or only in part succeeded, where a more delicate handling and wiser judgment might have prevailed. We made in those days—now getting rather far off—one cardinal error, that of expecting the very early *blanda* to prosper in the woodland, whereas, being a Grecian of the open breezy places, she languished for the sun of her southern spring. And with cousin *apennina* much progress was not really made until we managed to secure fresh roots, lifted before the foliage had died down in the early summer. These went away at once with such abounding vigour that they soon outstripped those raised from dry roots and quickly gave us wide colonies in all manner of places.

If there is one of these groups we like better than others it is that covering the ground beneath *Rosa Hugonis*. Should the one happen to be early and the other late, the effect may not come off. But that glorious blue, canopied by primrose yellow, would be something to be thankful for if it only occurred twice in five years, and we get it oftener than that. The Appenine anemone would be almost as beautiful under *Magnolia stellata* whose white ribbons flutter a welcome to the clearing skies of March, but lovely *Omphalodes cappadocica* holds that place with her opal-tinted azure.

A. blanda, shy but confiding little soul, does not naturalise in the hearty manner of the other. But she makes amends for this by a peculiarly winsome grace of flower and leaf and by giving us several varieties of especial charm. *Apennina* offers some colour breaks too, but these are not generally so pleasing or so reliable as the type (the white, rose and pinks are the best), none of them, for example, presenting the marked distinction of *A. blanda scythinica* whose pearl-white sepals have a sapphire reverse. *A. b. Ingramii* is very, very attractive in its deep prussian-blue, many shades richer than the normal and there are lots of intermediate hues.

A. ranunculoides takes us to the nemorosas. This little windflower makes up for its small size and unassuming manner by giving us flowers of a buttercup-yellow. Sometimes, deeming that an insufficient distinction, it carries two on a scape, and there are, if you know where to find them, plants of much finer form than those commonly seen, as well as a double. This pretty thing is a first-rate coloniser and it is easy anywhere. It is in flower with *blanda* in February—gold and blue in perfect unison—and has given us a delightful daughter in *A. intermedia*. This, supposed to be the result of a cross with *nemorosa*, is unique in the pale sulphur-ivory of its flowers, but we find it slow to increase.

Our own beloved 'wooden enemy', *A. nemorosa*, is in all its many manifestations so beautiful that one hesitates to make comparisons. Is there anything more affecting in the records of spring than its ripple of laughter which trembles across the crystal whiteness of some woodland glade in answer to the breezes of March? In the garden this anemone may be troublesome enough when it gets among its coloured sisters, or when it invades the rock garden with that wilful determination which is so great a virtue in the wild. Even so, forgiveness comes readily to a pest so pleasant, and there is something so bewitching about wood anemones when they are white that one longs to possess that super-white (is it *Leedsii* or Dr. Lowe's?) of which one can only read. The double-flowered white, however, is really good, so good that it is one of the few double flowers which are admitted to our woodland sanctum.

Blue forms of *A. nemorosa* abound. One may pick them up almost anywhere between the Pyrenees and the Arctic. The splendid *Robinsoniana*, large-flowered and a soft lavender-blue, is admirable always, and Blue Bonnet, which I believe originated in Wales (as did several others including *coerulea*) to make her debut from Daisy Hill, is another joy. Blue Bonnet is one of the best of the blues (not quite up to Blue Queen, perhaps, for which I believe we have to thank Mr. Mark Fenwick) and the firm, strong-textured flowers often do not appear until the others are going over.

We have from time to time brought in a good many diminutive Blue Bonnets and pink bonnets too, from the slate districts of N. Wales in particular, but these do not prosper in our humid glen as they do on their breezy upland sheepwalks. But the handsomest of Blue Bonnets, even the superb *Robinsoniana* itself, must yield place to *Allenii*. The biggest and bluest, latest and best of all these wood anemones, ample in leaf and with flowers as wide as a wild rose, there are surely few plants in the spring woodland to compare with the enthralling beauty of *A. n. Allenii*. We grow this exquisite thing in various places, it being particularly happy among flame- and orange-tinted azaleas and the fine old yellow *A. pontica*. But it touches its highest note of excellence perhaps on a westerly bank. There the lowering sun does not only clarify the blue of its ethereal lavender, but it induces the flowers to open wide at that hour the broad sepals as if the better to display the wreath of gold which it wears at its heart with such a masterly finesse.

All of these nemorosas are satisfied and sweet-tempered in any light woodland soil with some shade, though they have no real objection to full sun. But, as with the others, he who would create broad drifts of them without having to wait for the plants to settle down should secure them in clumpy masses and plant before the drooping leaves announce the termination of spring. And the same holds good regarding *A. trifolia* which takes the place of *nemorosa* in the more southerly of the eastern ranges of Europe. This is one of our first favourites, not only because it is one of our earliest, giving a long season of flower, but because it is so steadfast. Then there is a marked distinction about the firm, broad leafage which is less deeply cut and not so prone to variability as that of our own nemorosas. The flowers also, each held well erect above the green trefoil, are a true milk-white and the plant, spreading with seemly restraint, does not invade unduly either by seed or rhizome.

Farrer tells us how, 'in the woods round Misurina', he found *A. trifolia* varying 'unexplainably into the most lovely tones of soft clear blue, sometimes looking as if a large hepatica had got hung by mistake above the leaves of a fine and solid *A. nemorosa*', and Mr. Clarence Elliott (*Rock Garden Plants*) goads our interest in the same way. *A. trifolia* being such a very special pet of ours, was it surprising that we developed an absorbing desire for the same thing in blue? There were times, indeed, when the yearning to possess this alpine fairy developed into a passion so intense that there seemed to be nothing for it but to pack-up and go to Misurina to fetch it. However, our good friend Ingwersen came to the rescue just in time to avert what might have proved a fruitless quest. Some few years ago he found and brought home with him from the uplands of Greece none other than our long-desired treasure. And, knowing that it was a three-starred item on our list of 'wants', he immediately sent us a potful of roots. So the plant is now well on the way to being established and that in an honoured spot, which is at the foot of a youthful but always flowerful specimen of that best of all double white peaches, Russell's *Prunus persica flore albo pleno*, and no shrub ever more richly deserved so magniloquent a name.

There are few really high alpines, perhaps none among the anemones, that is quite so good a garden plant as *A. vernalis*. And there is none to challenge the 'Lady of the Snows' in that spell of mystic beauty which she wears. All over Europe from Spain to Scandinavia, over many of the Central and Southern Alps and away into Russia and the Caucasus, always at great heights and always, it seems, at the gates of the melting snows, eager to usher in the urgent spring of her lofty world, reigns this most gracious of alpine anemones. *Alpina* may be 'the Great King of Glory in the race', but *vernalis*, whose very name suggests the spirit of spring, has the braver heart and mounts to still higher planes where few or none may even question her claim to supremacy.

Now it is a curious fact that *A. vernalis* should succeed at all in gardens such as ours, which is low of altitude and muggy in winter. Such conditions, indeed, are so resented by most high alpines that we long ago gave up attempting to grow them. They were so unhappy always that efforts to keep them seemed hardly less inhuman than caging a lark. But *A. vernalis* is a striking exception. She will prosper with the best of good will, prove long-lived and never give one a moment's anxiety. This, always provided you treat her generously. Being assured that this was a moraine plant we once made a moraine mainly for her. A grievous job it was and the Snow-Lady disdained these our efforts by a polite but quite obvious disapproval. Then some seedlings were put in a gritty, but good old-fashioned kitchen-garden loam to 'do or die'—and they immediately 'did'. They waxed fat and comely and they are still there. Good living, in a word, suits *A. vernalis* as well as it does cousin *pulsatilla*, upon whom a slimming diet is too often imposed under the impression that she enjoys it.

A. vernalis is one of those plants which make you thankful you are a gardener. Others—there are hosts of them—may be as beautiful, but when spring calls forth those cones of tawny-brown monkey-fur, lit with little glints of gold in the April sun, when these split asunder to disclose the iridescent nacre which lines them, when this goblet of gold and silver, of opal and pearl and costly silk has opened like Aphrodite's shell and deep from the heart of the flower there rises a circlet of purest gold, then the garden has no gem so utterly beyond price.

It may be that the reason why one so seldom sees *A. vernalis* in cultivation is that already given; and our own experience tells us that the difficulty so frequently encountered with *A. pulsatilla* is due more often to starvation than anything else. At any rate, since we have grown the Pasque anemone in a good honest loam which never gets really dry, though the drainage is without fault, it has been eminently satisfactory.

The Easter anemone exerts much the same fascination as does *vernalis*. All swaddled in a pelt of silver, the adorable flowers rise on ten-inch stems from the same carroty leaves which *vernalis* affects, but they are infinitely variable in colour, size and form. From white to palest lavender and mauve, from mauve to purple, plum-red, ruby-brown and sombre, deep-toned crimson do they range, with ever the bold wreath of gold within, the ineffably graceful poise and that air of classic charm which has weaved around them so much legendary lore.

There was a time when, with a diligence worthy of a better end, we attempted to round-up the various clans of the *pulsat-*

illa household, to sort out and earmark these cattle of a hundred hills—Mrs. van der Elst, Mallenderi, Moeckler's, Farrer's, Dykes' and native forms among others—but none of them did we ever find really reliable from seed. Garden life may have demoralised them. They may, as Sir Arthur Hort suggests in his delightful book, *The Unconventional Garden,* have intermarried with some of the *pratensis* group, with the rare *Halleri* or some other. However, when visitors ask to see *A. pulsatilla* at its best we now introduce them to the whole gamut and invite them to make their own choice. Occasionally one may raise a mean and squinny flower, but that is not often. We weed these out, consistently sow from the best and are satisfied and more than that with our mixed company. Like *vernalis* and *alpina,* which we have never got satisfactorily agoing, *pulsatilla* yields in summer those seed mops of silk which, like spun glass, seem so fitting a climax to the loveliness of the flowers.

From the haunts of these higher alpines to *A. narcissiflora* is no great step, for this handsome woodlander will join *alpina* on the lawns above alpen tree-level. But it will also descend to much lower sub-alpine copses, and so cosmopolitan is it that its range girdles almost the entire Northern Hemisphere. New World or Old World, it is all the same to this comfortable, uncomplaining herb which you will find looking as contented just above the burning aridity of a Colorado desert as it is where Northern Asia all but touches the Arctic's eternal snows.

Why Linnaeus gave this anemone such an absurd specific name one can not even guess, for it bears not the remotest resemblance to any earthly daffodil, unless it be one of the cluster kinds. A willing doer in any light to medium loam, preferably with a little shade, the plant, which is herbaceous, puts up in spring a sheaf of stout stems of a foot to twenty inches in height. These carry aloft a broad ruffle of pale green, deeply lobed leaves which are covered with a nap of silvery silk. Above these appear, in an umbel, cup-shaped blooms, generally white within and stained with pink on the reverse which makes them look so much more like apple-blossom than even a bunch-flowered white narcissus.[1] There is a delicate beauty in this alpine anem-

[1]Yellow, pink and red forms of *narcissiflora* have recently been found in the Caucasus (Dr. Giuseppi, *A.G.S. Bulletin,* No. 23).

ANEMONE HEPATICA var. ALBA

ANEMONE APENNINA

THE GLADE IN THE MAKING
Early days by mill-stream and alders

'A LITTLE HUMP-BACKED STONE BRIDGE SPANS THE
STREAM . . .' (p. 24)

one, a quiet refinement which gives it a very special claim as a woodlander. It is, moreover, a reliable perennial and possesses that other attribute so desirable in woodland plants—a readiness to do its own sowing and thus become naturalised. All of which virtues belong to its winsome cousin, *tetrasepala*, of the Himalaya.

A. rivularis is a hearty waterside herb that will grow to a couple of feet with something of the likeness of *japonica*. It is a little disappointing in size of bloom, but some forms are better than others, and those glistening white saucers which have a blue reverse are centred with violet anthers. These are borne from late July through August when anemones in flower are few, and, once established, the plant will live for ever in any coolish spot. And near this on higher ground we have the choice little *parviflora* from the far north whose solitary flowers are a cold blue-white.

Yellow anemones, as has been noted, are uncommon but *A. palmata*, mainly of N. Africa (I have seen its leaves in one or two places in the Var, S. France), makes amends for this family failing by cresting its six to nine-inch stems with golden buttercups of much splendour. This fine thing, with its lowly, broad and fleshy leaves, we have grown and lost, also its pure white variety. In other places with conditions similar to ours it flourishes, and it seems more than probable that it was some murdering fork that did for it what once it did for our finest patch of *Sanguinaria canadensis major*. At any rate *palmata* being too good a plant to be without is being re-established, and a similar but more encouraging tale might be told of *A. sulphurea* of the alpina household.

But we are not so hopeful of having any success with *A. sylvestris* which, when it is A. s. Spring Beauty, or *major*, is a plant of undeniable quality. It is, of course, a runner, after the manner of *japonica*, but our results with it have so far given us scant cause for alarm in that respect. Farrer tells us (*My Rock Garden*) how the snowdrop anemone also disappointed him until he secured the *major* form which not only ramped but flowered abundantly both in spring and autumn. However, following the lead of better men, we are about to try again to coax this shy and fretful lamb to become the ravening wolf that it is in some gardens. After all, the satisfying of a sulky plant is often only a matter of finding the right spot, and that may be but a yard or two from the scene of failure.

If I had attempted to treat these anemones in their seasonal order of flowering *A. Hepatica* would have been placed at the head of the list instead of at the tail. Then it would have served as a piquant *hors d'œuvre* to the feast. But, as it will, with its mid-winter start, accompany some four or five months of the opening year, it will be doing it no injustice to regard it as the good wine of spring's sequence of anemones.

A. Hepatica, for some wholly inexplicable reason, is not so popular in gardens as it deserves to be. Nor does it seem to find much favour with the nurserymen. Some of them present a goodly list, others—even those who make a speciality of rock-plants and who profess to be up-to-date—do not so much as mention it. *A. Hepatica* deserves, I say, more than this not only because of its long season and its engaging manner and beauty of blossom, but because it is, if you give it the right place and let it alone, a plant of such amazing endurance that the older it gets the finer and better does it appear.

Our first hepaticas were white. They came from an old Scottish garden some thirty years ago and they are to-day more vigorous than they were in their youth. Moreover, they have given us more colonies of offspring than any other and these, cropping up where they will, have not shown any inclination to deteriorate or revert to the typical blue. These whites, by the way, are large in flower and having many segments to the corolla, they escape the starry effect of some. Why a plant such as this, having parted with its colour, should show so marked a fecundity I do not know, but there are places in Southern Europe where, even in the wild, *A. H. alba* is as fixed a variety as it is in the garden.

A. Hepatica (*triloba* some call it) opens fire here about Christmas-time with the whites. These are followed by the single blues and pinks, both of them pure and rich in tone, which are succeeded by the buttony doubles in the same colours. The double-blue is, for some unaccountable reason, a more difficult plant and consequently costly, as is the best of the double whites which is also none too amiable. But the double pink is quite amenable to any reasonable treatment and it is one of the prettiest. Hepaticas, however, have not improved their appearance by this doubling process, since one misses in them that freckling of white anthers which is such a telling attraction, especially in the blues.

The above by no means covers the wide range of colours and forms adopted by this versatile anemone. But if those unmentioned have comparatively little garden value *A. angulosa*, once included in the tribe of *Hepatica*, demands special notice. This Transylvanian is larger in all its parts than the others. It seldom loses its leaves, which are broader, greener and less glossy, and they often have a dimpled surface as an accompaniment to wavy, scalloped margins. *A. angulosa* is usually later than *Hepatica* with its bold blue flowers. These may vary a little in depth of hue and in one form (*lilacina*) which Mr. Clarence Elliott used to list, the blooms, ruffled in green, leafy bracts, are an exquisite shade of cool slaty lavender—a plant of rare loveliness. We also grow the American *H. acutiloba*, but it has not the garden merit of the European.

The whole of the hepaticas seem to have a partiality for limestone but they will do quite well without it. They are, above all else, sociable creatures, so much so that many of our oldest and best clumps are sitting firmly in the heart of some other plant, having seeded there of their own choice. They delight in a cool, deep, well-drained root-run and love to be among the smaller spleenworts and bladder ferns (*Cystopteris*) of shady retaining walls. They also delight in being wedged in between stones and this can always be provided at planting-time. But while these cheerful and faithful little friends will respond to careful division in the later spring the golden rule always is to leave them severely alone.

CHAPTER III

The Making of a Glade, with Notes on Autumn Colour

AN EARLIER volume, *A Garden in Wales* (Arnold), gave an indulgent public a brief insight to our garden as it was up to some six or seven years ago. Since that time several extensions have taken place. Offsets have appeared from the parent stock, the most important of these being a small meadow which adjoined our westerly flank. The acquiring of this addition has meant much. It has given us as an annex to our dry slopes not only a considerable area of deep alluvial sandy loam which required no levelling to speak of, and practically no drainage operations, but freer access to the millstream which had hitherto been little more than a boundary on the meadow side. This means that the stream now flows through somewhere about the centre of the garden and that we have its two banks to play with instead of only one, while beyond it, on the further side, our new westerly boundary, is a very much larger stream for the most part flanked, like the other, with alder and other native trees.

Yet another advantage, apart from gardening possibilities, we gained was this: Before the meadow became merged into the garden it was not possible to obtain a landscape view of the precipitous slopes of the old garden which rose abruptly from a path skirting the banks of the little stream. We were too close to them to get that distant, general effect which is so helpful in the making of a garden, so essential to a true estimate of results. Incidentally, if we ever do 'fall off the ranch', as once we were often in danger of doing, when working on the said slopes, we shall now at least land on our own property.

Having become possessed of this new vineyard counsellors wise and unwise dropped in to offer advice or satisfy curiosity. They looked at it, poked it with sticks, dug holes in it, said things about the weeds which lay ambushed in the turf, about the roots of the elms which were devouring the soil. But we had

THE LONG LAWN

LEANING ALDERS AND RHODODENDRONS FLANK THE GLADE

EUONYMUS
PLANIPES

Orange seeds hang beneath a blood-red canopy ($\frac{1}{2}$ nat. size)

ENKIANTHUS
CAMPANULATUS

A worthy representative of a distinguished family

already decided what we were going to do and that was to make
a glade. 'Not of grass!' they gasped. .... And strong men turned
pale at the prospect of mowing and rolling a lawn one hundred
and fifty yards long. Being good friends as well as strong men
they warned us of the hard labour with which we should be
punished for such a plunge. But we were not unfamiliar with
grass—or its alternative, cultivated land. We were determined
to have our glade, determined to have its longest sweep carpeted with grass, kirtled on both sides with trees and shrubs,
and abide by it. And events have proved that we were right.

Since the initial scything and rolling, the original meadow
turf has yielded to the mower with such surprising results that
we now have as fine a lawn as we desire. It may not be of Mac-
donald quality but it serves our purpose, and every dry summer
since its inception it has been the envy of less fortunate neighbours. Nor is the labour any greater—it is considerably less—
than that entailed by the arable ground. True, there have been
times when the brave Prometheus may have felt the strain as,
pursued by midges and heat of a summer evening, he drove the
mower over that belt of green. But was not that lawn his pride
and his joy, the offspring of his own sweat and thew? To him it
was an object of a regard so profound that even when midges
in battalions were in massed assault he could turn and look upon
its increasing sweetness with something of the thrill which
moved the artist whose 'cold marble leapt to life, a god'. But
every succeeding year the grass area—and the mowing—grows
a little less owing to the trees and shrubs having grown a little
more, and that is only another way of saying that each year our
ambition to create a garden glade comes nearer realisation.

This idea of a glade was no idle fancy or mere covetous desire. The term suggests perhaps an ambition a trifle pompous
for a small garden, but there is none other. And after all a glade
may be measured in square yards as well as acres, always provided proportion is given its due regard. However, our determination to make a glade the key feature of this new possession
came to us because it seemed the right—if not the only—thing
to do with the place. That narrow strip of meadow, running
roughly north and south, was, indeed, already a glade, fringed
as it was on both sides by trees. Nature's fingerpost had shown

us the way and it was for us to carry on where she had left off. And if we were able to develop our little valley without violating the gathered grace of a thousand years or hushing the pipes of Pan we should ask no other reward.

There have been times when we have felt that our glade garden was in jeopardy of losing those, the most precious, of its charms. We were afraid lest we should offend the 'large utterance of the early gods'. But such evil visions—perhaps no more than symptoms of an over-worked anxiety—have been fleeting. The streamside alders, leaning and hoary, ever reassured us. The mossed rocks and wild fern of the tumble-down wall by the larger river comforted us. The skylark's lyrics which the dipper repeated down among the water-tossed boulders of the glen, the heron who still stalks the garden with confidence unshaken by our changes, and the gambols of red squirrels on the lawn—these have restored our complex and given us courage.

Small matters these, perhaps, but big matters to us to whom the gospel of gardening, as we understand it, has ever consisted of a deep regard for the spirit of the place as nature made it. To follow nature in all her ways is no part of our policy. Those ways are often not our ways. Nature errs and commits extravagances not only against the canons of good gardening but often against herself. But it is possible, given such conditions as ours, to steer a course that, while the best and truest traditions of gardening are being maintained, will not affront the decencies of environment. To err is human, to do the wrong in gardening very easy. And nothing is more difficult to put aright than a too hasty step. A false judgment, if it concerns only the felling of a single tree, may not be rectified in a generation. Wherefore, ever since we first hedged-in the old garden and called it our own, it has been our constant pleasure to foster the natural in every possible way, knowing only too well that beauty, the beauty of common things, is too often sacrificed on the altars of false gods, that—

> The world is full of woodmen who expel
> Love's gentle Dryads from the haunts of life
> And vex the nightingales in every dell.

And it is in autumn more than at any other season that we enjoy the fullest satisfaction, the most ample returns for what we have attempted in this new garden. The long lawn is never quite so green, its texture never so alluring as it is when the patterned trees, borrowing a more velvety darkness from the sunshine's riper gold, steal across the sward with that dusky softness which seems so inseparable a part of the quiet that autumn's armistice brings.

But, arresting as thus it may be in such transient moments, the lawn has something more tangible to give. It is of all backgrounds for autumn colour the best—with the single exception of conifers rightly chosen and happily placed—and for autumn colour we have always had an appetite bordering on intemperance. In our modest way we have directed much of our energy towards this phase of gardening. We have yielded to the spell of the enchanter and indulged in extravagances in its name. Yet our indulgence was no wanton escapade. Those subtle and mysterious effects which accompany the slow surrender of the leaf have afforded us gratification in brimming measure. Individually and collectively they have yielded a satisfaction not to be estimated in words. But behind all this was the conviction that if we were ever to achieve our objective and build up our garden fabric in a manner that would be as much in sympathetic accord with the natural environment as it was humanly possible as gardeners to make it, then we should lay our foundation very largely on the firm ground of green and autumn colour.

That, at any rate, was a working principle. It gave us something to go upon in overcoming the difficulties which come to most who have to make a beginning from the raw, and it has not yet led us astray. After all, in the autumnal hues of trees and shrubs one rarely finds a false note. They conceal few traps to ensnare the unwary. They blend with one another in gracious unity, and the quarrelsome discords one knows in the border are not among them. And, what is more, the tints of the exotic will associate so happily with those of the native that we never need be afraid of vexing the nightingales of our wild wood by the introduction of the most gorgeously apparelled stranger from China or America. So in the bringing-up of our glade, as in the earlier planting of the woodland, have we been able to say of Old October, 'Thou wert my guide, philosopher and friend.'

Then there is that sense of maturity which autumn brings. Maturity in the garden is what we all strive to attain. It is the good hostelry which we hope awaits us with comfort and satisfaction at the journey's end. Yet of all the sylvan fairies whose confidence we would win this is the most hesitant and shy. Albeit, no matter how painfully new your garden may seem, autumn and autumn colour will soften its lines and sweeten its tones if anything will. Even no more than that litter of fallen leaves which is so distressful to the tidy mind will urge forward that ripening influence with kindly persuasion and magical effect. And perhaps that is why that good gardener, H. Avray Tipping, who was still making gardens when long past the Psalmist's span, so earnestly desired to 'discipline tidiness' when it came to the matter of sweeping up leaves. And how delighted he was when he discerned behind the swishing besom a laughing elf who, 'summoning light airs to her assistance', would send every leaf dancing back again !

The main way to our glade garden leads over a little hump-backed stone bridge which, made by the clever hands of Prometheus, spans the stream. Near this bridge, one on each side, stand two trees. One is *Liquidambar styraciflua*, the other *Eucryphia pinnatifolia*. They are still youthful, yet tall enough to be impressive, and throughout the autumn they guard the gates of the glade garden like flaming swords. The liquidambar's maple-like leaves are the first to colour and so kaleidoscopic is their display that there is scarcely a tint on the palette of autumn which they do not show. From palest ivory to yellow and orange, from rose to crimson, blood-red, claret, purple and bronze, the Joseph's coat of this sturdy American accompanies the slow trend of autumn with its changeful splendour, and few leaves are so resistant to wind, so indifferent to frost. The eucryphia glows into a pyre of orange, flame and crimson when its companion is about half-way through its performance, so that from these twin sentinels alone we get pillars of riotous colour for nearly three months.

Pyrus arbutifolia (especially varieties Brilliant and the columnar *erecta*) and *Vaccinium corymbosum* are shrubs of the highest merit in autumn colour. Both are rather transitory, their only fault, but they would command our esteem if they flaunted their glory only for one splendid hour. Wet with the dew this October morning the leaves of these shrubs were an almost dazzling crimson-scarlet against the soft green of the lawn, and that astonishing colour proved to be no ill companion for the cool azure of some belated blooms of *Clematis atragene* and *C. columbianum* which had been invited to use the shrubs as a support.

Also at the margin of the long lawn, with that most elegant of conifers, *Cupressus nootkatensis pendula*, behind it, is *Berberis Sieboldii*, here by a long way the best of barberries in leaf-colour. In early September its tips change to a vivid scarlet, and leisurely the entire bush assumes that guardsman's glory hue, every leaf holding until the first sharp frost of late November. *Parrotia persica*, no more than a lusty shrub as yet, was slow to take part in this parade. But our patience—most precious of virtues in a garden—has been rewarded, and parrotia is to-day a conflagration of bronze and gold with every beech-like leaf-spray terminating in a drooping pennon of carmine, bitingly brilliant.

It is not easy always, especially in a small garden, to curb one's inclination to press the accelerator and push along more speedily. And there are, it is only too true, occasions upon which one finds valuable time and space have been lost on objects which would never be anything more than second-rate. But our parrotia rubs in the lesson that to make haste slowly is the wiser policy, and *Nyssa sylvatica* has been no less convincing. One sapling, the tallest here, of this fine tree gave us nothing more exhilarating than a dirty green until this year when it suddenly became aflame with orange and crimson. Had we taken the advice of others who told us we had got hold of a 'non-colouring form', or that the tree was in too wet or too dry a soil—had we allowed our impatience to get the better of our judgment—that specimen might never have attained its present perfection. Of *Rhus cotinoides* a similar tale could be told, a tale of long waiting and yearly disappointment over the beggar's robes in which it sat through the feast of autumn. But, left to go its way, it has at length decided to retrieve its reputation, and its fine big leaves are, at the moment of writing, expiring in magnificent shades of orange, scarlet and wine-red.

But good as *R. cotinoides* can be it has to be very good indeed to exceed *R. Cotinus* in leaf colour here. Other shrubs may be more brilliant, but the spoon-shaped leaves of the venetian sumach on their long and slender bright-red stalks change from their glaucous green to a warm and generous blend of apricot, orange and scarlet which is rarely equalled. House decoration is no part of our curriculum, but a branch of *R. Cotinus* in its autumn dress, having been accidentally broken, was placed in water and its leaves retained their freshness and colour for six weeks. In the garden this admirable shrub is not less persistent. But growing it in poor, dry soil with the object of obtaining the best possible leaf tints is not conducive to successful flowering. Our shrubs moult their smoke-coloured panicles soon after these are formed, so it would seem that we cannot have it both ways.

R. C. atropurpurea, the 'Burning Bush'—or rather one of them—with its purple-tinted foliage and a 'wig' delicately tinted with the same hue is, I think, eclipsed by *R. C. foliis purpureis*—as a foliage plant at any rate. The rich burgundy-red which is the all-season wear of this variety may not appeal to those who suffer not gladly shrubs of that colour. The Lady of the Garden is one of those who would ostracise all of such, and so decided are her views on the subject that I have more than once lapsed into unpopularity for having smuggled-in that or the other 'red-leaved thing'. But this red sumach is so eminently attractive, especially seen against an evening sun, and it plays so dramatic a part on the autumn stage, that even in her animosity I perceive a weakening towards a toleration that borders on admiration.

The same story might be told of the claret vine which, wearing a dismal reddish green all summer, burns away in a ruby-crimson of glorious hue, which streams not only into the leaves but the branches and bonny bunches of grapes. *Berberis Thunbergii* is an old-timer but still one of the very best of its genus for leaf colour, and its *atropurpurea* variety, in every way worthy of it, is so distinct and handsome that we find a place for both. But for purple-leaved shrubs in general I myself have no great love. *Berberis vulgaris*, to give an example, is a fine old plant at its best, but garbed in plum-colour it seems to lose in every essential character. There is also many a good thing in the

Prunus and *Pyrus* tribes—notably in the plum and crab sections—which, in general planting, would be more pleasing had it not adopted a dull bronzy-red for regular wear.

Acers when they are maples have not been much of a success with us. Many have been called but few chosen, so few that most of the earlier planted have been cleared out. There remains a tall fellow with leaves nearly a foot across which turn a yellow which is not good enough to compete with a liriodendron close by. This maple came from America, a stowaway in a newspaper, but I am not at all sure that that is sufficient justification for our continued hospitality. Then there is *A. griseum* which, if slow of growth and stumpy in figure, must be numbered among the elect. *A. septemlobum Osaka-ʒuki*, perhaps unchallenged by any other in its early and late mantle of matchless scarlet, will always hold its place. And in addition to these we have a crowd of seed-raised infantile palmatums from which, it is hoped, a selection worthy of the tribe will some day be made, while coming on with every promise are several of those charming species with striated bark—*Davidii, pennsylvanicum, rufinerve* and others.

Euonymus alatus occupies a place on the lawn near a taxodium whose beautiful foliage does not acquire its foxy-red here until winter is nigh, the explanation probably being that the sapling is too busy growing. But the spindle, a well-rounded bush of some six feet, surrenders early and gradually changes from a dull bronzy-green to a riot most brilliant of crimson, scarlet, cerise and rose-red. *E. sanguineus* may put up a brave show with its larger leaves, *E. planipes, latifolius* and *yedoënsis* hold their own among the best with blood-red fruits swinging in the golden radiance of their yellowed leaf; *E. europaeus* is often as excellent in foliage as it is in fruit, especially the varieties *aldenhamensis* and *fructo-coccineo*, in which latter the capsules are ruby rather than coral, and there are other worthies in this engaging family. But in leaf colour alone none we have yet seen can ever hope to rival *E. alatus*. In the grey light of a misty November day the ardent flare of this excellent spindle against green turf suggests a lively bonfire, and much the same effect, but with the deeper glow of fanned embers, arises when *Fothergilla monticola* has joined this panoply of colour. The big, hazel-like leaves of this species develop a more varied colour than those of *F. major*—deep orange, old gold, mulberry and blood-red—and its creamy-white, powder-puff flowers in spring do their part in making a really attractive shrub.

Cercidiphyllum japonicum was for several seasons a disappointing shrub. The tender beauty of its early leaves, lovely as a dove's breast in colour and gloss, got pinched by spring frosts, the fuller leafage puckered in summer drought and in autumn withered away in ashen melancholy. But since the plant has become established in a new spot near the stream, as it is grown to such perfection by Mr. Mark Fenwick at Abbotswood, it has yielded more promising efforts to live up to its great reputation. *Disanthus cercidifolia*, on the other hand, made satisfactory progress from the first. This is one of those more costly and untried things in which one indulges with a sporting spirit, for in addition to its rarity it came with a warning that it was none too hardy. However, the sweep in this case has 'come off', for the plant has grown well in a deep, cool loam prepared with sphagnum peat for the dwarfer heaths which accompany it, and from frost it has not yet suffered.

This relation of the witch-hazels seems to have little to promise in the way of flower or fruit, but its heart-shaped, long-stalked, highly-polished leaves make full amends for this by distilling an autumn dye of remarkable splendour. A warm orange suffused with an elderberry purple, the two tints blended in a glowing intensity, is as near as I can get in describing their entrancing hue. We get much the same effect from that beautiful little rose, *Rosa hispida*, which dwells in an adjoining bed of similar make-up—the only rose known to me which can claim an even leaf colour of that particular shade.

Many of the smaller deciduous ericaceae and vacciniums we grow among the alpine rhododendrons and heaths which will be roped in to this garden story later. But some of the former are so invaluable as contributors to the autumn leaf show that they cannot be omitted here. Conspicuous among these from September to the first frosts are the members of the enkianthus clan. The red-flowered *E. campanulatus var. Palabinii*—a gift from that keen lover of good shrubs, the Hon. Vicary Gibbs—is one of the earliest to colour, every leaf becoming a pure and vivid scarlet. But the type is not far behind in foliage if not quite so brightly coloured in flower. *E. cernuus*, which also bears clusters of swinging bells which, in the variety *rubens*, gleam like rubies when seen against a lowering sun, is no less brilliant in its scarlet livery. And these again are challenged by the splendour of *E. perulatus* and *pallidiflorus*, an almost white-flowered variety of *campanulatus* which burns away in orange and gold. *E. himalaicus* and *chinensis*, both of Wilson's introduction, have not yet made much of autumn. The former has very large bells—primrose with red shadings—but we are told that the Chinaman, when it comes to bloom, will eclipse the older species in flower colour. Both of these are still rare. Their merits have yet to be proved here, as are those of the last to arrive, *E. nipponicus*. But this pretty red-barked shrublet is already making great promise by staining some of its leaves a bright cerise.

So I might proceed and risk straining the reader's patience by drifting into a catalogue of names. But those fascinating little shrubs, the gaylussacias—especially *G. ursina*—deserve a passing recognition for the share they take in autumn's passing show. Most of these say their farewells to summer with blood-red leaves which are retained for weeks, even months, and *Pieris Mariana*, quite a small shrub, is no less rich in colour and equally persistent. Then there is *Vaccinium pennsylvanicum* whose highly-burnished leaves develop a brilliant crimson scarlet, and these, usually not at their best until mid-November, will be with us until winter is nigh.

Most of the azaleas are so splendidly generous in their leaf colour that a selection of them would more than earn their keep if they had no other recommendation to offer. Not only are they unsurpassed in the magnificence of their autumnal garb, but they present an infinite variety of tints, and with no more than a modest collection one may rely on some of them being in full-dress parade from late August to December. The first to surrender here is *A. Vaseyi*, one of the loveliest of the race in spring. It gives us six feet of glowing ruby-crimson which prevails until the massed bands of *A. pontica* open fire on the woodland slopes, to be followed in quick succession by the wonderfully beautiful *Schlippenbachii* and the ghent *mollis* and *sinensis* hybrids which, with *pontica*, are grouped for the most part in the old garden. All of these give us a long season of glorious colour. So lavishly do they spill their wealth into the lap of autumn that the grandeur with which they greet the maturing spring is not more impressive. And the colours they display are so extraordinarily varied, the leaf change so erratic in point of time, that even in a species like *A. pontica* every bush of a group will often stand out with its own individual tint. This admirable shrub, the old yellow azalea as it is affectionately called, we planted years ago more extensively perhaps than was wise on so limited an area. That was before gardening for us became the all-time pursuit it is to-day. But those well-tried friends, now fully grown, we would not willingly exchange for any other shrub in the garden.

Viburnums, often so glorious in berry and leaf in the Midlands, are not for our light, acid soil—not as autumn shrubs at any rate—and the thorns and pyracanthas do not flourish as they do where they get a taste of lime. Our finest cherry in leaf colour, if not in flower as an early, is *Prunus yedoënsis*, possibly because it is the oldest. *P. Sargentii* is every year getting nearer that fiery crimson and orange with which it helps to maintain a reputation for being among the best half-dozen flowering cherries, but the fragrant *Shirotae* is equal to it. One mountain ash, secured on Mr. Marchant's recommendation as *Pyrus Aucuparia gracilis*, is a slender tree of well under the usual stature of such things, but in its leisurely way it is going to make a charming feature on the grass. It began bearing its large orange fruits at an early age and the pinnate leaves kindle so rich a crimson and hang so long that it looks like challenging a stripling of the Knap Hill scarlet oak. Upon all these, and a few others, weighs the heavy responsibility of representing autumn as specimen trees in and about our grassy glade, and those others include some birches.

I believe the birches give us greater pleasure than any other of the taller occupants of this part of the garden. One of the most beautiful of them is *Betula verrucosa dalecarlica*, the cut-leaved Swedish birch, which, its white bole rising to nearly thirty feet, is an object of peerless symmetry and grace. *B.*

japonica mandschurica (*szechuanica*) with a bark of cream and orange, promises to be no less elegant. *B. Ermannii*, its stem peeling from amber to a milk-white, its branches a gleaming golden-brown, is another tree of arresting beauty, and to these may be added several selected saplings of *papyrifera* and our own charming native.

For a small garden this assembly of birches—and there are more coming on—may seem to the busy side, but our immoderation, if so it be, has its reasons. In the first place these trees are in perfect harmony with the tone of the landscape. They grow very rapidly yet are so slender and light in build that they suit a smallish garden better than most tall trees. Then for giving slight shade where it is needed for rhododendrons, primulas and the like we have not met their equal. Along with these more or less practical considerations there is their faultless elegance and balance, their leaf colour and well-bred refinement. Whether they are veiled in the tender verdure of April, shimmering tremulously with light flashes in the soft airs of summer, draped in the golden raiment of autumn, or finely etched against a wintry sky these birches are infinitely beautiful.

Roots? Yes, they all have roots, but these are not the terror to us that they are to some. Indeed, we often find these roots exceedingly useful in helping to drain and dry soils that are to the wet side. And I will go further and suggest—having no little faith in the influence of root-association upon plant welfare—that birch roots seem to be peculiarly agreeable to most of those ericaceous and other things which, often grouped in the lists as 'peat plants', have for us an irresistible fascination.

CHAPTER IV

Winter Colour, mainly Evergreens

SINCE THERE is no off-season in English gardening the prerogatives of winter must be accorded their due, and these consist not so much of those flowering plants which bring the colour and sweetness of more genial climes to our northern land, but of those hardy trees and shrubs whose foliage persists the year round.

One of our oldest and best friends among these is a golden Scot's pine (*Pinus sylvestris aurea*) which, though twenty-five years of age, is still barely eight feet high. This charming shrub is, during summer, a neutral green, but when autumn comes its needles gradually become yellower until mid-winter when they gleam with the colour and lustre of polished brass. So the little tree remains until spring is on the way when its golden wealth melts away and it re-assumes its workaday cloak of green. All evergreen conifers, green, grey or gold, become a brighter hue in winter, and what is true of that little pine is true of *Cupressus macrocarpa lutea*, the yellows of the *Lawsoniana* group and others. But in none do we get so dramatic and complete a change from summer green to winter gold as in the wee Scot.

This miniature was given a few years ago a stable-companion in the person of a sprig of juniper brought from a Perthshire hill. As is the way with natives of that northern land once they cross the border, a determination to get on in life so obsessed this juniper that it is now nearly as tall as its neighbour and so obviously developing a bow-window below the waist effect that the Lady of the Garden—in the interests of decency she tells me—has corsetted it in wiry busks. However, it is its colour that matters, for the steely blue-grey which assumes so silvery a tone as mid-winter approaches is just right with the gleaming gold of its companion.

Years ago, before gardening had become the absorbing in-

ROSA HISPIDA
One of the most beautiful of the dwarfer wild roses in foliage, blossom and autumn leaf colour

RICHEA SCOPAR

*With its four-inch spikes of oran
and vermilion blossoms*

THE COFFIN JUNIPER

*The gracefully drooping foliage, a glossy
cucumber-green, is in striking contrast to
the bright red-brown twigs*

terest it is to-day, the good fates persuaded us to plant a number of Lawson cypresses. These are now stately trees, they are all eminently graceful and no two are quite alike. Their green may not be so bright as that of *Pinus radiata*, the beautiful *Cupressus nootkatensis pendula* and many another, but it is a generous and hearty thing to look upon on a winter's day, especially among our venerable oaks, and it makes as telling a background for both the silver and golden conifers as it does for autumn colour. Then the more or less columnar habit of the Lawsons has very great advantages in a place of limited area, and one must mention in passing the striking beauty of these trees, including the variety *Wisselii*, when their dark foliage is padded with the ruby-crimson inflorescences.

With the exception of those mentioned and one or two more our hospitality to golden conifers ceases. We have the same feeling about them as woodland trees as we have about the purple-leaved shrubs referred to, and they are even more difficult to place. We love them not, save in the right setting, and the goldcrests which visit us share our views, for their whispered appreciations, both at nesting-time and in winter, are rarely heard in any conifers but those of the deepest green. But with the blues it is a different story. Their charm is irresistible and they will fit in almost anywhere and never disregard the canons of good taste. Always first among these is *Cedrus atlantica glauca*, and if our specimen is a mere stripling of thirty feet we were fortunate in securing a really good blue. Rising against the Lawson's sombre umbrage, the cool glacier emerald of its spire and minarets seems to suit the delicate grace of line and leaf with that perfect accord one sees in frosted gossamer, while in the little fellows what is so blue as *Juniperus squamata Meyeri*?

Abies Lowiana glauca, *A. nobilis glauca* and *A. Pinsapo glauca* are also among the more striking of the maturer blue-leaved members of rather a juvenile collection of conifers. But a further reference is due to *Cupressus Lawsoniana Wisselii* and *Allumii*, for both are good blue-greens of columnar style. The former's curiously short, tufted and contorted branchlets are distinctly attractive and it grows so slowly that a specimen of thirty years old is still only about fifteen feet high and flowers regularly. Yet one more of the more adult conifers must be noted and that is *Cryptomeria japonica* which was started with the Lawsons in the early days. There is something of the dignity of *Sequoia gigantea* in the erect and stately bearing of the red-brown stem, the droop of the branches and their bunchy, up-turned tips of lively grass-green in this fine tree and it makes a most imposing pyramid. Here in the humid west it is particularly happy, but it seems to prosper under any conditions that suit Douglas fir and Monterey cypress. A more handsome and satisfactory tree in every way than *C. j. var. elegans* which is more often planted.

Later additions to our coniferous family include that crowning triumph of the genus, *Abies Forrestii* (or is it *Delavayi?*) a silver-fir of peerless distinction, the beautiful *Picea Breweriana*, an eight-foot coffin juniper making a foot each year, *Fitzroya patagonica*, moss-green and supremely elegant and *Taiwania cryptomerioides*. These newcomers and others are no more than a few feet in height and some are still on their trial here. But the youth of these things matters little to us, nor does the fact that posterity will enjoy their maturity ever shadow the pleasure they give us. It has often been said that it takes two generations to make a garden, but I am confident that the greater satisfaction comes not to those who succeed to the work of others but to those who do the initial spadework. However, we are content, and more than content, with our little trees, and in these saplings of forest giants there is a charm and intimacy so delightful, a responsiveness and hopefulness so encouraging, that we shall plant and go on planting so long as we can wield a tool and space allows.

Winter is parade day, not only to conifers, but to all ever-greens, the one season in which their welcome verdure stands out in pleasing contrast to the grey of naked boughs and those harmonies of rusty fern and fallen leaf which carpet the woodland floor. And I might fill this chapter with a running commentary on the burnished grandeur of the winter holly, that 'vulgar but incomparable tree', which was to old John Evelyn, as it ought to be to every one of us, the best of all broad-leaved ever-greens. I might extol the peculiar beauty of the tree-heaths' moss-green plumes, more especially those of *Erica lusitanica*,

Veitchii and *arborea alpina*, the dusky green with which the orange-berried stranvaesias are draped, the highly polished, coral-beaded wreaths of *Danaë Laurus* and the appeal of the bamboos whose pennoned wands, so matchless in grace of line and gentle movement, seem to invoke the garden peace with the caress of their silken rhythm.

That bonnie little evergreen, *Azara microphylla* might also be roped-in to this eulogy, the flash of its deep green, well-glossed leaves accorded their meed of praise along with metallic oleasters and sage-green cistuses, viburnums and berberis. The many greens of the dwarf ericas, flushed with the rusty-red of their withered bells, as well as those heaths with silver, coppery, orange and rose-tipped foliage could claim no slight notice. Even the common cherry-laurel, most abused of evergreens, might be applauded with so much eloquence that people who have the space, which we have not, would be inspired to grow it unmolested until it became a noble woodland tree, unsurpassed in symmetry and in winter without a rival in its own peculiar green.

But I must pass on. *Arbutus Menziesii* is at its best to-day. Its leaning stem, rising to thirty feet, is a warm terra-cotta red, soft and smooth as kid. This beautiful stem, with the equally red branches, makes a most effective contrast with the large bright green leaves gleaming in the thin sunlight. The tree flowers but does not fruit in our humid glen as it does with more openness and a harder life. It is too much occupied in growing, often making two or three feet in a favourable season. But the madrona, which Bret Hart saw as a sylvan masquerader in scarlet hose and Robin Hood cloak, is nevertheless one of the goodliest of our winter trees. A hybrid arbutus (probably *A. Unedo + Andrachne*) which stands near the Californian, reaching to about half its height, rather loses by the presence of so distinguished a comrade. Even so, it is handsome enough with its bold foliage and rough cinnamon bark to embarrass one's view of Robin Hood.

The placing of these two trees too close together was one of those errors for which most gardeners must repent at some time or other. Easy enough would the remedy be were one of the two so inferior that it could be spared without a wrench.

But when, as in this instance of the arbutus trees, neither of which could be sacrificed lightly, I am invited to deliver a sort of Solomon's judgement as a way out of the dilemma, no glamour of judicial dignity fills my anguished soul. Once we did decide to fell the hybrid and in a moment of rash but dauntless intrepidity I declared myself able and willing to do the deed. In any event, I would hold the coat of Prometheus while he acted as executioner. But when the hour appointed approached the Lady of the Garden, who had promised to second me with moral support, could not be found. She had suddenly realised that she had an engagement with the mountains to fulfil—well, there the story ends for the tree still stands, a living testimony to the folly of injudicious planting, an evergreen reminder that some mistakes can, by their very inadvertency, be rather comforting.

Few trees are more delightful at any season than the eucalypti, but it is in winter that they excel. Here *E. Gunnii* has shot up to thirty-five feet since the last severe frost gave it a setback. It flowers and fruits freely and its slender spire of drooping boughs and quivering silvery leaves is the last word in delicate grace. Other kinds, including *E. pauciflora* and *Cambagii*, are getting along so nicely one's feelings that many of these beautiful trees are much hardier than they are supposed to be are gathering proof year by year. Eucalypti grow so rapidly and are so charming in their youthful stages—often more so than when grown-up—that one gladly takes the risk of loss. And so it is with the mimosas, so fascinating in the forms and colours of their leaves, so unsurpassed in easy poise. *Acacia dealbata* may only be able to carry its buds through two or three winters out of five here, but even so it would always pay the rent. And that *A. Baileyana*, with its still more beautiful foliage, is going to be even more trustworthy we have some reason to hope, for a stripling of nine feet has just given us six weeks of lovely blossom.

Another evergreen of the not-too-hardy list which we value highly is *Escallonia macrantha*. There may be better ones as flowering shrubs—most of them owing their primary merits to this species—but *E. macrantha* wears such a full and generous green, its aromatic gum is so delicious as you brush past it, that it must take precedence as a winter shrub. *Piptanthus tomentosus* is also singularly attractive when the colder season brings out the silver down which swaddles leaf and twig. *Cytisus Battandieri* may run this Chinese laburnum close in leaf colour and eclipse it as a flowering shrub, but the latter has for long been very pleasant at this season up against the sombre green of another evergreen of quality, *Eucryphia cordifolia*—loveliest of all our autumn blooming trees. And we get a like contrast where the emerald and white of *Teucrium fruticans* is clambering over a wall draped by the dark verdure of *Vitis striata*.

Guevina Avellana is a distinguished-looking evergreen which an old botanist visitor, momentarily dropping his scientific attitude, described as 'a well-dressed shrub', and it is. Our specimen is only some six feet or so. It has never been injured by frost (even 25 degs.) and its broad and handsome pinnate leaves, often well over a foot long and of a rich glossy green and good texture, together with the golden-brown fur which clothes the young shoots and a stately carriage, make this Chilian a most imposing tree even as a youngster. Its relations, the lomatias, have also been so far hardy. *L. obliqua* with its large, ovate leaves of a slightly greyish green with red stalks, midribs and twigs, has never flinched under the severest tests and to wind it seems indifferent. *L. ferruginea*, having deeply and much divided leaves of a full-toned rusty olive green, is even more attractive as an evergreen. We have not had this nearly so long as *obliqua*, but it is evidently hardy and at Bodnant annually produces an abundance of its curious golden-buff and crimson flowers. With still more narrowly cut greygreen leaves is *L. tinctoria* which has defied some punishing winters and yielded its creamy white flowers every spring.

It is, of course, disrespectful to the big guns of authority, the nursery lists and all that, to regard not the warnings given us about the tenderness of shrubs. But we put out pretty well anything, that is, which is not generally recognised as hopeless in the open. And if we have often got our reward in the way of a prompt loss during the first frost, we have, on the other hand, been able to grow successfully quite unprotected many a shrub which is not even attempted in gardens with a milder climate than ours.[1]

Winter-worthiness, it seems, is largely a matter of soil, especially drainage, and there are possibly other factors which no one knows anything about. Plants generally regarded as useless outdoors may be seen flourishing in one garden, while in another where conditions appear to be much more favourable they are a failure. And this is not one of those instances in which a plant, grown with full exposure to all the elements and no coddling protection, so hardens its tissues that it is better able to resist frost and biting winds. Other influences seem to be at work. Wherefore, in the absence of any reliable guide on the subject, and holding on to the conviction that you never know, within reasonable limits, how plants—especially the untried—will behave, we shall continue to indulge in experiment. After all, gardening is fundamentally empirical. Our vast stores of knowledge, our sum of experience, the very foundations of the colossal horticultural temple which we have built up have all been acquired by trying it on the dog.

Now for a final paragraph or two on rhododendrons in winter. To anyone who grows these fascinating shrubs in any quantity the season is filled with interest. At no other time does their foliage exert such a pronounced effect upon the garden, whether it is the little ones crowding the open places like heaths, the species and hybrids of more average size which fringe the woodland, or the big-leaved kinds which assert their claim to the denser shades. In all of these leaf colour and leaf form are to-day at the peak of their beauty and then, along with these, one enjoys the excitement of looking-out for the evidences of incipient growth and flower, of watching the development of blossoms which, in not a few of the newer seed-raised plants, have yet to see for the first time the light of an English sky.

The years rush on as if even they had been caught up in the whirl of speed which possesses the earth, but we do not forget the thrill with which, after long waiting, we saw, one wintry day, our first *R. orbiculare* breaking into its green flower buds.

---

[1]*Richea scoparia* and that botanical curiosity, *Baurea rubioides* have so distinguished themselves that I may, incidentally, use their names in support of that statement.

And it was only yesterday that the Lady of the Garden came along on top gear urging me to go at once to *R. Falconeri.* Fully expecting to see the noble creature blown over or perhaps about to explode from blood-pressure, I hastened to the woodland to find instead that a great flower bud, as big as a plover's egg, had appeared at the topmost shoot. To some, this may seem a matter of small moment, but when you have reared a plant like *R. Falconeri* from an eighteen-inch infant, when, after some twenty years, still without any expectancy of flowers for some considerable time, the shrub suddenly greets you with bulging signs of maturity, your feelings touch something deeper and more gratifying than exhilaration. You have achieved an immense reward, the greatest reward that a gardener can reap.

These large-leaved rhododendrons we have planted more with the object of adorning shady wood bottoms with their handsome foliage than with any hope of ever seeing them in bloom, and for such a purpose they are admirable. The massive grandeur of their leaves, which may be a yard in length, the wide diversity these leaves display in line and texture, in veining and port always excites one's admiration. Then there are their wonderful greens, dark and medium, glossy with a metallic burnish, or roughened with a mat surface, which, as often as not, have in sharp contrast the cream or rusty felting of their undersides. And if these are commanding in their dignity in winter their spring foliage, rising above the ribboned leaf scales—often an intensely bright crimson—is in not a few of them and others so exceedingly beautiful that many a rhododendron would easily earn its place did it never produce a flower.

Compare the large leaves of *R. sino-grande* with the thyme-like foliage of little *R. telmateium* and we shall have a study in contrast which borders on the grotesque. Moreover, while the former are a green of profoundest density those of the Tiny Tim are so pale and yellow a green that they gleam like gold-washed emeralds in the light of winter. But most of the lapponicums have a leaf coloration so charming and so diverse that a thicket of them at this season will rival the heaths. From the thinnest and coolest blue-greens of some of the *hippophaeoides* and *scintillans* groups to the sombre *russatum*, reddened with rusty fur, one gets an infinite variety of tones, not only of leaf but of bud and bark and hair.

Here, for example, is beautiful *R. intricatum*, a symphony of tender green, frosty emerald and dove-red, and there *R. impeditum*, its mounds of full-toned green against the distinctly hoary cloak of *fastigiatum*. *R. pemakoënse* is a tight little hummock of grass-green warmed with a glow of vermilion from its swelling buds. *R. cantabile*, rivalling *russatum* in its sullen verdure intensified by a heavy red tan, has for neighbours a company of ripariums which make amends for an indecisive green by veneering their aromatic leaves with an iridescence of silver, golden-buff and dove-grey. In striking contrast to these last are those other saluenenses, *keleticum* and *radicans*, so glossy and hard of leaf, so entirely different in their lowly habit of growth. And again in this series there is the squat little *R. calciphila* with wee leaves of an emerald so glacier cold on its hazel twigs that it gleams with a luminous radiance on a grey day. Our lepidotums, mostly comprising a collection of seedlings under number, are also all very comforting to look upon with their bronze-tinted foliage, but in the beautiful *R. imperator* this breaks off into a mat of dark, highly-burnished green. And again, one gets in that queer little plant, *R. myrtilloides*, of another series, a close dense mat of lustrous plum-red.

Then there are the distinguished members of the sub-series Haematodes, of which a seed-raised family group of *R. chaetomallum* K.W. 6805 is singularly handsome in its winter dress. In these the large and raspy leathery leaves are an olive green of the richest dye, their undersides felted with a rusty-red which in some forms glows with a fiery hue. The twigs are bristly with red-brown hairs and in these, intensified to a chestnut verging on vermilion, are the shaggy buds wrapped. Almost as striking in foliage are some forms of the same species of Forrest's collecting, notably *R. c. var. glaucescens* and *var. hemigynum*, the vivid iron-mould of the leaf undersides appearing as if it shone through the green of the polished surfaces. In strange contrast to these and the type *R. haematodes*, as opulent in foliage as it is in flower, is the thin glaucous lettuce-green of the leaves of *R. erileucum*, a triflorum with underparts of a vivid chalky white. Again, here is a *R. floccigerum* of Forrest's whose narrow, cucumber-green leaves are nearly as white underneath as the last and tufted with little nubbles of golden brown like bits of sponge. Near-by is what promises to be hardy *Boothii*, a *R. deleiense* of Kingdon Ward's, whose curiously thick-stalked, strap-shaped leaves, a medium, lustrous green above, are under-stained with a rosy-tinted violet-powder, and to this you may add a touch of mahogany-crimson lipstick to pedicels and buds.

R. Bainbridgeanum may be a dull creature alongside some of the foregoing, but his plain bottle-green, rather soiled under-clothing and unshaven stubble have earned for him the distinction of being 'the ugliest rhododendron in China', which is something. This dismal individual has a half-brother under number whose clothes are marked by the cut of a rather better tailor and he is a little less seamy in the epidermis, but a *Bainbridgeanum* he remains. It is not quite nice of them, but one cannot get away from the impression that some of Bainbridgeanum's companions do not hesitiate to turn his misfortunes to their gain. But for the grace of God there go I, you can hear them say—and not without reason, for compare Bainbridgeanum's most commendable efforts with that of his next neighbours, *R. Fargesii* and *cyclium*, with *R. Souliei*, *Williamsianum* or *orbiculare*, *Thomsonii*, *Fortunei* or *campylocarpum*. Not only in leaf colour but in leaf shape do these blazon their superiority. Indeed they carry a foliage that is so vivid and abundant in its healthful green, so full of quality and breeding in line and texture, so exquisite in the purity of the icy whiteness or delicate transparent verdure which films their undersides, that such shrubs as these would always earn their space and a deal more merely as evergreens.

And so one might ramble on only to be pulled up ever and anon to give, perhaps, some form of *R. glaucopeplum* a nod of recognition for its cheerful combination of cedar-red and bay-green. Here, again, is a *R. scyphocalyx* whose broad, blunt leaves, a yellow-stained green, have underparts of a nacreous white flushed with rose. There is bushy little *R. Makinoi*, its crinkly dull green leaves making amends in number for what they have lost in width. But these mere strips of leaves, rendered narrower than they need by their inrolled margins, reveal, on being turned over, a lining of exquisite apricot-fawn, soft as velvet.

Then what is there among all these, even among lacteums, whose foliage is more arresting in its charm of refinement and good taste than *R. Wightii?* The large leaves of this distinguished species are a lovely apple-green, even-toned and unpolished yet as smooth as finely-dressed leather. Their undersides, in sharp contrast, are a golden-chamois while the buds which crown the yellow-tinted green of the young shoots are sheathed in silver suede. But there are any number of these larger-leaved rhododendrons whose winter worth as evergreens deserves eulogies of praise—the decorums and discolors, *fulvum* with its sombre green lit by an under tomentum of flaming orange, and *campanulatum*, the *Aucklandii* aristocrats of which we happen to possess a few, the splendid *R. calophytum* whose leaves have an architectural beauty in line, substance and poise, and the estimable *sutchuenense*.

I am conscious, in giving so meagre a handful of names, that this magnificent genus is not being accorded the importance it merits. But the fact that I write only of what our own modest collection contains must be my plea and at that it must suffice. To wind up, however, there are one or two blue-leaved rhododendrons which must be mentioned and among these are few, if any, more beautiful than one we have labelled *R. lepidostylum*, F.24633. This lowly, spreading little bush is a distinctly better colour than others of the same birth certificate. Its silver-haired foliage, fringed with white bristles, gleams with an electric-blue luminosity in evening light or a dull day. Those beautiful old azaleodendrons, *Smithii aureum* and Glory of Littleworth, also have radiantly blue leaves which in early winter stand out with remarkable emphasis among the greens. Some forms of the excellent *R. oreotrephes*, notably the pink-flowered *R.o.* Rock 59591, are not far behind in blueness of their foliage, and the frosty lacquer which varnishes their dainty leaves contributes in no small measure to the beauty and interest of the year's darkest hours.

CHAPTER V

Hardy Heaths: Some Winter-Spring Bloomers

TO ALL the ericaceae we are wedded by an indissoluble bond. Of these, the heaths were the first to claim our homage, the first to win us over to their infinite and subtle charms, their all-the-year-round usefulness and willing adaptability. We were heather fans before we were anything else. Since the second baby came in the person of a rising temperature in rhododendrons the heaths may not have enjoyed so undivided an attention. But none can say that our loyalty to them was shaken by the appearance of a rival in the field. On the contrary, we are now, and have been for some time, planting more heaths than we have ever done. Increased space has afforded an opportunity for increased indulgence in them, and if rhododendrons and the rest of the allied genera continue to grow in numbers, as we hope they do in prosperity and virtue, the areas devoted to heaths get larger as the years pass.

A dozen good reasons might be given by way of explaining our affection for heaths. In the first place there is the peculiar fascination of their flowers, foliage and habit of growth. They have a glamour about them, a romance touched with that sense of the untamed moorlands where grouse are chuckling and curlews call, of wide spaces, sanctuaries of untroubled and abiding peace. Born of our own soil, as most of the heaths are, and associated with those aspects of nature which, in the midst of a distracted world, still seem as inviolate as a poem of Keats, they bring into our gardens something of their unspoiled purity. Yet, even though our heaths in all their varieties and forms have come to us direct from their native sod they are among the best behaved of garden plants. That final test of good manners, the apparent absence of all manners, is theirs, so that the greenest debutante from the shaggy slopes of the far north or Cornish cliff wears the same unaffected grace as those which have been for generations under garden culture. They have

43

lost nothing and gained nothing, beyond an increasing admiration, by exchanging the wild and woolly for the luxuries of an easier world.

Not many plants represented in gardens as large genera have escaped the ministrations of the hybridist, few have resisted the temptation to respond to the cultivator's zeal by diverting from their ancient tribal laws. But the heaths we grow to-day are as fresh with the breezy delights of their own mist-swept moorlands as if they had never known the softening influences of a cultured life. They are the virgin gold of nature's own mint, and so devoutly do they cling to their ancestral conservatism that the diversions of a cocktail age have no attractions for them. In the garden their racial traditions have never shown a lapse. If, among themselves, they have at remote intervals allowed the bar sinister to cross a family shield, if goings-on of a matrimonial sort have occasionally resulted in offspring which bear unmistakeable testimony to the fact that illicit unions between clan and clan have taken place, that is entirely their own affair, and their loss, if it be a loss, has been our gain.

To the unique appeal which heaths as flowering plants exert, one may add the fact that with even a moderate collection it is possible, rather, easy, to have some species or variety in flower throughout the year. Our own natives alone give us seven months of blossom, but, include the winter bloomers and the tree-heaths, and there need not be a single break in that chain of blossom with which these plants will girdle the year from January to December. That is a very great achievement for any one genus. Indeed, I know of none other which can challenge such a remarkable claim. And there is this about these heathers: Never at any season need their blooming be a half-hearted affair. At no time do their blossoms suggest by feebleness of effort that they have a difficulty in maintaining the reputation they have won. Whether it be the darkest hours of mid-winter, under the trials of a blazing August sun, or at any other moment of the year, one or other of the heaths will be giving colour in bountiful profusion.

Among the manifold uses to which heaths may be put in the garden there is none quite so satisfying as massed planting. They are sociable creatures, delighting to grow in crowded

companies from which they doubtless gain no little actual bene-
fit of a mutual co-operative nature. For a good many years we
were unable to give our plants that space and detachment which
suggests the amplitude of a heath garden. But by segregating
the various kinds on open woodland slopes and dry banks, by
running the smaller ones among the lesser shrubs of the rock-
garden and mixed borders we have found it possible to give all
species and most varieties a fair representation.

Our ambition to have a heath garden worthy of the term has
yet to be realised, but the glade has provided us with oppor-
tunities for a much fuller use of our favourites than ever we
were able to attempt in previous days. We can now grow the
tree-heaths in groups large enough to do them justice. We can
satisfy the desires of the callunas for a loam that never gets
really dry, which was rarely possible on the hotter slopes.
Erica Tetralix and its hybrids can be disposed with liberality as
a ground-work for magnolias and other trees where the soil is
still stiffer and cooler. *E. vagans* and *carnea* can be invited to
create broad drifts of foliage and colour and thus afford pleasing interludes between the taller shrubs and trees which abut
upon the main sweep of lawn.

Now this massing of heaths brings me to another virtue that
may be claimed for this engaging family. I refer to the fact that
heaths are among the greatest labour savers that ever came into
a garden. Not only do they prosper with a minimum of cultural
attention, taking entire care of themselves for an unlimited
period, but they keep down weeds. Once your heaths have all
but covered the ground hoe and cultivator may be hung up for
good so far as they are concerned. For so dense is the foliage of
most of them that they will soon smother any weed venture-
some enough to invade their territory. Fertilisers, mulches and
the like they never need, pruning is seldom required, and so
permanent are they that an old and worn-out heath garden is as
rare an object as a dead donkey. Blessed are the labour savers
in any garden ; in one such as ours which is very largely kept
going by our two selves they are thrice blest.

One word on the matter of soil. There is no doubt, whatsoever, that a few years ago many people were deterred from
growing heaths because they had been led to believe that peat

was an essential to success. But that old idea having been exploded, these plants have steadily increased in popularity among gardeners of all kinds. We have learned that they actually do better in a free, medium to light loam than ever they did in peat, and since the most casual observation of heaths in the wild will at once disclose the fact that very few of them grow in peat if they can get anything else one wonders how the notion became disseminated.

Given such a loam as I have described, the highest possible results can be obtained with heaths with practically no expenditure beyond ordinary cultivation. But one thing is very desirable and that is a nice friable tilth, and it should, in most soils and situations, be given something that will tend to increase and maintain the friability, or texture, and at the same time retain moisture in dry weather. Up to a few years ago we relied on leaf mould and decayed vegetable refuse to achieve those ends. But ever since sorbex came on to the market we have used it almost entirely, not, be it known, because it is a peat but because it is probably the most efficient moisture absorber and retainer in the shape of humus ever manufactured in the laboratories of nature or anywhere else. Being composed of sphagnum moss in a state of arrested decomposition this is not surprising, nor will it be surprising to anyone who knows anything of sphagnum to learn that this moss peat is infinitely more durable in the ground than almost any other available form of humus.

We have used it for breaking-up and warming a cold and cloddy clayey loam, and it has been worked in to very light and hot sandy slopes which, without it, quickly dried-out in summer, and after three or four years the moss peat in these soils was still there, still doing its good work. But I must say no more, or I will be credited with having an 'interest' in sorbex. (I only wish I had!) My object at the moment is to draw attention to a principle as much as to any particular factor in the promotion of that principle, and in chanting the praises of sorbex I do so with a sense of no little gratitude for having come across a weed-free, pest-free material which has in so many ways helped us to attain what we are all seeking—the best possible results for the least outlay, especially in labour.

While there are good reasons for regarding the heaths as xerophytic plants, our experience teaches us that it is the exotic rather than the native species which are the more suitable for growing on hot and arid, sun-beaten banks of thin soil. *Erica cinerea* in all its many varieties is a great drought resister. Once it has covered the ground it will endure the most grilling tests. And *E. vagans*, having got its roots well dug in, is nearly as good. But even these do not seem to be able to stand up to such severe ordeals as *E. carnea* or the tree heaths, to which no soil is too parched, no sun too fierce. *Calluna vulgaris*, the well-loved ling of Scotland, is, as I have suggested, impatient of dryness and a burning root-run. It will put up with it, but until we were able to give it the deep, sandy, often stony loam of the glade garden we never enjoyed such splendid growth, such bountiful sprays of blossom. Here we have had the magnificent *C. v. Alportii* well over three feet high, emerald-leaved *Serlei*, the finest of the whites, only a little less, whilst that other excellent white heather, *C. v. Hammondii*, has equalled *Alportii* in stature and flower trusses.

Then what suits the callunas will suit *E. ciliaris* and *Tetralix*. Indeed, these appreciate still cooler conditions at the root, and if, as happens occasionally where such conditions prevail, frost is apt to pinch the former, there are the hybrids to fall back upon. To these hybrids between the Dorset and the cross-leaved heath I have already alluded. They are 'nature's bastards' but, none the less, plants of exceptional value in the garden. This because they give us in happy mixture the delicate grace of *E. ciliaris* with the indestructible hardiness of the other. Their flowers, if a little smaller than those of the Dorset heath at its best, are larger than those of most dwarfs and, beginning earlier, they maintain a prolific crop of bloom into late autumn. Even as I am writing, with the first blooms of *E. carnea* telling us Christmas is fast approaching, some broad plantings of the admirable H. Maxwell, *Watsonii* and Dawn still have their downy green freely dappled with their cheerful rose-lilac bells.

The numerous named varieties of heaths now available have already been dealt with in detail in some of my books, and those nurserymen who specialise in these plants issue such complete descriptions of them that I do not intend to strain the reader's patience by repeating them all here. But, while some of the newer introductions certainly demand notice, continued experience with others has, in some cases, yielded results that I think might be a helpful addition to this commentary.

We always regard late autumn as the opening date of our heather season. It is then that *E. hybrida darleyensis* first flecks its sombre green with shell-pink, but the earliest varieties of *E. carnea* follow on so quickly that hummocks of Winter Beauty and Queen Mary will be flushed with pink before the end of the year. After these comes the splendid King George, probably the finest rich red, mid-winter variety, to link up in early spring with *atrorubra*. This last is a prodigious bloomer, the spikes are long, the colour a peculiarly brilliant crimson-carmine and it will continue flowering until spring is well advanced. *Atrorubra* is so good that if we were ever doomed to grow but one *E. carnea* I think this would be our choice.

E. c. Vivellii, sent out by Messrs. Ruys of Dedemsvaart in 1925, must not be passed by, for its deep green foliage (bronzed in winter), dwarf habit and rich red flowers together form a make-up that gives it a place by itself among these heaths. Then there is another which, ushered in under the name of Urville, so closely resembles *Vivellii* that I should not like to have to decide which was which. Indeed one wonders whether there may not be some truth in the story that the plant originally called Urville was actually intended to be labelled 'Vivellii', but its sponsor wrote so badly that the name was deciphered as 'Urville'! More impossible things have happened. However, *Vivellii* has a successor which, though fashioned upon the same model, is distinguished enough and good enough to merit a place in any collection. This is Ruby Glow and that name it earns, for the flowers, larger than those of *Vivellii* and more flagon-shaped, are a warm yet bright ruby-red. It blooms throughout the early spring.

There are, of course, too many named coloured varieties of this winter heath. Several of them are so much alike, no one being able to tell 'tother from which, that it would be no great loss were one-half of the so-called Backhouse Hybrids (which are not hybrids at all) eliminated from the lists. We should still have left a selection of first-rate varieties capable of giving us an unbroken sequence of all the outstanding colours from November to May.

The only weak point in *E. carnea* up to a few years ago was its white variety, *E. c. alba*, a feeble affair and quite unworthy of the species. Then from the Broadstone Nurseries came the greatly improved white, Cecilia M. Beale, with larger blossoms and more of them in generous spikes held well erect. But Cecilia was destined to have her nose put out of joint by an infinitely superior white which was first issued by Mr. John Stormonth of Kirkbride bearing the name of Springwood.

This remarkable heath, certainly the most important addition made to the carnea group for a long time, was found by a lady in Italy some years ago. I hesitate to be more informative, both as regards the lady's name and the place of her discovery for obvious reasons. But this much of the plant's history may be added: When it was found—quite accidentally—some sprays were sent to Mr. F. J. Chittenden (then Director of the Wisley Gardens) for identification. He at once pronounced it to be the finest white *E. carnea* yet seen and bestowed upon it the name of Springwood after the lady's house in Scotland.

E. c. Springwood is a heath of splendid vigour with a bright green foliage and spikes of six to eight inches closely packed with blossoms. These flowers, slightly yellow in bud, are a dead white with chocolate anthers and, being fully half-an-inch long, they rival in length, as they do in fullness, the best of the coloured forms. The flowering spikes, moreover, are held upright and yielded with extraordinary profusion. Our plants are at their best from early February to the end of March, and here I must put in a good word for the deposed Cecilia. It has been suggested that the latter would be entirely superseded by Springwood. But, superior in every way as the newer variety indubitably is, Cecilia flowers so much earlier (at least two or three weeks) that there is room for both. Further, C.M.B. is such a dwarf compared with her Italian rival that she can be used in a variety of ways for which the other would be less suitable.

Since the coming-out of Springwood a coloured *E. carnea* appeared as a seedling in the Scottish garden referred to. As this stray was found close to a clump of the original Springwood it is believed to be a seedling from that variety. Sent to Wisley for propagation, this plant appears to have been labelled Springwood Pink to distinguish it from the other, upon which the true Springwood began to be known as Springwood White. Later on the latter was put up for an Award of Merit at Vincent Square under that name, and having secured that honour, it has since had the appendage 'White' attached to its baptismal name. This change may have struck some of us as undesirable and unnecessary, but there it is. Springwood Pink promises to be a fine heath in every way worthy of its forerunner.

Late autumn brings *E. lusitanica* into flower and there is nothing more beautiful than this. Taking foliage and habit of growth into consideration, as well as blossom, we should be hard put to place any of the taller heaths above this one in garden value. And because it is always so pleasing, whether in flower or not, always so fresh and delightful in its delicate verdure and finely plumose branches, always so adaptable, cheerful and well looking, we grow *E. lusitanica* in various ways. It is grouped in open woodland, on dry sunny slopes and serves as a background for some of the dwarf heaths of the glade. As to its hardiness, it has here withstood over 20 degrees of frost with no more than slight injury to the tips, those plants which are grown hard, quite in the open, being especially resistant.

The cylindrical bells (those of *E. arborea* are globular) of *E. lusitanica* are slightly fragrant and a dead white. But as the unopened buds are red, the style and stamens a vivid pink, a shrub in full bloom has its whiteness warmed by a rosy flush. Commencing with a few open flowers in November, this splendid heath gathers an increasing loveliness with every spell of mild weather until late spring when the bushes will be sheeted with bloom. Under average conditions we expect to get at least seven months of blossom from *E. lusitanica*, an achievement rarely equalled by any other shrub. Then there is this also to be placed to the credit of the Portuguese heath: It does its own propagating by yielding self-sown seedlings. These are hardy, independent little things, so well able to take care of themselves that *E. lusitanica* has become naturalised over wide areas in Southern England.

E. Veitchii, originated many years ago at the nurseries of

ERICA CARNEA var. SPRINGWOOD
*The finest white carpeting heath and one of the most beautiful of all
the E. carnea group*

ERICA AUSTRALIS var. MR. ROBERT

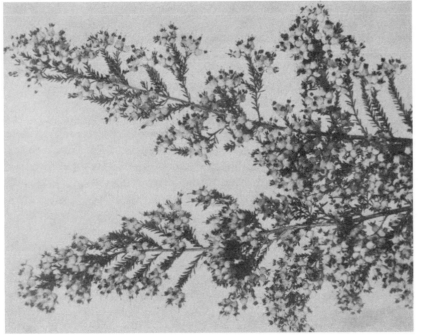

ERICA UMBELLATA

Messrs. Veitch of Exeter, is doubtless a hybrid between the foregoing and *E. arborea*. It is almost identical with *lusitanica* in its rose-flushed flowers, but is more of a spring bloomer. The beautiful fox-tail branches are the same delicious green but perhaps a trifle looser in growth. Some consider it hardier than *lusitanica*, which it may be, and the flowers it bears with equal freedom are certainly more sweetly scented. *E. arborea*, the most tree-like of all these taller heaths, is a noble plant when fully mature and the rich vanilla fragrance of its abundant blossoms is given with prodigal liberality. One hesitates to make comparisons where so fine a shrub as this is concerned. But the slightly ashen tint that pervades its flowers and the smoke-grey which often dulls the green (more pronounced in some forms than others) of its foliage rather detract from the appearance of *E. arborea* as compared with the two just mentioned and the form known as *E. a. alpina*.

The latter, which comes from high altitudes in Spain, is a more erect shrub of closer, more stocky, build. Its denser leafage is a strong grass-green and the sweetly-fragrant flowers it yields so freely in spring are a purer white than those of the type. *E. a. alpina* does not often get much above six or seven feet, and whereas *E. arborea* is certainly rather to the tender side for bleak districts, its alpine understudy, which seems deserving of specific rank, is as hardy as an oak. Fifteen years ago, when the mercury dropped to zero, this excellent heath came through the ordeal without a wince, and that in various parts of the country. For all these reasons *E. a. alpina* must be regarded as superior to the type for general planting. We still keep our old bushes of the latter, including some with distinctly rosy-white flowers raised from cuttings brought from the French Riviera, but all future plantings of the species will be confined to *alpina*.

Grouped along with the above heaths we have that charming miniature *E. mediterranea* known as Brightness. I should place this high up among the best of heaths for it makes a shapely, rounded shrublet of two or three feet with a deep green foliage, while the flowers are a full-toned rosy-red, keen and bright. These sweeten the winds of spring with that honied fragrance so characteristic of the six-foot type which, by the way, attains its top note of splendour in the variety *superba*. The white-flowered *mediterranea*, also much dwarfer and denser and darker in foliage than the typical species, is a prolific bloomer often starting before March is in. We find it makes a useful companion for Brightness, but as the only white-flowered heath of its stature (about two feet) and season the services one can claim from it are many.[1]

With heaths as with other things—with gardening itself—there is always some Parnassus whose heights, holding unattainable treasures, for ever beckon to us in the valley below. One might fondly believe that all the hardy heaths, of Europe at any rate, had found their way into our gardens long ago. But it is not so. There are, I am convinced, good forms yet to be found and, as for species, we are only now getting the beautiful *E. umbellata* established and *E. multiflora* we have only just acquired. True, many a good half-crown has been spent on plants alleged to be the latter species, but these all turned out to be *mediterranea* or something else. Oddly enough, I am inclined to think that a heath recently acquired may be *E. multiflora*, though under quite another name, but time must give proof of this. If it, too, turns out a deception we shall pack up for Southern France, make a raid on the strongholds of *multiflora* and bear it home in triumph. There are places on that sunny coast where this species ranges as widely as heather on a Scottish moor, where we have seen it sweep across the rocky slopes, a stain of crimson against the pansy-blue sea. There are reasons to believe that *E. multiflora* may prove a good limestone heath.

The Mediterranean slope has, however, given us one good heath which is, or was, something of a novelty. This is a winter flowering form of the Scottish ling, and we have called it *Calluna vulgaris hiemalis*. The plant our strain came from was found flowering in early February on the coast of the Var. Cuttings brought back with us did all that was expected of them and we now have a stock of plants which, about eighteen inches high, carry a profusion of pale lilac spikes from the end of November onwards. Severe frost not intervening, this show is maintained

[1]We have just had the new white *mediterranea*, W. T. Rackliff, a two-foot shrub with exceptionally fine blooms, a plant of great promise.

until well into the early year and the plants make a charming link of colour between the latest of the autumn and the first of the winter flowering species already mentioned.

Since this bantling of ours made its debut other winter blooming callunas have appeared. Mr. W. J. Marchant has one—much like ours but slightly earlier—and then came Mr. Ingwersen with a star performer he happed upon in Portugal. In colour this form is rosier than ours, but its most striking feature is the length of the flowering spikes which, entirely unbranched, may be over twenty inches in length, beautifully tapered and arching and flowered from base to tip. Put up at Vincent Square this conquering hero of the winter lings secured the Award of Merit, its name being officially sanctioned as *Calluna vulgaris elegantissima* and most elegant it certainly is.

CHAPTER VI

Hardy Heaths: Summer and Autumn Flowering

ERICA AUSTRALIS is always in such haste to greet the spring that our bushes are often opening flower in March. This is generally acclaimed as the finest of the tree-heaths, and of the other than white it undoubtedly is, for the bells are fully one-third of an inch in length, a vivid rose pink and borne in amazing prolificacy. With every one of the little side sprigs, which bristle along the yard-long growths of the previous year, tipped with blossoms, usually in fours or eights, the entire branch appears as one great raceme of blossom. Indeed, this output of bloom is so copious that the branches are much inclined to flop over even when grown with full exposure, and this is the only failing—not a grievous one—that we can place against this handsome species.

The hardiness of *E. australis*, which comes from Southern Spain, appears to offer support to the statements already made that you never really know how winter-proof a plant is until you have tried it. Years ago, acting on the advice of authorities, we used to treat *E. australis* as if it were little hardier than a Cape heath. But time proved that all our fuss and anxiety had been expended for nothing, since *E. australis* is able to endure our winters quite as well as any of the tree-heaths. As a matter of fact frosts which have mortally wounded *E. arborea* and singed the moss-green fur of *lusitanica* have left not a trace of injury upon this species here. It may, of course, be possible that plants of earlier introductions were more tender than those distributed later. The former, being frequently cut back or lost, would give the species a bad name. It would be starred in the nursery lists as one needing winter protection, and writers would recommend it only for the most genial south-western counties. All this would be quite enough to explain why so beautiful a shrub was with us for something like 150 years before it began to be planted generally in gardens. Indeed, I am inclined to think that there is something more than conjecture in this, for if I am not greatly mistaken the plants of the old days—which certainly were rather tender from what one can gather—were of a different model to those seen to-day, the difference being most apparent in the wider-mouthed, fuller corolla.

However this may be the *E. australis* we grow to-day is a superb garden shrub, a rapid grower and good doer in any average light loam with full openness, and the white Mr. Robert is worthy of it. There are some who contend that this variety is hardier than the type, but our experience is just the contrary. If we get frost severe enough the tender tips of this white heath may get injured, whereas those of the typical plant escape untouched.

It was Lieutenant Robert Williams, a son of Mr. J. C. Williams of Caerhays Castle, who first discovered this white *E. australis*. That was in 1912, and it took him ten days hard searching over the hills of Algeciras to find it. At Caerhays this heath is now, I am told, nine or ten feet high and, having proved its merits as a first-rate garden shrub—undoubtedly one of the most beautiful and largest flowered of all the white tree-heaths—it has found its way into every garden where choice shrubs are appreciated. The story of the introduction of this plant is unhappily touched by grief for Lieutenant Williams never saw the fruits of his discovery established on English soil. The Great War took him and he was killed near Loos in the autumn of 1915. Since he was known as 'Mr. Robert' when a young man at home the Kew authorities decided to commemorate his name by attaching it to the shrub he introduced.

Erica Tetralix, that comely little heath whose white or rosy waxen bells and glaucous leafage are generally seen occupying the more boggy parts of our moorlands is one of our favourites among the dwarfs. It does not need bog and will often put up with fairly dry slopes of light soil. But we please it best by giving it raised-up places above water, yet near enough to the latter to enable its roots to reach constant moisture. The *mollis* varieties of this heath are all very charming and they are usually the first of the natives to flower. Pink Glow is one of the most attractive, the clustered heads of shell-pink hovering over a foliage of silver filigree. Silver Bells, with an even clearer pink, is new but full of promise, and an old friend we should not like to be without is *Lawsoniana*. I strongly suspect a hybrid influence in this last, but that matters not; it is a dense, lowly grower and its blush-pink, short-legged flower clusters over its rug of frosty emerald make a combination of rare beauty.

Although *E. Tetralix* will often be in flower in early May it carries on pretty well all summer, even into autumn, that is provided it gets enough to drink. Before it has touched its top note *E. cinerea* opens fire, always beginning here with some old plants of the deep blood-red, very dwarf *coccinea*. *E. c. atrosanguinea*, also small and compact, runs the latter close in colour but it is rather later. In both of these the blooms are enriched by a touch of orange-scarlet which is uncommon in heaths. Another splendid dwarf is Mrs. Dill which covers its little hummock of deep-toned green with bright carmine-cerise bells. This is such a good bloomer, so neat in growth and so pure in colour that it has here superseded the larger Frances, but I rather think the new Startler will prove a serious rival even for Mrs. Dill.

In mid-season pinks *E. cinerea* is abundantly provided. For the old *rosea* we still find a place, but Rose Queen, with even finer spikes and an all-summer display is better. This and the ruby-red *atrorubens* are probably the finest of all the pink to red bell-heathers, the latter continuing its non-stop production until November frosts call a halt. C. D. Eason, a ruby-red of a deep, warm tint, is a variety which we should place in the shortest selection, and of those which still wear the family blue in their red is P. S. Patrick. As a full-blooded royal purple I know none quite so good as P. S. P. It is, indeed, so good that we have planted a drift of it on a sunny bank with a few plants of the almost white *pallida* running into it for contrast. A good white *cinerea* still being among the 'wanteds', *pallida* (or Apple Blossom) must serve as a substitute, and it goes very well along with the darker shades. Domino, with its white corollas and ebony stalks and sepals, is the best white we have, but it has not yet given us the satisfaction we anticipated. What the bell-heather does want is a plant that will do for it what Springwood has done for *E. carnea*, and that such an one exists, only awaiting some happy discoverer, one does not doubt.

Although *E. cinerea* lives cheerfully enough on some of our hottest slopes, gallantly draping ground disdained by almost every other herb and shrub, it gladly responds to more generous conditions. At the same time, and adaptable and willing as it is in a general way, there are places in our glade garden where, the loam being a little less sandy or perhaps colder in the subsoil, it has turned its face to the wall and refused to be comforted. Bell-heather has perhaps a fiercer passion for the sun than any of the British heaths. It also has a more profound horror of cold feet. But give it the happy medium, a really free soil (stony if you will) with a leaning to the dry side, and no heath will render a more generous return for so many years and that without asking a moment of your time for cultural attention.

E. umbellata, a species of south-western Europe is, as I have said, a newcomer to us and to most gardens. Its hardiness has not yet been conclusively proved here, but a colony raised from seedlings has come through some fairly sharp frosts without any complaint worth recording. In any event this is a heath so charming in its pale green, linear leafage, in its lax and graceful manner of growth and beautiful sprays of blossom that it is worth any amount of care. It has not exceeded eighteen inches with us, growing in a free sandy loam in which *E. lusitanica* thrives, but it sprawls about with an abandon of its own and flowers with unrestrained freedom during May and June. The flowers of *umbellata*, borne in clusters at the tips of short laterals, often in twos, fours or eights as in *E. australis*, differ from those of most heaths in being almost globular. They are abruptly and much contracted at the mouth, from which protrudes a wisp of purple-tipped stamens. In nature the colour of *E. umbellata* varies considerably, even to white, but we had the good fortune to make a start with the Bodnant strain in which the corollas are a lovely shade of pink, bright and pure in tone and without a trace of blue. It was a Bodnant plant which won the Award of Merit for this species in the spring of '34. *E. umbellata* comes freely from seed, it strikes readily and rooted cuttings grow away with remarkable liveliness. Our seed-raised plants have all retained the parental colour.

The callunas, of which the winter bloomers have been mentioned, are our great stand-by in heaths during the later summer. Coming into colour towards the end of July they increase in splendour for at least two months and flower well into autumn. Even then, and throughout the winter, the faded flowers which bleach to shades of grey-white, buff and hazel-brown are very attractive, especially in such dark-leaved kinds as *C. vulgaris Hammondii* and *Alportii*. Reference has already been made to some of the taller of these and to their appreciation of moisture during summer in particular. But the lings are a sturdy, thrifty, uncomplaining folk, always ready to make the best of their circumstances and so steadfast in their duty towards God and man that it is obvious they have lost nothing in piety by their association with Scotland. Still, if ever we do have to plant them on ground that may be rather dry for a thirsty race we bear in mind the advice that Cromwell gave to his soldiers before crossing a river. He suggested that while it would be well to put their trust in the Almighty it was up to them to keep their powder dry! That is to say, instead of relying wholly upon the natural resourcefulness of these plants in places where they may feel the pinch of drought, we start them off with an equipment for water storage, a generous lacing of porridge in the form of sorbex.

None of the heaths are so prolific in variations from the type as *Calluna vulgaris*. There are, indeed, so many named kinds in the lists—especially whites—which closely resemble one another that any attempt to sort them out would soon land me in the institution in which the compiler of Bradshaw took refuge. I have already referred to the superb *Serlei*—the choicest of the white heathers—and to *Hammondii*, another grand white. But as the latter is an early bloomer and the former one of the latest the pair afford an illustration of the wisdom of growing both. Mair's Variety (mid-season) is another admirable white in this section, a plant of near three feet putting up a great crop of erect, finely-tapered spires of unusual length and snow-white. Then there are lots of much smaller whites, *pumila*, *rigida* and *tenella*, all being cheerful little plants for a foreground or the late summer rock garden.

C. v. C. W. Nix is said to challenge *Alportii* in the depth of its red, but this novelty is still on trial and it does not look like making so tall a shrub as the older one. The low-growing Mullion must be ranked among the peers of the lowlier carpeting callunas, for it is twiggy and close in habit and the freely-branched spikes are busily packed with lilac-pink flowers. The taller, but semi-prostrate, *tenuis* with its maze of slender interlacing branchlets still earns its keep among the more crimson and dwarf varieties, and from *Serlei* one may often pick up coloured seedlings of beauty and distinction. These, while inheriting the growth and leafage of their parent, bear rosy or purple flowers and some of them have been named and listed by specialist nurserymen of enterprise.

A calluna variety which always attracts attention here is *C. v. tomentosa*. This must not be confused with the white sometimes listed under that varietal name. It is a tall, loose but elegant plant, of Perthshire origin I think, whose leaves and stems are so densely clothed with silky hairs that the entire shrub has a smoke-grey appearance, with which the pinky-lilac flowers do not go amiss. Among other curiosities which we grow is the variety Mrs. Pat whose foliage tips are a vivid carmine in winter—rather suggesting a nasty turn of dyspepsia but not inimical to the lady's charms.

Yet another oddity is Winifred Whitley which, sent out by Messrs. Maxwell and Beale, seems to be a natural child of *E. cinerea* and *C. vulgaris*. I am not sure, but believe this to be the first evidence that has ever come to light of these species hybridising. Other kinds, we have seen, think lightly of lapsing from the path of virtue, but calluna has never before to my knowledge thus fallen from grace. Never had it offended against its historic family name by going off the square. But Winifred has appeared and she means to stay, and if she is not endowed with good looks she is unusually interesting for her flowers show a striking originality in not only being larger than those of either parent but they are made up of quite separate ray-like petals. Botanists regard Winifred with an interest so stimulated by curiosity that the Lady of the Garden tells me their intimacy often threatens the borderline of decorum, but I am content to leave it at that.

The most important addition made to the callunas for a long time is the double-flowered *C. v.* H. E. Beale which was introduced a few years ago by the firm just mentioned. The old double variety was, and still is, a good thing, its rosy-lavender flowers being delightful in the mass, and because it is earlier than the newcomer we shall always have hospitality for both. But H. E. Beale excels over the other in the enormous length of the flowering spikes. These may be as much as fifteen inches long, they are beautifully tapered and arched and adorned with blossom from the tip to the base, from which a crop of secondary flowering sprays shoot up. The blossoms of this magnificent heath are so closely packed with petals that, seen through a pocket lense, they look like replicas in miniature of the old pink monthly roses. The colour, if not quite a rose-pink, is very near it and it has the softness of tone one associates with some carnations. H. E. Beale is a grand heath with plenty of vigour. It is just a little late, perhaps, in this wood-girdled garden, but it begins to bloom in September and we find it makes an admirable background for drifts of *Gentiana-sino-ornata* and *G. Macaulayi*. Even after the flowers are over they retain their pinky hue and this is often noticeable until winter is far advanced.[1]

The Dorset heath (*E. ciliaris*) displays features which mark it with a distinction of its own. It is normally a trailer with long, slender and flexible branches, and the leaves, instead of being linear, as in most heaths, are ovate. These, owing to the silvery down which covers their gentle green, have a hoary appearance which makes a telling setting for the rosy bells which swing from tall, erect stems in autumn. Beautiful as it is, the average Dorset heath is not such a good garden plant as its rose-pink variety, *globosa*, and the typical white is a squinny affair compared with the excellent Stoborough. In both of these the flowers are fuller and fatter, the habit is more erect and here they always begin blooming earlier (August) than the type. Mrs. C. H. Gill, with full-toned rosy flowers, we can find a spare bed for, and then there is *Maweana*. This last, a Portuguese form, has the largest flowers of all, and these, borne on bold spikes, have in the mat of dark olive-green foliage a most effective setting for their bright rose-carmine.

[1]Among the more recent additions to this section are two dwarf double lings of the highest merit—County Wicklow, practically a miniature of H. E. Beale, and J. H. Hamilton in a pure soft pink.

E. ciliaris is a moisture lover like *Tetralix*. In fact it bears a superficial resemblance to the latter in so many ways that one is not surprised the two species are more ready to inter-marry than any other ericas. To some of the results of this union reference has already been made, but the fact that the *ciliaris* + *Tetralix* hybrids are better plants than the typical Dorset for everyday wear will bear repeating. Dawn, H. Maxwell and *Watsonii* are extremely floriferous, their bright pink flowers, in bold umbels, are large and well-rounded and the plants are better able to stand climatical extremes than *E. ciliaris*. I know of nothing of the kind quite so pleasing as these for carpeting between widely spaced trees which, like themselves, enjoy a cool root-run, and one of the most attractive features of our autumn garden this year was a broad sweep of *E.* Dawn alongside a colony of *Rhododendron hippophaeoides*. The latter broke into a shimmer of delicate mauve in early autumn, as it often will, and this colour made a most harmonious accompaniment to the bluish-pink of the heaths.

In spite of novelties and heaths of more demonstrative qualities our loyalty to *E. stricta* remains unmoved. Its peculiarly soft, medium-toned apple-green is its own, as is its stiffly erect habit, and if its terminal umbels of shell-pink in the later summer and autumn are not in the front rank, the bright foxy-red of the withered bells gives to one's winter garden a touch of warm colour that is singularly pleasing. Add to this beautiful green and rusty-red the brilliant colours—steely-blue, crimson and jet—of bullfinches, which prefer the seeds of this heath to any other, and the darkest hours of the off-season will not be lacking in inspiration.

A low hedge of *E. stricta*, growing in the most arid of dry soils, is one of the most satisfying of our heath joys. It is near the windows and to it the gay bullfinches come. But this is a hedge plant that must be carefully pruned rather than sheared. *E. vagans*, on the other hand, seems, as a hedge plant, to enjoy being clipped, to which it will respond by developing the density and firmness of yew, and the process does not greatly impair its flowering propensity.

Of all the Cornish heaths *E. vagans kevernensis*, found some years ago near St. Keverne by the late Mr. P. D. Williams, is still our choice in this species. There are, unfortunately, a good, many spurious forms of *kevernensis* going about, seed-raised masqueraders which do the reputation of the distinguished beauty no good. This fine variety has won our admiration because of its splendid length of flower spike and the exquisitely clear pink which goes so well with the lustrous, deep green foliage. Even so, one does not attempt to compare *kevernensis* with the newer Mrs. D. F. Maxwell. The latter, a really noteworthy plant, has struck out a line entirely its own, for the fine trusses of bloom are a curious, but very taking shade of rich cerise warmed by a slight suffusion of brick-red. Thus these two are so different to one another that they defy comparison and every heath grower must have both. Nor will he omit to work into his groups some plants of the excellent Lyonesse, a white of outstanding merit and distinction. Big stuff, all of these, asking abundant room so that they may make vast mounds of colour, each six to eight feet across. And one does not know what a grand autumn shrub *E. vagans* can be until it is treated in this way and given a deep sandy loam in which to develop its splendid proportions.

We recently acquired from the Donard Nursery Company a variety of *E. vagans* labelled, Miss Waterer. This is evidently close to *kevernensis* but it is reported to have even larger flower spikes. Our plants have not been sufficiently established to say more, but they inspire bright hopes and I rather think the colour will be a shade softer in tone than that of *kevernensis*. The enthusiastic heath grower of Ludgvan, whose name it bears, appears to have found the variety near her Cornish home some twenty years ago. She also made another discovery in heaths, this being what is virtually a prostrate form of the *E. vagans* + *Tetralix* hybrid, *Williamsii*, found long ago by Mr. P. D. Williams near the Lizard. This interesting variety, now called Giravas, has the same fine moss-green foliage as the other, but it grows flat, making a dense mat of beautiful verdure. The bright pink flowers on some rooted layers Miss Waterer kindly sent to us appear to me to be larger than those of *Williamsii*, perhaps nearer those of *Tetralix*. In any case, this looks like making a very useful and beautiful autumn-flowering carpeting heath.

So with the Cornish heath does one complete that cycle of

L. G. INTERVIEWS A NOVELTY AMONG THE HEATHS OF THE
ALPES MARITIMES

DABOËCIA (POLIFOLIA) CANTABRICA var. ALBA

DABOËCIA AZORICA

CALLUNA VULGARIS var. H. E. BEALE

colour and interest with which these ericas embrace the entire year. But one comes to a conclusion on the threshold of winter only to find the endless chain beginning all over again with those late-flowering callunas, the carneas and others with which these chapters opened. There is, however, still one more whose appeal for notice must not be unheard before I switch off and that is the Connemara heath, *Daboëcia polifolia*, and this is a shrub so admirable in every way that it seems fitting it should conclude my list as the good wine of the feast.

The latest edition of the Kew *Hand List* calls this plant *Daboëcia cantabrica* K. Koch. One supposes there are good reasons for upsetting recognised and established names, but this continual re-shuffling of our botanical nomenclature undoubtedly tends to aggravate the difficulties of life and it is manifestly injurious to the peaceful progress of gardening. Queer folk, our mentors the botanists, and one's devout prayer is that some day they will have decided what each plant is to be called and stick to it. To the average gardener generic and specific names are often troublesome enough, even after long use, but to eliminate from the panel of authority a good name just when the world has become accustomed to it and to substitute another (and this has been done in wholesale fashion just recently) seems to be an inversion of what is reasonable, a process that renders confusion worse confounded to the gardener. And, after all, it is the gardener and not the botanist who is mostly concerned by this matter.

Daboëcia cantabrica, to use the name resurrected from the tomb, has already suffered many vicissitudes in so far as its nomenclature is concerned. Shortly after it was first discovered in Ireland (about the year 1699) by Dr. Edward Lhwyd of the Ashmolean Museum the plant was called *Erica S. Dabeoci Hibernis* in commemoration of the Irish saint, St. Dabeoc, who seems to have lived in the fifth or sixth century. Fifty years later when Linnaeus introduced his botanical classification the species was named *Erica daboëcii* instead of *E. dabeocii* as it ought to have been. How the great classifier passed that very obvious slip we shall never know, but the error became established, for when David Don (1834) robbed the *Erica* family of this, one of its most beautiful members, and placed it in a genus of its own, he perpetuated the Linnaean spelling by calling it *Daboëcia* rather than *Dabeocia*. Now the anomalous part about all this is that while we are presumably bound by rules of botanical nomenclature established by international agreement to adhere to any name that has once been officially given—even the repetition of errors being condoned—our plant nomenclature appears to the garden mind to have been pitched into a more chaotic state than ever it has been in the history of gardening.

By way of illustrating the inviolability of the Rule of Priority in scientific nomenclature I am reminded of a story which relates how a loyal and patriotic zoologist, innocently enough, once applied the ex-German Emperor's name to a singularly loathesome marine creature. On hearing of this the 'All Highest', instead of regarding the matter as a mark of honour, was moved to ferocity and at once ordered the removal of the offending name. But it was too late. That unbending Rule of Priority no living being dare infringe and the name of the ex-Kaiser is still attached to that revolting haunter of the deep sea's slime!

St. Dabeoc's heath (observe we have for once got the English name right if the botanical one is wrong!) grows freely in Connemara where it associates with ericas and *Ulex Gallii* on many a moorland, preferring the drier slopes. The shrub is also a native of Spain where it endures severe winters on the higher altitudes of the Pyrenees. Thus in Ireland it constitutes part of that Lusitanian Flora—*Arbutus, Erica vagans* and *ciliaris* and *Saxifraga umbrosa* (London Pride)—which, so one supposes, once occupied territory, now submerged, extending from our south-westerly shores to the Iberian Peninsula.

Daboëcia differs from *Erica* but little in general appearance. Its most marked peculiarity is its habit of shedding the spent corollas intact instead of retaining them as a brown winter overcoat for the seed-vessels as other heaths do—a commendable example of thrift. It is a hardy shrub—hardy enough for most places anyway—with glossy green, rather broad, ovate leaves with white undersides. The flower spikes, often nine or ten inches long, stand erect above the well-rounded hummocks and bear from May or June onwards a profusion of unusually large, egg-shaped, drooping flowers which, in the typical species, are a beautiful bright lavender-mauve. But, handsome as the type undoubtedly is, *D. cantabrica* attains its greatest perfection in the white variety which, if you get a good form, will bear still larger flowers, more than half-an-inch in length. The whiteness of these is exceedingly pure and it is accentuated by the richer green of the leaves, and, commencing earlier (often in April) than the type, the plant will bloom continuously until December.

This white heath is one of the most precious treasures of our garden. It never gives any trouble, in the wilder parts it seeds freely—and true to colour, oddly enough—and the only help what may be called specimen plants ever get consists of the removal of the old flower spikes. The Lady of the Garden, possessing the greater fund of patience, performs this shingling operation with diligence and a pair of scissors. This event takes place usually in early spring and about an inch of the older wood is removed with the spent racemes. The plant flourishes in any of our light, lime-free soils, with full sun, and although it will put up with a deal of drought on the hottest of banks our finest results are obtained from a deep, but sandy, loam which never gets really dry.

Next in order of merit to the white daboëcia I would place the variety, *globosa*, which has the largest flowers of all. These are more cylindrical than oval, their colour is a clear rosy-mauve and they are borne on stately spires of nearly a foot in length with abundant flowering laterals at their base. Then we can always find a good and prominent place for the old purpurea, which has a dark, bronzy foliage and bells approaching a deep crimson. That oddity, bicolor, so-called because it bears blossoms of three (not two) colours—white, pink and crimson —all mixed up as if it had not yet made up its mind which it liked best, always appeals to lovers of the curious. Yet another variety is one just sent us from the Donard Nursery. Of this it is too soon to express an opinion, but there is both attractiveness and distinction in its finely-drawn, flesh-pink blossoms with their bright red sepals and pedicels. We also like the ruby-crimson coccinea, given to us by Mr. Smith of Daisy Hill, a very attractive plant, quite unlike any other.

The latest arrival in daboëcias is *D. azorica* which Mr. E. F. Warburg introduced in 1929 from the island of Pico in the Azores. Since it had proved hardy in Sir Oscar Warburg's garden near Epsom we had little doubt about its winter-worthiness here. However, so as to run no risks with the precious little stranger we put it in a snug spot on the higher ground of the old garden where dwell other treasures not yet to be trusted on the lowlier levels where lurks the

> ... *envious, sneaping frost,*
> *That bites the first-born infants of the spring.*

There the plant has done well, coming through an exceedingly trying winter, with 18 degrees of frost, without a complaint.

D. azorica looks like making a denser, more prostrate plant than *D. cantabrica*. Its leaves are smaller and blunter, distinctly silky and felted with white on the undersides, and the flowers, egg-shaped, a quarter-inch long and carried in erect racemes of four to ten blossoms, are a deep red-crimson without a trace of purple.

One more recent arrival must be given a brief notice and that is *Erica Pageana*. Not having had any real success with *E. canaliculata* we were rather mistrustful of trying this S. African. But on the strength of Mr. W. J. Marchant's experience with it a plant of *Pageana* has been installed, and those gardener's hopes which so rarely admit defeat are centred upon this beautiful heath. There is something of the moss-green of *E. stricta* in the closely-whorled, linear leaves of *Pageana*, and the flowers, as the many who have seen W. J. M.'s plants at Vincent Square will not need reminding, are a wonderful butter-yellow with chocolate anthers.

A HYBRID
HELLEBORE

*Primrose buds and
nodding bowls of
rose-stained ivory
with an inner freck-
ling of wine-red*

THE STARCH-WHITE
STARS OF THE
WINTER PERIWINKLE
(VINCA DIFFORMIS)

CROCUS
TOMMASINIANUS

*Raises its wine-
glasses of rosy-
amethyst to the
February sun*

ANEMONE BLANDA

CHAPTER VII

Some First-footers of Spring

AMONG THE earliest and best of our pre-vernal woodland flowers are the hellebores, and a better investment we have never made than a collection of these curiously fascinating things. A few odd plants we had had for years, but at one of the winter shows in Vincent Square we saw such an enticing array of these strange herbs that several dozens were forthwith ordered. Not one of these plants has ever let us down. They asked a year or two to get settled in, but since that they have increased in vigour and charm with every recurring season, and we can rely upon them to yield a succession of blossom from November to May. Throughout the darkest days they fearlessly put forth leaf and flower whenever the weather is tolerably mild. Should sharp frost come along their sappy growths will collapse as if mortally wounded, but they are only shamming. With the return of more genial days they resurrect those flaccid and prostrate stems and carry on as if nothing had happened.

These hellebores we grow in the woodland and among plantations of rhododendrons, and for such places there are few hardy perennials to equal them. Not only do they flower throughout the darker months of the year but their leaves are bold and handsome. Moreover, this broadly-fingered leafage is evergreen, the great majority of species and hybrids exercising the admirable precaution of preserving their old suit until the new one is ready for use. Although they dislike moving and insist on having a couple of years in which to forget their grievance at being interfered with, when they do get away nothing will make steadier progress. The clumps increase year by year and continue indefinitely not merely to gather size and amplitude of leaf, but the older they become the better do they seem to bloom. They are said to be lime-lovers and we know that Canon Ellacombe did them very well at Bitton where the soil is distinctly limy. Our natives, *Helleborus foetidus* and *H. viridis*, also seem to be more at home in localities having a calcareous soil. Notwithstanding this we have had unqualified success in our acid loam, all plants doing well in stiffish ground or light, in sun or shade. One thing they resent is wind, which is apt to break their leaves and give them a tattered, unhappy appearance. Hence the wisdom of grouping them among evergreen shrubs or in quiet wood bottoms.

H. niger is doubtless the most beautiful of the tribe, but the average gardener has still to realise the merit of this lovely plant. It is a species which varies enormously in quality—as it does in season of blossoming—and selected forms, many of which have been named, are incomparably finer in size of blossom and their peerless whiteness than the mediocre specimens which too often do duty as Christmas roses. The explanation is probably this: A Christmas rose, even if a third-rater, makes such a touching appeal to our senses and imagination that its charm remains unchallenged. To indulge in comparisons before a flower of so delicate a beauty at that season would seem odious indeed. So the old clump lives on in the old, old garden, the merit of its flowers unquestioned, its perfection accepted.

Which is of course all wrong, however right it may seem in sentiment. Wrong because it is as easy to grow the most beautiful varieties as it is to perpetuate the less beautiful—and surely wiser—and once you have known the former you will wonder however you endured the others. Then there is every good reason why the season of a plant so enchanting should be extended. In its native sub-alpine woods, especially of the Italian Lakes, and away eastward to the Carpathians, Christmas roses —if one must use the term—flower from early autumn to spring and this they will do in our gardens, giving, if we take the trouble to get them, finer flowers of a more immaculate whiteness than most of us have yet seen.

The other hellebores we have, and already referred to, are mainly comprised of hybrids raised for the most part from *H. orientalis, lividus, colchicus* and others. But the splendid *H. corsicus* deserves individual mention. This, making a big bush of three or more feet, with three-lobed, long-stalked leaves, stands out as a most decorative object at the margin of the woodland. Its branches are a pale emerald and above the rich green of the smooth but leathery spine-margined leaves it raises copious clusters of the characteristic bowl-shaped flowers in a subdued yellowish-green. A smaller plant we possess, with the likeness of *corsicus* in blossom but with a more glaucous trifoliate leaf, is probably a hybrid with a strong leaning towards *lividus*. These two are the best of the bunch in our green-flowered kinds, but they are not quite so early as the majority of the *orientalis* hybrids. The first of these will show colour in autumn and the latest will be with us until spring is surrendering to summer.

Any attempt to describe by their colours these hybrid hellebores would be tedious and bewildering. They are there in the lists in scores. They bear the names of kings and queens, of classical heroes, milkmaids, fairies and gods, and they carry with them a guarantee to give long and faithful service. There is only one thing they will not do and that is they stubbornly decline to live as cut-flowers.[1] At least, most of the coloured ones do. So utterly and promptly do these resent this sort of abasement that, having gathered some sprays for photography, they will often hang in limp dejection over the rim of the vase before I can get the camera adjusted. And, after all, why should they suffer this indignity? We have been assured that bruising the ends of the stems with a hammer before placing them in water will make them behave more agreeably. And another tells us that if a panicle is cut after its first flower has shed its trumpet-shaped nectaries (petals) the rest of the blooms will survive as long as a Christmas rose, which may be kept in water for six weeks. But we have not tested these assertions and in all probability never will. It is enough for us to see these lenten roses (another ill-chosen name since their flowering overlaps Lent at both ends) challenging the wintry earth with their robust vitality and unflinching courage.

Beautiful in colour these hellebores may not be, but enthralling they certainly are. From green to white and cream, from cream to rose-flushed ivory, pink, amaranth and red, from red to purple, plum-crimson and a velvety darkness that is almost

[1]Floated like water-lilies in a crystal bowl blossoms with an inch of stalk last long and make an attractive table decoration.

black, they range in an endless variety of shades. And, as if that were not enough, their finely modelled bowls indulge in all manner of strange freakings, frecklings, cloudings, stripings and blotchings, every individual flower a fantasia of its own caprice. Yet, just as over the colours of all of them one perceives a curious mistiness which subdues the hue even of the brightest, so over all there seems to hang the shadow of some inscrutable gloom.

They are really a little uncanny, these flowers. But need this be surprising in a plant whose very name in its Greek form means, 'food to kill'. In the blood of the whole race there lurks not the least deadly of the juices which rendered the herbs of the garden of Persephone so useful to those who once amused themselves by poisoning a friend or removing an enemy. And if, as legend records, it was a spray of hellebore which Eve was permitted to take with her when expelled from Eden, well, un-popular husbands with nasty visions of weed-killer in their minds are not likely to regard the incident with cheerful-ness. There seems to have been more than one creature in that first garden which excelled other beasts of the field in subtlety.

The vincas as a tribe are either misused or not used at all—not as they should be at any rate. But writing of hellebores re-minds me not only of how much we owe to them but of the fact that their principle flowering season—autumn to late spring—synchronises with that of those lenten roses. *V. major* we can do without, valuable as it may be in some gardens. Where space is limited—even in those shady, drippy spots of meagre soil which this uncomplaining plant so valiantly puts up with—something often has to go. Furthermore, this old periwinkle a few years ago developed a fungoid rust which swept through it like fire without, however, entirely subdueing its dauntless courage. That settled the matter for us at all events, for, fearing that the malady might attack other members of the genus, we did away with *V. major*.

Only one form of *V. major* have we retained and that is a curiosity bearing flowers with extremely narrow, dagger-shaped segments of a deep violet-purple. Having submitted this oddity to the scrutiny of Mr. W. T. Stearn he decided it should be described as *V. m. oxyloba*. On further investigation, however, he tells me that that name cannot be regarded as final. And with a perspicacity and thoroughness which sends my untutoured mind a-reeling he groups our *oxyloba* with *V. m. hirsuta, V. pubescens* and *V. m. pubescens* under the synonymy of *V. major* sub-sp. *hirsuta*. The taxonomy of plants bewilders and yet fascinates me. But it is interesting to learn that specimens apparently identical with this periwinkle of ours which so arouses the curiosity of visitors were run to earth by the zeal of W. T. S. in the herbaria of Berlin and some Italian cities, and that the range of the plant and its affinities covers a considerable area of S.E. Europe into Asia.

Having dry banks and walls in plenty, not to mention woodland slopes, we find *V. minor* a willing and delightful ally in helping to cover such places. Seldom out of flower it is at its best in early spring when nothing is more charming than its hardy, happy looking blossoms brightening with colour those arid spots in sun or shade which most plants disdain. The white form—a warm, milk-white with reddish stems is one of our favourites, but of the blues we have nothing quite so good as some selected forms brought home from the wooded shores of the Italian Lakes years ago. These are large in blossom, extremely free flowering and their colour touches a richness of blue we have seen in none other. Moreover, the segments being distinctly rhomboidal and sharply pointed the blooms have more character than the more rounded and podgy faces of the general run.

V. minor Bowles' Variety has the biggest blossoms of the group, and these, obtuse of segment and therefore full and compact, are a pleasing shade of soft lavender-blue. The plant sent out as La Grave, appears to be the same thing. The whole of these little periwinkles—white, lavender-blue, piebald, slate-blue, blue-purple and a deep-toned red-crimson, singles and doubles, have done all that we ever asked of them and more in clothing the nakedness of earth, blending with the native herbage of woodland or draping unsightly stonework. Slow to start they are so persevering that they will steadily overcome even rank grass and eventually reward you, as they have rewarded us, by creating broad carpets of growth which—in the right place—will ask no attention and, incidentally, prove the most efficient and permanent of weed-killers.

Along the Mediterranean shores *V. difformis* fills many a wayside ditch, creeping down the watercourses to the verge of the sea where, as often as not, it covers the mud flats beneath the pennoned spires of that most graceful reed, *Arundo Donax*, whose woody, cane-like stems, rising to a dozen feet, seem to be used by the peasants for every imaginable purpose from the building of a house or making a hamper to fishing rods and fences, water-pipes and mouse traps.

V. difformis (*acutiloba* or *media*) most ably represented here by the Riviera form, is much like *V. major* in leaf and habit, though it is not so rampant. But in flower it is very different both in appearance and season. With us it puts forth its starch-white, rather starred blossoms with the first autumn rains and these are yielded in abundance throughout the winter. Sharp frost may check its ardour and singe its tender shoots, but *V. difformis* knows no defeat; it goes ahead as merrily as ever with the return of milder weather. It is obviously desirable to give such a plant as this some shelter from cutting winds and this is easily provided since it rather enjoys the shade of an evergreen. But few things are more thrifty and easy going than *V. difformis*, to which the fact that one of our heartiest colonies is in a starved and stony soil around the base of a copper beech bears eloquent testimony. Curiously enough, the later flowers of this species—those yielded from about mid-March onwards—exchange their icy whiteness for a delicate blue.

We had long had a desire to secure the dark, or slate-blue, form of *V. difformis* and had almost decided to give up the quest and make an expedition in search of it in its native south, an excuse for a winter holiday. However, one day a precious bit of root arrived from Mr. W. T. Stearn who had secured a few collected scraps from a botanist at large in Algeria. I have never been quite convinced that the receiving of that little plant was sufficient to compensate the Lady of the Garden for her obvious disappointment in having that suggested winter trip put off by the quashing of the main objective. She has been quite polite and all that to the plant, but her hospitality towards it is as lacking in warmth as is her interest in my efforts to comfort the homesick creature. However, I have flowered it but not well. The blossom, a blue-lavender, clear and bright, is large—larger than that of the white one—but the plant is the least happy of our periwinkles. It grew enormously at first, putting out runners of four or five feet in a season, but did not flower and winter nipped its precocity. Now it is being tried in a sunnier spot with a poorer, more stony soil and hopes renewed.

V. difformis needs an occasional removal of the runners, or most of them. We generally do this once a year, just after the spring flowering, and *V. minor* may be treated in the same way whenever it is desirable to keep it within bounds. This does not merely prevent these plants from becoming a menace to neighbours, but it leads to more abundant flowers and does away with the unsightliness of a tangle of often leafless runners. As Sir Arthur Hort says, when writing of *V. difformis* in his engaging volume, *The Unconventional Garden*—'Like other plants which increase vegetatively, of which strawberries are the obvious example, it is trying to do two things at once: it will do the one all the better, from the grower's point of view, if it is prevented from doing the other.'

There is no lack of blue in the spring garden from the days when *Anemone blanda* braves the frost-traps of February until the scillas and muscaris are sinking into the rising herbage of May. But among things other than those usually catalogued as bulbs there is nothing in blue for which we have more reason to be grateful than the pulmonarias. That beautiful plant, Mawson's Blue, is one of the best of these. The authorities still seem to be in doubt as to what species it belongs, but this does not deeply concern us. It is enough for us to enjoy those masses of real gentian-blue which almost cover the thongy roots before the neat, comparatively small, unspotted leaves appear. Mawson's is a blue that fears few rivals even among scillas and chionodoxas. The plant is indestructibly hardy, its flowers as weather-proof as any flowers can be, and, though it lives for ever unaided, an occasional lifting and division is advisable. There is only one other blue lungwort which can challenge Mawson's and that is a form, probably of the same thing, which came to us with the honoured name of Munstead attached to it. This, and some seedlings we have raised from it, if not much better in colour, are definitely larger in flower and leaf and they seem more compact and slower to make offsets than the older plant.

These blue pulmonarias are not usually in flower until March, being preceded by the spotted-dog fraternity of *saccharata* and *officinalis* which, in spite of their 'towzled and morbid-looking heaps of leprous leafage' (Farrer) we welcome for the earliness of their flowers. Often enough these flowers, an indefinite purplish-blue and faded rose, are grievously weak in colour, but in days of early January too drear even to raise a smile in a winter aconite he would be ungenerous who could not give such courageous optimists at least a nod of approbation. Moreover, these spotted lungworts do occasionally aspire beyond the customary level of their excessive modesty by presenting flowers of larger size, of better and more uniform colouring, not to mention a more becoming leafage. One of these is a variety called Mrs. Moon whose flowers, nearly an inch across, have rather a sweet old rose tint. There is a good white form of *saccharata* and another of *officinalis*, a sky-blue whose connections I do not know, a pretty little *angustifolia + rubra* hybrid with rather small flowers of a clear low-toned pink without any purple and a few more. All of these carry us bravely through the opening weeks of the year until spring is well on the way which is the signal for *P. rubra* to appear.

P. rubra could claim originality if nothing else, for its blossoms, on stout nine-inch sprays, are of that uncommon mixture of scarlet, rosy-red and terra-cotta one may see in some of the pimpernels or *Rhododendron Griersonianum*. This fine plant is as amiable and trustworthy as any of the others, but it likes moisture better than most and is seen at its best in some part-shaded wood bottom where the feeding is good and the tap never dry. *P. rubra* has only one fault. Its summer leaves, which follow the flowers, are both large and coarse, as big as those of a prosperous dock, and these render it unfit to associate with the less stalwart species or plants of the rock-garden. But, given the right spot in which it can indulge in leafiness to any extent it pleases, and *P. rubra* ceases to be anything but one of the most charming of early woodland herbaceous perennials.

Anchusa myosotidiflora runs the same risk of forfeiting the honours it wins in spring by indulging in a summer leafage to which 'cabbagy' would be flattering. But, again, this is surely only a matter of placing for, given such a spot as I have suggested for the red lungwort—and the twain run in adjacent groups can be very striking—and this borage becomes elevated from an ugly nuisance to a woodlander of grace and distinction. After all, there are few blues so piercing in their purity and intensity as the gems which hover high above the dark knobbly crowns of the forget-me-not anchusa. These exquisite sprays are admirable with the red lungwort, but I think they are even more beautiful when associated with the crimson, vermilion, bronze and gleaming amber with which our uprising spiraeas and astilbes are stained. In these latter, too, the anchusa has a foe worthy of its steel. Along the margins of their territory it can aggress and battle with all its native ferocity, but summer brings to its neighbours a power of elbow which it cannot overcome. It is held in check just when discipline is most necessary and suffers no loss of dignity for its flowering days are over long before the foliage which threatens it has acquired its summer green.

Grown either in single clumps or in the mass, *Omphalodes cappadocica* is the most beautiful of its section of the early borages. Its flowers, half-an-inch across, are a forget-me-not blue of unsurpassed purity, their delicate tone is softened by a slight flush of rose in the bud, and they are borne on freely branched, nine-inch sprays of matchless elegance over the pointed, tongue-shaped, glaucous leaves. *Crocus Tommasinianus*, chionodoxas and lavender erythroniums, sweeping in a haze of rose-tinted blue beneath a canopy of forsythia glittering with golden bells, together create a scene of bewitching loveliness. But I think the azure carpet which *O. cappadocica* has laid beneath a large spreading bush of *Magnolia stellata* whose every twig is a-flutter even in March with snow-white ribbons, is equally arresting. We have no woodland flowering herb of its size and season good enough to challenge this Cappadocian forget-me-not. The taller *O. nitida* has flowers of a keener blue on slenderer stems of a foot or so, and it will often begin earlier and stay later. Then there is the creeping verna which, like the lesser periwinkles, rambles about our woodland places, jewelling its prostrate growths with a charming blue and a white of the whitest. But, unkind as it is to make comparisons between beauties who are all so fair, *O. cappadocica* bears a hallmark of quality to which none other can attain. And one may add to its long season of flowering and gracious comeliness a willingness to take care of itself, to bring up its own seedlings, and to increase by offsets with such restraint that it never abuses the hospitality granted it.

Few of the comfreys (*Symphytum*) can claim the gardener's friendship. We find quarter for *S. bohemicum*, said to be a form of *S. officinale*, for it is only some two feet, not seriously invasive and from its unfurling croziers drop earrings of ruby-crimson. *S. asperrimum* (or is it *peregrinum?*) is also a plant whose noble stature of four or five feet, handsome leafage and endless shower of turquoise bugles are a recommendation one cannot ignore. This giant, moreover, will put up with any sort of a life and so gallantly that we find it useful for filling a draughty, shady corner by one of the garden sheds. But these belong to later days and my sole excuse for introducing the genus here is to air the merits of a species which came to us as *S. grandiflorum*.

It is as a woodland carpenter that this comfrey excels. The foliage, considerably smaller than that of most kinds, is evergreen and it carries just clear of this to a height of about nine inches sprays of ivory-yellow bugles vividly tipped with crimson. These flowers may not earn the specific name of *grandiflorum*—if, indeed, that is the plant's name—but in thin woodland shade they never fail to arrest the notice of all who see them and the plant is commonly in bloom from February onwards. In a mild winter it will be out a month earlier, and I have known it to put up a non-stop performance the year round. A robust, but not rapid creeper it will overcome almost anything in the way of weeds and woodland herbage and it has no fads about soil. The rust common to symphytums sometimes attacks *S. grandiflorum* until not a leaf is left. But it takes more than that to kill a comfrey and the plant soon recovers and goes on as merrily as ever.

The handsome sub-shrubby spurge, *Euphorbia Wulfenii*, is an early bloomer and its huge mass of tropical-looking foliage makes an imposing object at all seasons. It prepares for its spring show in autumn by elongating and bending over the tips of its flowering extremities. As this proceeds its terminal leaves become veined with red, and the rest of its younger growths veneered with a rosy glaucous sheen. By February or early March the plant has thrown off its appearance of bored despondency. The bloom shoots rise from the now erect tips of the leaf-frilled branches and quickly break into great panicles of greenish-yellow flowers. These inflorescences may be a foot in height and they will prevail for at least three months. We have not had this magnificent spurge taller than some four feet, but a neighbour near the sea has a specimen which stands at nearly six feet with a circumference of fifteen feet at least.

There are more beautiful spurges among the hardier giants of this mighty and baleful race, notably *E. dendroides* which is such a fine feature on many a sea cliff of Southern Europe. But *Wulfenii*, the Dalmatian, is the only one of these big evergreen fellows which we have found winter-proof and that seems to be a general experience. For its spring foliage—olive-green leaves, stalked and ribbed with bright red—we also grow a spurge labelled, rightly or wrongly, *E. sikkimensis*, a stately thing of two or three feet. *E. polychroma* we also like for, from February onwards, its sheaf of leafy eighteen-inch stems is crowned with broad rosettes of a lemon-yellow so potent that it runs down the stems to permeate the upper leaves with its biting hue.

One more early flowering woodlander with which I may round off this rambling chapter is *Saxifraga ligulata* which arrived here bearing the label, *S. Stracheyi*—as it has a way of doing. The latter is really the better garden plant for it has the wisdom to defer its blooming until most of the other bergenias are in colour and risk of spring frost is departing. Even so, there is a peculiar joy in seeing *S. ligulata* in bloom while days are still brief. The flowers are exquisitely beautiful, pink and pearl-white, delicate as a shell, and they are clustered with their red buds on sturdy little red stalks before the highly glossy leaves are half awake.

These blossoms, which seem even more susceptible to frost

than those of a rhododendron, arrive so suddenly that the knobbly crown which yesterday appeared so lifeless will to-day be breaking into colour. It is, of course, an easy matter to cover at least some of them with a handlight, but how often are one's good intentions turned to remorse by the discovery that they are too late! The moral of which is: Never grow, or attempt to grow, more plants than you are able to attend to. But the gardener who is likely to carry out such a counsel of perfection has not yet been born.

GAULTHERIA NUMMULARIOIDES
Draping a shady woodland bank

GAULTHERIA
HISPIDA

Its snow-white fruits
⅛ nat. size

GAULTHERIA
TRICOPHYLLA

The bird's-egg blue
'berries' shown are
⅔ nat. size

CHAPTER VIII

Gaultheria and Vaccinium

THOSE WHO have found themselves captivated by their magic spell will not need to be told that there is no other group of shrubs quite so subtle in their drawing power as that of the gaultherias. A craze for rhododendrons one can understand. The persuasion of the heaths is also comprehensible. But endeavour to fathom the depths of a gaultheria's bewitching influence and your efforts will be like trying to catch a flicker of marsh gas in a butterfly net.

Gaultherias have a racial antipathy for window dressing of any sort. Publicity they do not seek, garden popularity they would go a long way to avoid. Their flowers express the last word in modesty, and if in some the fruits are brightly coloured they, as often as not, do all they can to conceal them from the eyes of the vulgar. Children of the wild, they cling desperately to the ways of their own unfettered life. Disdaining to sink into the comfortable easy-chair of garden existence, to forfeit their birthright for any mess of luxury, they endure captivity on one condition and that is to carry on as far as may be with loyalty to the ancestral traditions of their tribe. And perhaps it is the spirit of the lonely places, some link with the great untamed, which in part explains the 'pull' they exert over us. Other plants possess that 'it' to some degree—vacciniums, *Cornus canadensis*, phyllodoces, menziesias, the beautiful little *Linnaea borealis*, schizocodons, shortias, alpine rhododendrons and galax. These never quite lose touch with their own pristine individualities, they never relax their grip upon our imagination.

Gaultherias have an extraordinarily wide natural range. They occur in eastern N. America and cross that Continent to the Pacific slope. They creep southwards from that point, following Rockies and Andes to the Magellan Region, thence to Australia, Tasmania and New Zealand where they appear, not as lonely outposts but as old settlers, in quantity, variety and prosperity. From Pacific N. America they also travel west, settling in Japan and China. Tibet knows them, the Himalaya is rich in species and a few have invaded Ceylon. But Africa they avoid and Europe can only claim them as cultivated exotics.

Yet, in spite of the fact that, as a wild genus, the gaultherias have rejected the soil of Europe, they are not really difficult with us. Some of them from warm southern countries and W. America are not reliably winter hardy, but most of them are quite up to the level of most evergreens in their toleration of our conditions. A lime-free soil they must have, and while that soil should be beyond suspicion regarding drainage it must have that humoid consistency which tends to maintain a uniform moisture and coolness of root-run.

Once upon a time we always herded our groups of these things in shade, partly because, in such positions, the trials of our summer dryness would not be so acute. But since we have acquired more low lying, moister ground the plants have been given considerably more sun, many being quite in the open where natural dampness is unfailing. This has certainly given us more blossom and fruit and, incidentally, the hardening of the wood and foliage which follows exposure has afforded the frost-tender stouter powers of resistance. The ideal situation is probably a gravelly-peaty (or leaf mould) soil with light shade from tall trees, such as one sees at Wisley.

Our first love in gaultherias was *G. tricophylla* and for this engaging little mite our affection remains unshaken. A three-to six-inch, semi-prostrate species weaving a dense mat of slender red stems closely furnished with wee oblong, dark green bristly leaves, *G. tricophylla* (once it has forgiven you for the root-disturbance it dislikes) will spread freely by means of underground stems. In some gardens it is none too amiable, but it is easily one of our best doers and every spring yields in abundance the pitcher-shaped rosy flowers which are followed by those wonderful fruits which alone place this Himalayan among the choicest of its genus. These 'berries' are normally pear-shaped, as large as horse-beans and a lovely bird's-egg-blue. We get a crop of these gems about mid-summer and the plants almost always yield another equally prolific show in early autumn.

G. Hookeri is a Himalayan of bolder growth, making a close-set bush of some three feet. The thick, leathery leaves, a deep glossy green and distinctly reticulated, are more or less oblong and up to four inches in length. The white flowers, which are borne in racemes, give place to indigo-blue fruits the size of small peas. This is a handsome plant simply as an evergreen. It is hardy and easy and here I may break off for a moment into the Chinese section and bring in *Veitchiana*, which suggests a geographical form of Hooker's plant. In this garden *Veitchiana*, so much like the latter in habit, flower and fruit, does not attain quite so great a height and the leaves are narrower, more pointed and a paler green, the flowers slightly rosy.

G. fragrantissima, rare a few years ago but now obtainable from specialists, we have found more tender than the above, probably because its range extends to Malaya and Ceylon. It is referred to as 'a large evergreen shrub or small tree' (Bean) but I have not seen it above about four feet. An attractive species of open, branching habit with narrowly oval, pointed, dull green leaves and red stems, *G. fragrantissima* holds its own with the other large-leaved kinds. The fragrant pale primrose or green-white flowers are rather a feeble effort, but the fruits change from a pearl white to a presentable blue. This fruit colour, however, is a variable quality in many gaultherias. It does not always arrive according to plan. Blues may be pucy purples, whites may be pink or pink white. And this does not appear to be decided only by soil or locality but often by season.

In the Himalayan, *G. Griffithii*, there is a pronounced family likeness to the foregoing in its reddish stems, oval-oblong toothed leaves, which are hard and olive-green, and the short racemes of blossom. This species is said to make three feet, but here it seems to prefer a lateral progress, for while it does not rise much above a foot or so, it ramps by underground stems and thus soon covers a square yard or two. Its mission is to be a woodland carpeter and as such it will always enjoy our encouragement. But as a bloomer it is weak, the flowers being a pale greenish-white and the fruits here have not developed beyond a glossy green, perhaps with a touch of plum-blue.

G. nummularioides is another of these N. Indian species which we esteem very highly as a woodland under-shrub. It makes a compact mass of its more or less procumbent, but often arching, stems along which the heart-shaped leaves are closely arranged in two uneven rows, tapering to the point as in the familiar moneywort. These leaves, as well as the growths, which are anything between six and twelve inches long, are covered with brown bristles which are golden in the younger shoots. A vigorous, but not rapid spreader this species will cover several square feet in a few years, and it is never more delightful than when flopping over the mossy boulders of some shady bank accompanied by dwarf ferns and other woodlanders of refinement.

G. nummularifolia, which we first had as a diminutive form of the last-mentioned under the varietal name of *minor*, is apparently a distinct species. It is a perfectly prostrate shrublet, its long thin branches, with red hairs trailing about the ground, being beset with the same double row of alternate olive-green leaves barely three-eighths of an inch long at their largest. Like *nummularioides* it hides wee bell-shaped, dull-pink blooms underneath its branches but these have not fruited in either species. This is not a particularly lively bantling but a delightful thing for a mossed stump or woodland bank where it will not have to contend with bigger stuff. What promises to be a much better garden plant is a closely allied introduction of Forrest's (G.F. 2522) with broken pairs of considerably larger egg-shaped leaves along its prostrate growths. These leaves are more distinctly glaucous beneath and more closely toothed than those of *nummularifolia*. The plant roots freely as it sprawls about, which its little cousin rarely does, but though its comparatively large, rosy-red flowers are borne freely they fail as do those of its affinities to develop further. Perhaps they never do, for all gaultherias do not cradle their seed in the inflated, fleshy calyx common to most.[1]

G. pyrolaefolia is still on our 'wanted' list. It is a Himalayan and, from what little I know of it, would seem to be a slightly smaller Indian representative of the Japanese *G. Miqueliana*,

[1]Since this was written G.F. 2522 has borne a crop of plum-purple fruits the size of buckshot.

still familiar to most of us as *G. pyroloides*. But whereas the latter—one of the most beautiful of the genus—has globular snow-white fruits those of *pyrolaefolia* are described as red. *Miqueliana* runs about by underground stolons, making pleasant little colonies with erect, nine-inch growths bearing aromatic, coriaceous, usually oval leaves and white flowers. These blooms (May), yielded singly or in racemes, being a quarter-inch wide, are only a little less attractive than the fruits which appear from late summer onwards and often persist into winter. *G. Miqueliana* is a willing, sweet-tempered, hardy plant that will prosper almost anywhere, and worthy to be coupled with it is *G. cuneata*. This Chinese introduction of Wilson's makes a neatly-rounded, wide-spread bush of a foot or more, very twiggy and amply endowed with narrowly obovate, hard glossy leaves about an inch long. It has been classed as a variety of *Miqueliana* to which it bears some resemblance in flower and 'berry', both of which are large and conspicuous, the latter often being tinted with carmine when exposed. *Cuneata* is as delightful as its ally and no less ready to make its garden life a happy time.

G. Forrestii,[1] one of Forrest's finest introductions in ericaceous plants other than rhododendrons, is said to attain four or five feet but the tallest specimens I have seen have not exceeded half that stature. We have not found this species quite so dependable as some, nor do the fruits which follow the waxen-white flowers always develop that wonderfully vivid and rich porcelain-blue which distinguishes this shrub in some gardens. Some sprays sent here by the late Mr. Bedford from a specimen grown at Exbury bore fruit of an amazingly brilliant blue, against which our best efforts looked a dismal violet. Some contend that this fruit colour is a question of 'form', seed-raised plants in gaultherias, as in other things, being apt to divert from the parent type. That may be so, but I am inclined to think, as already suggested, that such factors as soil and situation have a deal to do with it, and to that end we are giving Forrest's gaultheria a trial run in various parts of the garden.

[1]There seems to be some doubt as to this name. I refer to the plant which won the A.M. under that name at Holland Park, Sept. 28-30, 1927, and which was figured in *Gardeners' Chronicle*, p. 285, vol. lxxxii.

Other gaultherias sent in, I think by Forrest and Ward, are still in their infancy with us—*adenothrix*, *tetramera* (akin to *Forrestii*), *Wardii* and *thibetica*, as well as a few still under number. It is too soon to speak of these, but the first has given us some flowers of great promise and a passing reference may be made to the last-named (K.W. 6845) since it stands out distinctly among others in its very small, almost linear, crenulated leaves. These leaves are even smaller than those of *tricophylla*, they appear to be hairless to my second-rate eyesight, and their rich green wears a high polish. Though six inches high, an erect and healthy, branching little shrub which Mr. Marchant tells me does not grow any taller, we have not yet seen its flowers.[1]

Coming to those of Australia and Tasmania, *G. hispida* is the only one of which we have had a lengthy experience and that has not been invariably successful. We have had it two or more feet in height and marvelled at its white flower panicles and copious clusters of large snow-white fruits, but only for a season or two. Our winters it does not resent, its grievance we cannot discover, but it has a way of suddenly going off piecemeal. It behaves in this way in other gardens also and no one seems to know why it does so. But *G. hispida*, with its glossy, deep green, almost lance-shaped leaves and red wood is so handsome a shrub, especially in fruit, that the purchasing of a new specimen to replace the departed, becomes a more or less regular occurrence in one's routine, like buying a new hat.

Of New Zealand gaultherias our gardens have probably not seen the last. Perhaps they never will if these Antipodean alpines continue to indulge in those mixed marriages to which Sir Arthur Hill has referred, and which render garden identification difficult and embarrassing even to the botanists. *G. antipoda* is perhaps the best-known of these, a loose-habited little shrub of a couple of feet here, with thick, roundly-oval, or almost orbicular, toothed leaves of a glossy, rather dull green. The solitary, axillary flowers, small and indistinctly white, are followed by dark red fruits as large as peas which remain through autumn and part of winter.

G. depressa (or *G. antipoda depressa*), practically a miniature

---

[1] Since this was written the plant has bloomed well, the top-shaped flowers, very contracted at the mouth, being a rosy-green with broad red stripes.

GAULTHERIA FORRESTII
Fruiting branches of a typical form

GAULTHERIA
MIQUELIANA

*White fruits, often rosy-
tinted, ⅛ nat. size*

VACCINIUM
MORTINIA

*A charming little ever-
green with pale almond-
pink flowers*

of *antipoda* but with larger fruits, we have never been able to keep more than a few seasons. *G. rupestris* would appear to come near to these in botanical characters but differing in its racemose inflorescence. Since our plant under that name has not yet flowered its identity remains in doubt. Indeed, all of this little lot (*antipoda* presents many forms) seem destined to remain for a while outside the limits of recognition so far as we are concerned. Where *G. reticulata* and *G. fagifolia* (which hints at an affinity with *antipoda*) come in, I am not sure.[1] The former has given us urn-shaped flowers of unusual size, a lovely carmine, and rosy fruits, the latter dull blossoms and white fruits.

G. oppositifolia, now over a couple of feet, looks like proving a much better garden shrub than the above. In flower, it is described as 'the most ornamental of the gaultherias in New Zealand' (Bean) but our plant has not yet given us first-hand evidence of its charm in that direction. It is an attractive shrub as an evergreen, the stemless, ovate, or heart-shaped, opposite leaves being well over an inch long and a good hearty green. It promises to be one of the hardiest of these southern species and is said to grow to at least six feet.

Our star turn in New Zealanders, however, is *G. perplexa*, a specimen of which, now about ten years old, is three feet across and some eighteen inches high. Its mound of slender, tortuous, interlacing branches, with a meagre show of almost linear, bronzy-green leaves is not exciting, and its pale greenish-white flowers also err on the side of modesty. But when, in early autumn, the fruits begin to colour, *perplexa's* tangle of rusty wire is transformed into an object of great beauty, for the 'berries', as large as marrowfat peas and as crinkly, are a most vivid carmine. And these are of no fleeting splendour for they hang on throughout the winter and there will often be a few left when the plant is freshening for spring. Although more or less prostrate the branches do not root, nor do they take readily to layering. The Kew *Hand List* includes a natural hybrid between *G. perplexa* and *depressa*. This I have not seen, but it ought to be a good thing if it fruits.

In Americans, *G. Shallon*, whose edible fruits David Douglas

[1]*Gr. fagifolia* = natural hybrid *antipoda* + *oppositifolia*: Kew *Hand List*.

found so pleasant and satisfying, is well known. But I am not so sure that the meagre value often placed upon it is the true measure of its worth. As a thicket shrub for woodland and waterside it is extremely useful, and it is handsome in foliage, flower and fruit. Moreover, it is such a hardy, accommodating creature that it will grow anywhere in sun or shade, dry soil or moist, adapting itself to conditions by presenting a stature of anything from six inches or so to as many feet.

Then there is that pleasant little carpeter, *G. procumbens*, whose crushed leaves are redolent of wintergreen—and lumbago—and whose pink and white flowers and holly-red fruits are an unfailing delight. This happy woodlander we have in colonies which fend for themselves, even overcoming the native herbage. Occasionally *Cornus canadensis*, which is no less inveigling, contends with it for place and power, both running together and giving us one of those all-the-year-round features which are so comforting in their readiness to carry on without asking a moment of our time for cultural aid.

G. ovatifolia comes from British Columbia and the Rockies and is not too robust or easy-going in this garden. It has made some six inches and is inclined to a lateral or semi-prostrate habit. The stems are reddish, the leaves broadly ovate, glossy and about an inch long, and it bears cheerful pink and white bells and scarlet fruits which are said to be 'spicy and delicious' (Bean). Of these fruits our plants have borne a few, but who would be base enough to devour such rare comestibles? Near *ovatifolia* is *myrsinites* (*humifusa*) which might be regarded as a smaller, more prostrate version of that species. It also has flowered and fruited, but it is a shy little fellow, slow to make progress and somewhat to the tender side. On high elevations of the Rockies it weaves a low, turf-like mat, but it probably relies on snow for its winter protection there. One Chilean species I may bring in as a conclusion to these random notes and that is *G. furiens*, which the heavyweights of authority call *Arbutus furiens*. To what height this uncommon shrub grows I do not know. Our solitary individual has been a dozen years attaining three feet, and it was long before it decided to bloom. But it is only fair to state that this leisurely progress is in part due to a periodical snubbing by frost which, if severe enough, injures the tips. *G. furiens* is a rigid, stiffly erect bush with green, stubbly wood and narrowly ovate, bristly, two-inch leaves of a deep, sombre green and a texture that is leathery and tough. White flowers are produced in drooping axillary racemes in spring and these are succeeded by round, burgundy-red fruits. A distinguished, well-looking plant, especially in flower, which always catches the eye of the connoisseur.

The genus *Vaccinium* I approach with no little trepidation for it contains an enormous number of species and their identification presents difficulties which do not ease the way of even such a brief and unbotanical survey as this. However, one may simplify matters by dealing only with a select few, those which, having proved their garden value to us, are established as friends. Further, I am absolved from mentioning a large section of the deciduous species of the class to which our common bilberry belongs, for these we no longer cultivate. Having few claims of an ornamental kind and a more ardent passion for suckering than most, we are better without them, even in the woodland. This suckering may of course be a virtue in a thicket making vaccinium of quality, just as it is in a gaultheria. But if a plant which indulges too freely in that kind of fun has little merit to offer in atonement it has, if only in the interests of space, to suffer expulsion.

Among these deciduous species whose propensities for travel we suffer gladly is *V. pennsylvanicum*. This is a shrub no one who enjoys autumn leaf colour can do without for its glossy, lance-shaped leaves, referred to earlier, assume a most brilliant scarlet. This does not come on until November, the leaves hang so bravely that we often have them until Christmas is nigh, and throughout the winter the crimson twigs are distinctly atractive. The rose and white blooms with which the shrub is profusely laden in May are pretty enough to attract notice even at that season and they are followed by black berries dusted with a blue bloom.

For its leaf colour alone *V. pennsylvanicum* is a shrub to be grouped on a generous scale. It does not often exceed three feet. *V. canadense* is a deciduous species after the style of the above but lowlier. It also has pink-stained white flowers and blue-black fruits, but in leaf colour it does not aspire beyond a medium yellow. *V. stamineum*, which follows it in this last respect, is taller, going up to three or four feet. In flower it is dainty and delightful, the corollas, which are bell-like and widely spread rather than of the usual urn shape, being pearl-white with a bold tuft of yellow stamens and a muffling of leafy bracts.

Into the botanical labyrinth of *V. corymbosum*, its allies and synonyms, I shall not attempt to penetrate, beyond what usually passes for *corymbosum* in the trade, its variety *amoenum* and *pallidum*—which probably has nothing to do with the clan. *V. corymbosum*, as most of us know it, is not merely the best of this little company but it is certainly one of the best of all deciduous vacciniums. Making a spreading bush of anything from five to ten feet, this hardy eastern American is a good flowering shrub, attractive in fruit and so magnificent in autumn leaf colour that I make no apology for returning to what was said on the subject in another chapter. Indeed, a specimen on our own grass glade is an all-the-year-round satisfaction. In spring its tender leaves and young shoots are daintily tinted with amber, rosy-fawn and bronze. Then in May come the abundant clusters of urn-shaped flowers with their fresh pink-flushed whiteness, to be succeeded by edible berries as big as currants, their plum-black powdered with a blue bloom. In autumn one gets those wonderful leaf shades—scarlet, crimson, wine-red, purple and bronze—and even in winter the cinnamon bark of the old wood and the vivid red of the new will not pass unnoticed. So there you have a first-rate all-season shrub. It is one that never gives any trouble, asking no more than a fairly moist non-limy soil, and it only suckers from the base, giving a few young shoots to replace the old.

V. corymbosum var. amoenum is equally good and differs little in garden estimation from the type. As for *pallidum* of Virginia which Kew regards as a distinct species, our representative of this has made a stiffish, wiry bush with green twigs and bright green leaves which have glaucous undersides. This leafage is said to colour in some gardens but it has not done so here as yet. The flowers are a lively pink and the berries blue-black. *V. padifolium* of Madeira, often described as deciduous, is only partly so in our climate. It is a stiffish, erect bush of five or six feet in favoured spots, the ovate leaves being a full-toned green and fully an inch wide. Its bell-shaped flowers, borne singly or in short racemes, are a pale yellow flushed with purple and the half-inch berries are plum-black. Not a plant to make a fuss about, yet one we find interesting enough for a sheltered spot on our warmer slopes among other more or less touchy things.

It is *pallidum* that is often sent out as *V. Arctostaphylos*, why I have never been able to discover, for the one comes from the Canary Islands, the other from the Caucasus, and there is little more than a faint family resemblance between them. The Caucasian whortleberry which Dr. Fred Stoker does so well in his Essex garden, is only represented here by a stripling of a foot or so, it having been exceedingly scarce. A deciduous shrub of eight to ten feet, it may be distinguished by its uncommonly large, narrowly ovate leaves, these reaching as much as four inches in length, and white bell-like flowers flushed with a red-purple. The fruit is round and purple, the foliage presents a fine glowing red in autumn and the younger wood is crimson. A shrub of quality and breeding, *V. Arctostaphylos* will always earn a place among the élite of vacciniums and ericaceous shrubs. The spring flowering *ovalifolium*, also youthful as yet, gives promise of becoming a good shrub.

Among evergreen vacciniums *V. ovatum* is one of the best known. Here a bush of five or six feet, and still growing, it is a pleasing object at all seasons with its glossy, cheerful green and red twigs, and it flowers in September, putting forth racemes of white bells which are occasionally succeeded by black berries. Hardy and easy, we use this Pacific N. American for sheltering more precious things of the kind, as well as shortias and the like. *V. crassifolium* is a prostrate shrublet with oval leaves of a reddish-bronze and rosy flowers which we have not yet seen, but a better garden plant than either of these is *V. Mortinia* in which we have a shrub from equatorial regions that is hardy enough for most gardens. With us at all events, it has come through 30 degrees of frost, only suffering slight injury to the tips. As a matter of fact this is one of those instances in which elevation means more than latitude in estimating a plant's hardiness, for although *V. Mortinia* may be a native of the Tropics it grows at an altitude of some 10,000 feet.

V. Mortinia is a shrub to associate with the most elect. It grows to three or four feet. The broadly twigged and rather pendulous branches are amply adorned with half-inch ovate leaves which, with exposure and in winter, are a warm bronzy-red. The young spring growths are brightly tinted with rose and gold, pink and white flowers in elegant racemes are yielded in May and the red berries of early autumn will often be retained until mid-winter. In balance and elegance of poise, as well as in colour and charm of leaf and blossom, *V. Mortinia* will always assert its claim to a place of prominence among the most worthy shrubs of its kind.

A companion 'classy' enough to associate with this Ecuadorian treasure is *V. Delavayi*. A short, stiff and stubby, little bush packed with glossy, leathery box-like leaves, notched at the blunt tip and of a deep and sullen green, Delavay's whortle-berry is a striking contrast to the other's light and colourful grace. But the plant cheers up in spring when the bright red cone-shaped young growths terminate every sombre twig and these remain in colour for several weeks. This is a species which believes in doing things slowly. It has taken nearly twenty years to attain the dignity of flowering in this garden, but now that it has made the great plunge it performs annually. The racemes it puts forth are usually terminal, about an inch long, and the urn-shaped flowers are ivory-white, sometimes flushed with pink. The fruit is a deep plum-red and the size of small peas.

V. nummularia might be likened to the last in its thick-set foliage, the dark green leaves being heavy in texture, blunt and rounded. But their stalks, as well as the young wood, are bristly and the plant is considerably more enterprising. Thus it will often be carrying its pink flowers when in the cuttings frame, it runs about freely by means of underground stems and is ready to abound almost anywhere. But it likes a coolish bed of vegetable soil where it can be permitted to make a colony after the way of *Gaultheria procumbens*. In this way it can be most useful as a woodland carpeter for it seldom attains a foot in height and the crimson new growths in spring are, as with

Delavayi, by no means the least pleasing of its characteristics. Then we have in *moupinense* a Chinese species of rather over a foot with a close resemblance in leaf and habit to both the foregoing, but the flowers are a dark red. Since this and *nummularia* are partly epiphytic in nature they ought to suggest exciting possibilities to those people who indulge in stumperies, a phase of gardening to which we have not yet fallen.

The evergreen, white-flowered *bracteatum*, which was known a century ago, we grow and it makes a goodly bush of three or more feet. *V. fragile*, a lowly carpeter, is here also but still untried, and the handsome *V. Dunalianum*, having only been in the open a couple of seasons, must be passed with the briefest of reference. Mr. Smith of Newry sent us this species with a strong recommendation, but I fear a severe winter will try it. A tree-like plant in the Himalaya and W. China, *Dunalianum* has bright glossy green, narrowly oval leaves, often four or five inches in length with a long, finely-drawn apex which Mr. Bean well describes as 'tail-like'. Its white flowers are not in the first class but as an evergreen alone the plant is earning its keep on the warmer of our woodland slopes.

Our engaging native, *V. Vitis-idaea*, we should not like to be without, for it is a willing little carpeter for open woodland or associating with heaths, and its pretty pink and white flowers are as welcome as the bright red berries. There are various forms of this moorland waif, one diminutive (*minor*) not yet exceeding two or three inches in poorish soil with full exposure. With her unbounded faith in the innocence of the small the Lady of the Garden has invited this little creature to share some of her alpine rhododendron beds. But time only will prove whether luxury and a fat living will not, as I suspect it will, so demoralise this child of the lonely crags that it will develop into a ravening monster to the undoing of its neighbours and the confusion of L.G.

There is yet one more species to be included here and that is *V. glauco-album*, perhaps the finest garden shrub of the genus. If *corymbosum* merits a leading place among deciduous kinds, this excellent Himalayan might well claim the same precedence in the evergreen section. *V. glauco-album* slowly makes a bush of some three or four feet (our old specimen is four feet, six inches) with a width greater than its height. The ovate leaves' over two inches long, are a pale green on their upper sides, the underparts being blue-white. In summer, urn-shaped flowers a quarter-inch long and a fresh shell-pink, are produced in abundant three-inch racemes. Delightful enough in themselves, these blooms are enveloped in large bracts of a rosy-flushed white and these are retained for a long while after the flowers have fallen. By autumn the berries, which are the size of currants, ripen and, though black-skinned, they are so heavily coated with a vivid blue-white, waxy bloom that they gleam with a radiance almost electric in its luminosity, especially of an autumn evening.

Many vacciniums can boast of ornamental fruits but in none that I have seen are the latter so brilliant as in this choice shrub. Moreover, though these berries are not unpleasant to the taste, rather like a sharp bilberry, birds do not touch them. What is even more remarkable is the fact that they are so frost resisting that here they remain on the bush all winter, often until late spring. The plant itself is also tougher than it is supposed to be, especially if grown hard with full exposure and in rather a dry soil. We have ours on a warm heath slope and it has endured 20-30 degrees of frost without much injury. The only attention it ever gets is an occasional mulch of sorbex and leaf-mould.

So here endeth what is little more than a commentary upon the more distinguished of the world's whortleberries, as represented by our modest collection. They are not everybody's plants any more than gaultherias are, but anyone who likes the ericaceae will like them, and conditions that suit the one will suit the other. I believe, though I have not tried them with lime, that an acid soil is essential and patience will also be demanded. In common with the allied family they dislike root disturbance and nurse a resentment so bitter towards interference of the kind that they will often take years to settle down. But, planted carefully from pots, or in clumps, which is better still, one need not anticipate any trouble in that direction. And once they are established few things will be more permanent for, after the manner of most suckering plants, they have discovered in that process a means of maintaining a perennial youth.

VACCINIUM
GLAUCO-ALBUM

*Its vivid blue-white
berries ($\frac{1}{2}$ nat. size)
photographed in mid-
winter*

GAULTHERIA
(ARBUTUS)
FURIENS

*Gleaming white
blossoms against
a leafage of dark
and sullen green*

PRUNUS COMMUNIS var. POLLARDII

The largest in flower, most beautiful and fragrant of all the almonds

CHAPTER IX

Early Days on Sunny Slopes

IF I were to attempt to make the contents of these chapters follow the progress of the seasons I should very soon be in difficulties. But it is not my intention to venture upon such a course and one good reason is this: There are plants of importance which belong to no one period and of these I can think of none more likely to upset a seasonal programme than *Lithospermum rosmarinifolium* and *Coronilla glauca*. These may be in flower by mid-autumn, continue through the winter and accompany the spring to the brink of summer. And it is not possible to say at what particular time such plants will be at their best, for their blooming is entirely a matter of weather conditions, not only from autumn onwards but during the previous summer. Nor is there any guarantee that the two will be in colour simultaneously, since circumstances which affect the one may not affect the other.

At the moment of writing, however, we are enjoying both. The year is still not a month old, yet a broad drift of brilliant blue is adorning one of our many dry, walled-up slopes, whilst immediately below is the beautiful yellow of the coronilla, tumbling in copious masses over a low retaining wall. Bring in to the scene the clarifying light of a winter's lowering sun— the plants having a westerly aspect—and fill the sun-warmed air with the fragrance of broom blowing over the rising bracken of May, and you will agree with the conclusion that has just come to both of us that at no season has the garden ever given us anything more beautiful than that of this January afternoon.

L. rosmarinifolium comes, as everyone knows, from the marble-white cliffs of Capri. Its flowers, a long way larger than the largest of any other gromwell, are bluer than the waters of its blest island home, bluer than the blue of *Gentiana sino-ornata* whose latest blooms were still responding to the autumn sun when the rock-plant began. Hardy this Mediterranean

93

beauty may not be in so far as frost injury to its flowers is concerned, but in branch and leaf it will stand a good deal on a wall with a dry and stony root-run behind it. Then, even if it should have its loveliness marred, it is so full of energy, so anxious to make the best of its adopted home, that recovery is rapid and it will soon be going ahead as bravely as ever.

The coronilla is, on balance, perhaps the less trustworthy of the two. It, also, will quickly repair the ravages of a wintry spell if not too severe, but we have had large bushes destroyed by bark-splitting. *C. glauca* is as charming in its own way as its companion. There is a delightful harmony not only between its soft yellow and the gromwell's blue, but the former blends very happily with its own glaucous pea-green foliage, while in its careless elegance it has few equals. A better seaside flowering shrub than this I do not know. There are plants six miles nearer the sea than this garden which are a dozen feet across, and I have seen these ablaze with blossom from November onwards. There is a pygmy form of *C. glauca* which, though not a new plant, seems to be rare. How it compares with the type and whether it will prove to be worthy of the latter for rock-garden planting I do not know, our solitary specimen being still in the cradle.

Rosmarinus prostratus is often associated with *Lithospermum rosmarinifolium* for it also is said to have come from Capri. But diminutive and prostrate rosemarys can be found on many an Italian hillside. We once came across a great colony on some slopes near San Remo, every plant of which was not only gnarled and stunted, but the branches, having made a height of a few inches, drooped earthwards to push flat along the ground. And this was odd seeing that they were among other shrubs and not subjected to great exposure though the soil was gravelly and lean.

Here we cannot give this sweet little rosemary the openness and abundant sunshine it loves. In yearning for these it grows soft and lax, loses character by reaching up in search of light, and in this sappy condition easily succumbs to frost. Given full exposure it often grows hard enough to resist frost as successfully as the typical rosemary, but our conditions render it even more susceptible than the lithospermum mentioned. However, the prostrate rosemary is such a dear little shrub, yielding its azure blossoms at almost all seasons, that it will always be given the best of what we have to offer. A more attractive shrub for draping a wall it would be difficult to name and we have never seen it doing so well nor used with such admirable effect as in a famous garden on the Mediterranean. There, planted behind the top of a sunny retaining wall some four or five feet high and thirty yards long, it had crept over and clothed the entire wall with a close dense curtain of its fragrant, blue-decked green.

When *Erica carnea* is challenging winter's coldest steel with cushions of carmine and the shrubby milkwort, *Polygala Chamaebuxus*, is hastening to freshen up its mats of lustrous green with lilac and gold, the earliest of the brooms will be starting on their long career. The familiar *Cytisus racemosus*, often known as *Genista fragrans*, is not much of a success here. It will come through an average winter, its flowering period covering that of *Coronilla glauca*, then comes a frost to put an end to all its glory. Still, it is so easily raised from cuttings that it is always worth that risk.

A better garden shrub than *C. racemosus* and one that serves as a most efficient understudy for our old greenhouse friend, is the Porlock broom. This is a hybrid between the pretty *C. monspessulanus* and *racemosus*. It was discovered by Mr. N. G. Hadden of Porlock some years ago but its great value is only just being realised. Put briefly, the Porlock broom may be regarded as a hardy *racemosus*. It has the same rich leafiness, the same elegance and the same long and slender racemes of bright yellow flowers. Its beautiful blooms often begin to appear in February and, gathering splendour with the increasing sun, the bush is a blaze of golden-yellow from March to May, or later. The only quality lacking in Mr. Hadden's hybrid is fragrance, this being comparatively faint. But since *C. racemosus* is often as scentless when growing in the open, especially in winter, that failing is of little account in estimating the respective merits of the two shrubs. The Porlock broom is easily raised from cuttings and these will often begin flowering when a foot or so in height.

C. monspessulanus, which we have had over eight feet high, is another of these wakeful southern brooms which begin to anticipate the spring in the early days of the year. Said to be untrustworthy elsewhwere, including Kew, we have never had it seriously injured even by 25 degrees of frost. It does well anywhere with us, and there is such a charm about its fresh and luxuriant leafage, its easy grace and masses of little gorse-yellow flowers that we have it in generous groups and invite it to serve as an informal hedge or background to some of the beds and borders. This is one of the few of our brooms which naturalises freely, and its seedlings crop up so abundantly that we always have plenty of stock for replacing the old and worn-out. *C. monspessulanus* is a species with a natural range so extensive that it is possible we may have a hardier form than the one commonly grown.

C. hirsutus is an early broom and not one whose merits would earn it much approbation in the gay days of May. But the warm orange of its comparatively large flowers, whose standard petal is adorned with a flare of golden-brown, is welcome enough along our open woodland walks before the first of the wild anemones are awake. *Calycotome spinosa*, also a precocious member of this family, is a cheerful evergreen of four or five feet. Its little trefoils, being a lively glaucous green, make a good setting for the fairly large, bright yellow flowers. *Calycotome* earns its specific name for it is armed with ferocious spines. Along the seaward slopes of Var it covers many an arid acre much as gorse does here, and when associated with *Lavendula Stoëchas*, as it often is, one may enjoy a splendour of purple and gold rarely equalled by any other two shrubs.

The lavender, whose blue-purple cockades, cresting its rather gloomy inflorescences, are so telling against the hoary grey of the foliage, we have been unable to keep very long. But its neighbour of the *maquis* seems hardy enough in a dry, meagre soil and takes a mischievous delight in stabbing the nose of anyone unwary enough to inquire into its delicate fragrance. Thrifty peasants of S. Europe, who find a use for most things, often make their fences of *C. spinosa*, and the drying of the branches so increases the fierceness of its highly-tempered needles that it is almost as nasty a thing to meddle with as a barrier of prickly-pear.

Along the dry, westerly slope occupied by this mixed com-

DAPHNE
CNEORUM

DAPHNE BLAGAYANA IN EARLY FEBRUARY

THE MARBLE-WHITE
SPATHES OF
LYSICHITON
KAMTSCHATKENSE

PODOPHYLLUM
EMODI VAR. MAJOR

*Apple-blossom flowers
crest the lustrous bronzy
leaves in April*

pany whose yellows and blues drift on until they blend with the lovely pink of that superb almond, *Prunus communis Pollardii*, there will seldom be a mild day between November and March upon which *Daphne Dauphinii* (*hybrida*) will not greet you with its delicious scent. This sweetness it has inherited from the beautiful *D. odora*, and, since the latter is only just on the borderline of hardiness here, the hybrid makes a very satisfying substitute. *D. odora* we still keep on trying in various places for it is too precious a shrub to abandon lightly, but, meanwhile, its comely daughter (*sericea* being the other parent) plays the part and does it very nicely with clusters of plum-red blossom and that exquisite fragrance. A still more reliable daphne which will start away even in February is *D. Fioniana* which some believe to be a hybrid, while others call it *D. collina var. neapolitana*. This makes a neat little rounded bush of two feet or so with narrow, dark-green leaves and terminal clusters of deep-toned rosy flowers, very sweetly scented. *D. Fioniana* does much in the way of sustaining one's garden faith which, in a race so notoriously fickle as this, is often rather badly shaken. It will prosper almost anywhere and usually repeat its spring blooming in early autumn.

Daphnes are not plants for ground that may quickly dry out in summer, but the more frost-tender kinds we must grow on our sharply-drained slopes or not at all. And some do not resent this treatment. The finest plants of *D. Cneorum* we have ever had occupied exceedingly poor, sun-baked ledges for many years, making masses three to five feet across. Even so, now that a cooler and deeper sandy loam is available, with more space, they are promising to do still better, and the same change over has brought an equally generous response from *D. Mezereum*. This grand old shrub has not, within my memory, been accorded its due recognition in gardens. The cottager has always cherished it and, as if it were determined to impress upon us its hardy and adaptable nature, it has become naturalised in woods of this country and others, including N. America. At the moment we are making some amends for our own neglect of so valuable a shrub, and hopes run high of one day deriving from it such broad masses of colour as those with which *Rhododendron praecox* and *Erica carnea* carry us through the latter half of winter. *D. Mezereum* is not less worthy than these; it is not less reliable, and it yields, in addition to colour in abundance and a good show of berries, a wonderful perfume—not to mention self-sown seedlings.

Some find fault with the rather heavy purple of this old daphne. But the plant is variable in colour and there is reason to believe that with a little careful selection, one might raise varieties in clear shades of flesh pink, both dark and light. Our ancestors did so and some of these colour forms were named. But if *D. Mezereum* is rather on the wrong side of its luck these days, when so much time and money and energy are spent on novelties—often, perhaps, of inferior garden merit—its day will come and we shall applaud the virtues of a spring bloomer —and autumn fruiter—of sterling qualities.

The regrettable feature of this neglect of old things, however, often means something more than a passing loss. They are like so much frozen capital, and worse, for there is always present the risk of their being entirely lost. Of this we have abundant proof. The roads which our garden story has traversed are strewn with the victims of indifference and neglect, some of them precious things which never can be recalled.

Even *D. Mezereum* offers testimony of this for, unless I am much mistaken, the colour varieties which once were cultivated under name seem to be no longer obtainable (one or two may still occur in some lists). Then there is *D. M. autumnalis* (*grandiflora*) which, just like the type in other respects, flowered from October to February. This was a most valuable plant and some years ago we possessed it. But it eventually went to where all good daphnes go and we have never been able to replace it.[1]

D. Mezereum alba is a good milk-white at its best, and it offers double-flowered forms of which the finest was Paul's White, but it is long since we had this and I know not if it still exists. By what devious means a species is determined by the botanists is a mystery that has not yet penetrated my dark mind. But it appears to me that *D. M. alba* might put up a fairly sound claim to specific rank. Of its botanical characters my ignorance is abysmal, but from the point of view of an

[1]Through the kindness of Mr. Hillier this priceless antique has just been reinstated.

ordinary observer this shrub seems to differ in a very marked degree from the type. With us, at any rate, it is considerably more robust than the purple. The leaves come earlier, as do the more densely packed flowers, and there is a difference in the scent. The blooms are not only white without a trace of purple, but seedlings have in my experience invariably come white. This constancy is impressive, and then, to wind up its season, *D. M. alba* produces, not rich red fruits, but bright yellow. I am told, moreover, that these yellow fruits and the unfailing determination of the plant to yield seedlings after its kind are as steadfast a feature in the wild[1] as in the garden.

D. pseudo-Mezereum, evidently an old species recently introduced from Central Japan, is still on trial. It has given us a crop of its chocolate and green trumpets, but its habit of leafing and flowering very early in the year does not make its prospects very rosy. The golden *D. aurantica* is also on the 'try out' list. But a weakness for the uncommon, plus an affection for the whole tribe of *Daphne*, is our excuse for indulging in such plants as this. And so it is with *Edgworthia papyrifera* (or *Daphne chrysantha*), an early, yellow-flowered Asiatic. This shrub lives and languishes in one of our warmest corners, an object of chronic resentment at all our seasons, all our weather, and all we do towards the amelioration of its great unhappiness. And one of these days it will go hence, unregretted. If there were a Society for the Prevention of Cruelty to Plants we should probably be cast into a dungeon for inflicting so much misery upon creatures like this. But so long as kind friends give you such things with the firm conviction that your climate is much more kindly than it is; so long as you yourself endeavour to explain a quite incomprehensible desire to attain the impossible by the argument that you really do not know how a plant will behave until you have tried it—which is true enough within limits—for so long will your garden have nursing cases to deal with.

But gardening, after all, would lose much of its fun and sporting interest if all were easy and straight sailing. And what is more, we have good and comforting testimony to prove that had we abided by the warnings of the less adventurous, or been

[1] It is plentiful in Switzerland and some of the more Eastern Alps.

influenced by the records of meteorology, we should never have known what it is to enjoy scores of plants which, often regarded as hopeless under such conditions as ours, have been a surprising success. *Acacias dealbata* and *Baileyana* which, as I have said, sometimes adorn their steely blue-grey foliage with golden honey-scented powder-puffs, may be easy prey to the first frost that comes along. But it is much if we can only occasionally enjoy these stolen sweets, if only at odd seasons we are reminded with the gratification of reality of those beautiful words: 'Come, thou South! And breathe upon my garden that the spices of it may flow out.' Even should these charming saplings of fifteen feet or so entirely succumb to frost, mimosas grow at such an amazing pace—either from seed or stump sprouts—that flowering specimens may be raised in an incredibly short time.

But a policy of trial has a wider application than that relating to winter worthiness. There is the much more difficult and perplexing matter of soil worthiness, or whatever you like to call those often entirely inexplicable causes which induce a plant to flourish in one spot and which deny it existence in another, even though the two places appear to offer entirely similar conditions. In this affair one could not desire examples more illuminating than some of the daphnes. We know *D. Cneorum* when it comes to us from Holland in a lump of peat is very apt to expire before its roots can effect a change-over to, say, a sandy loam. That can possibly be understood and explained, and rhododendrons will often behave in the same way. But why does *D. Cneorum* flourish in our shaley soil and utterly decline to have anything to do with the same brand of soil, the same general conditions, in a neighbour's garden? No one has yet answered that question.

Then consider *D. Blagayana*. It is possible to grow this lovely plant without any difficulty, but he would be fatuous indeed who assumed that anyone who adopted the conditions under which it prospers in one place could reap the same success in another. With all daphnes tribal law is guarded more zealousy than it is with most plants. But *D. Blagayana* cloaks its family secrets beneath inviolable shade. It conceals its mysteries in a darkness so obscure that it has baffled the best of us. Where it flourishes it flourishes, and if it decides to have nothing to do with us, all the teachings of science and the gardener's cajolery and patient care will not avert a languishing death.

D. Blagayana, exasperating enigma, once surprised us by displaying a most remarkable liveliness under conditions that seemed impossible. That was on one of the driest ledges of the dry slope with which this chapter deals. There it abounded most amazingly and every February for many years its green rosettes were centred with its ivory-white, deliciously scented flowers. Each spring it had the same top-dressing, layering and other attentions and it looked like making a really permanent job of it. But there came a day when it began to wear the pallor of decline. It developed a galloping anaemia and in a few weeks it was in a better land. A successor reigns in its stead and is prospering with abounding promise. It has just given us sixty-seven trusses of bloom. Even so, to-morrow it may turn its face to the wall.

Daphnes are like that—not excepting the exquisite *D. petraea*, darling of the rock-gardener's heart. You never know how they will behave until you try. One day they will send your spirits sky-high in a triumph of exhilaration and anon cast them into a pit of darkness and dismay. Which, to round off rather a lengthy parenthesis, is not an unfamiliar example of what an empirical pursuit like gardening has in store for the faithful. For our sins these thorns and thistles may have been given us, but life would be dull without them. The daily round would lose much of its stimulating romance and it is very largely to them that we owe what little knowledge and skill we possess.

To return to the thin and rather stony soil of our westerly banks upon which most of the aforementioned plants are growing, this is, as I have inferred, the first to be warmed-up by the increasing sun. It is here that we look for that engaging mite, *Cyclamen balearicum*, for the awakening of *C. repandum*, the earliest anemones and the broad emerald blades which embrace that super snowdrop, *Galanthus Elwesii* and its even bigger and more glaucous-leaved variety, *Whittallii*. It is here that the first leucojums break asunder their sheathing green, here that the first *Hyacinthus azureus* shakes out its little peal of china-blue bells. It is along these goat-track walks that *Iris reticulata*, spearing a carpet of *Hypericum reptans*, raises aloft its pennons of royal purple and gold to hasten the retreat of winter with its sultry violet breath. And here that *Scilla bifolia*, the lovely *taurica* and richly apparelled Spring Beauty of the *sibirica* group will be rivalling *Chionodoxa sardensis* and *Tmoli* some weeks before these and the muscaris are running in pools of blue between the erythroniums of the turf below.

With these pre-vernal messengers come the forerunners of the daffodil clan among which we have none so steadfast and permanent in miniatures, none so exactly what a pocket-edition daffodil ought to be in proportion and colour as *Narcissus minimus*. *N. cyclamineus* is equally early and exquisitely beautiful with its perianth so sharply reflexed from the rich yellow trumpet that the segments cross their tips as they hug the swan-neck stem. Some of the bulbocodiums and jonquils are not far behind as to date, and there are others among which the cyclamineus hybrids are exceedingly dainty if a little tall to rank with the smallest. But few, if any, of these can rival *minimus* when it comes to staying qualities, reliability and steady increase.

N. nanus, a very early bloomer, is a charming miniature of the typical daffodil and the colour is good. But it will top the three inches of *minimus* by at least another two inches. *N. minor*, still a trifle taller, is also a little daffodil of precocity with prettily twirled perianth and a full-toned yellow. But, delightful as these are they don't quite touch that refinement of grace and proportion which belongs to the sweet-tempered *minimus* whose fanfare is so delicately attuned to the tender ears of the infant spring, nor do they attain that perfection of form, colour, balance and poise which belongs to the peerless Queen of Spain.

It is, however, so odious a business making comparisons between these brave and blithesome heralds of the opening year that I must take refuge among the crocuses. Here our trump card is *C. Tomasinianus*, for we have never had the like of this cheerful little fellow for taking care of himself and naturalising by seed into broad drifts. And what is lovelier than those slender, finely-drawn shell-grey buds which crop up in an eruption of ardent, trustful and expectant life just when the Greek anemone is raising its bowed head to greet the February sun? And what is more chastely beautiful than the silvery lavender, warmed by the slightest flush of rose into an amethyst of infinite delicacy with which the outer parts of the elegant, long-drawn wine-glass flowers are stained, while the inner petals deepen to a delicious violet? And then, within, there is that telling dash of orange-scarlet. Tom. will, moreover, give you variety in its numerous offspring, seedlings which range from the refined purple-amethyst of the type to a parma violet with a decided touch of ruby in its blue. And all you have to do to raise this adorable little creature in plenty is to plant a handful of bulbs in a few sunny places where the soil is tolerably free. In two or three seasons these will prove what a successful colonist this species is by increasing an hundredfold. It will pop up in all manner of places, even in grass, with that engaging unexpectedness which is one of the great rewards of informal gardening. Explain it I cannot, but *C. Tomasinianus* is one of the few 'croci' which are left alone by mice. That it is immune in some way is extremely doubtful, and it may be that its safety is due to its excessive numbers. As the cat ceases to prey on mouse when the latter swarms, so mouse may turn in satiety from the inexhaustible legions which this crocus brings forth.

C. biflorus we also regard very highly, for it is a good stayer though it does not increase by seed. Like other plants long subjected to the luxurious ease of garden life it seems to have drifted into sterility. Even so, the Scotch crocus is a great lad. Its large flowers of a warm white are deftly feathered on the outside with a sumptuous purple, it is scented and will carry on for years and be out with the firstlings of spring. A changeable species this, and the lists offer varieties differing a little in colour from the type. And so it is with *C. versicolor* (Cloth of Silver) which brings the news of spring to the Maritime Alps with its white chalices ornamented with crimson-purple and ruby-red freakings in fantastic diversity, these breaking away from the crocus tradition by striping the lining silver of its inner segments. *C. susianus* is another of these fascinating bulblets we should not like to part with. It lacks some of the elegance of others perhaps, but earns its familiar name of Cloth of Gold by the lustrous fiery yellow of its brown-striped petals.

If you would have a really early crocus of the bluest blood

there are few, if any, to equal the exquisite violet-blue and fawn, *C. Imperati*—'sweet-voiced nightingale of the spring, peering up into the sere dark world when all the ground is rotten with death, and January, like sad Barsanti, weeps across the scene' (Farrer). On the other hand if your bank balance demands something at less than half the price, something that you can submit to the discomforts of an English winter with an easier conscience, there is *chrysantha*. Lovely enough to rank with the most precious is this beauty of Eastern Europe, and if her everyday wear is of purest gold unadorned, she will yield seedlings in a bewildering assortment of blue and white, pale and rich yellow, bronze and silvery rose, ivory and creamy citrons of moonlit pallor, all with or without lines and stipplings of contrasting colour. Many of these have been named, one of the best of them—and of all crocuses—bearing the distinction of being called after the illustrious Crocus King himself, Mr. E. A. Bowles, who has, with such enlightened enthusiasm and masterly craftsmanship piloted so many of us through the confusing labyrinths of the crocus world.

C. vernus is a happy plant under almost any conditions and very fresh and dainty she is in her spring frock of delicate mauve. But to this she is not any more constant than she is to her figure, for in both she is ever indulging in departures from her established style. But *vernus* has always that peculiar appeal which imparts to her near relation, *Tomasinianus*, so irresistible a charm, and it is said that it is she whom we have in part to thank for all those common or garden crocuses which for generations have done so much for the gaiety of our lawns and borders. And these opulent creations of the Dutch hybridists let us never despise. In refinement and breeding, in that grace of manner and line and often colour which marks the species, they may show a grievous falling-off. They are commercialised and prosperous, they blazon their well-fed affluence without restraint. They do and say things which nice people do not say and do. They are apt to be noisy, to forget the respect due to those who give them hospitality.

But, even so, it would be an ill day for English gardens—for all gardens—were these Dutch crocuses to be no more seen. They fill a place which nothing else could fill so well, and used in the right way they can be as delightful as any other flower of spring. Their irrepressible good humour is alone something to be thankful for. I should not know how to define what Mr. Punch calls the 'crocus feeling', but most of us do know what it is to enjoy the rollicking laughter of these jolly Dutchmen which shakes across the lawns of spring. We do know that there is a something in these common crocuses which speaks to us of the mirthful sunshine and warmth of the victorious sun, that their sturdy optimism is as heartening a thing as their friendly, homely smiles. Between these crocuses and ourselves there has grown up a living intimacy which sometimes in this age of speed and change seems to harbour and to succour a mellowing sweetness which is comforting.

Dutch crocuses, it is true enough, may easily seem all wrong in some gardens, striking a garish, loudly aggressive note which you feel is entirely out of tone without quite knowing the reason why. But here, I take it, much depends upon one's personal tastes and each may follow such inclinations as appeal to him. We have had these crocuses paraded in all manner of arrangement, and if one really definite conclusion has been attained it is the exclusion of the yellow from all lawn plantings, and especially from mixed groups. Even the latter are now reduced to the simplest conceptions and consist, for the most part, of no more than two varieties to each drift.

A good white like Kathleen Parlow, with the deep rich violet-purple of *purpureus grandiflorus* or King of the Blues, gives us a fine effect on grass under the leafing trees, and this has pleased us as much as any. The silver-white Margot, delicately lined with lilac, a beautiful crocus, goes well with Amethyst, and blue-purples in two distinct shades, dark and light, are always delightful, giving that hazy impression which suggests the wild hyacinths of May.

But in a garden of limited area these richly endowed confections can easily be overdone, and we endeavour to keep our Dutchmen not only to themselves—as the wise keep their hybrid rhododendrons—but sparingly, as well as irregularly, spaced. In this way they give us unqualified joy, and if they do not abound in increase as they do in some gardens, well, I am not at all sure that that is a matter for regret. Indeed, they tend to decrease which means that every year a few corms are put in to keep the population up to normal.

Yes, the Dutch crocus can be exceedingly charming—and almost gross if abused in treatment. At its best it ranks high among the most treasured tokens of spring. There is such pulsing ecstasy in its passionate zeal for sunshine and the glad young life of early days that it always reminds me of the late Mr. Gerald Gould's moving lines wherein he tells us how the returning light

> *Proclaims the day of pageant, laughter comes*
> *Along the watercourse, like beaten drums.*
>
> .   .   .   .   .
>
> *And colour linked with colour flows*
> *About the country like a tune. . . .*

A tune it is and one of jocund merriment which trembles across the crocuses of our grassy glade on the winds of March, and we are grateful to them for that.

CHAPTER X

Some Waterside Plants, of Spring and Other Days

S
O HOTLY do we pursue the novelty these days, so ready are we to perjure our good name as gardeners so long as we can wipe a neighbour's eye with something in a pot, that one wonders whither this zeal will lead us. Wholesome enough it doubtless is, for nothing keens up one's interest like a novelty. But to that there is another side which is this: We are too apt in being unbalanced by the latest arrival from Tibet to place rarity before that all-important virtue—garden merit. Plants that will never be of any use save as toys for the specialist are awarded high honour, their owners are the heroes of the hour. *Omne ignotum pro magnificum,* and the really well tried and worthy are passed by. Plants, indeed, which have little more than botanical interest are hung on the line, while those which have a loveliness which has charmed generations and a constitution that is beyond any doubt are left out in the cold of our indifference.

It may be urged that a good garden plant, like the blue poppy, will always make its own way into our gardens by sheer force of excellence. But if we are to be honest with ourselves and do the just thing by England's gardens it is as incumbent upon us, as Mr. Kingdon Ward himself has said, to rediscover the old as it is to discover the new, and in support of that contention I could hardly do better than call in the aid of *Primula rosea.* For here is a plant of unrivalled loveliness, of indestructible hardiness, a long-lived perennial of a short-lived family, a plant that will do well almost anywhere, never asking a moment of your time, never failing to reproduce itself from seed. Yet *P. rosea,* although it has been with us for a generation, is comparatively little known. We spend ourselves and our resources over primulas and others not more beautiful, often inferior, and this delightful thing is overlooked.

It might be argued that *P. rosea* is a bog plant and therefore unsuited to gardens that have no water. But, granted it enjoys bog or waterside, even shallow water, it will do, and do well, in any moistish border with not too hot an aspect. That good gardener, the late Sir Arthur Hort, tells us (*The Unconventional Garden*) how he used to grow it in ordinary cool soil with leaf mould and some shade, and incidentally drops the useful suggestion that, in the border, *Isopyrum thalictroides* should be grown with it. Thus, the maidenhair leaves of this wee plant will cover the leafless primula while its elegant little white anemone flowers will join the rose-carmine of its companion with charming effect.

So completely naturalised is *P. rosea* by our water that it takes care of itself, bless it! It has followed the runnel of water which feeds the pool from an intake off our old mill-race, and wandered all round the pool itself. And as early as February, if the weather be kindly, its barren looking clumps, so brown and mummied and wintered, will be studded with ruby buds. So our Aphrodite rises out of the cerements of death to hail the first hint of lengthening day, the very spirit of spring. Those vivid buds will, for at least two months, crop up with surprising prolificacy, the flower-clustered stems will grow longer and longer and it will be May before the last bit of colour announces the conclusion of rosea's round. And the excellent Brockhurst Variety is no less satisfying.

P. rosea, having given me a lead, suggests an incursion among other early bloomers of the water garden, one of the more precocious being that great aroid, *Lysichiton americanum* which used to be called *L. kamtschatkense*. The big butter-yellow hoods of this noble plant, thrusting forth from the cones of polished ebony which rise well above the soil like those of *Lilium giganteum*, follow one another in brave array for several weeks. Established plants will put up a dozen of these splendid golden callas which go so well with the rosy flush of the yellow-eyed primula, which, however, must not be too near the arum since the latter's flowers are followed by enormous banana-like leaves of imposing proportions in a cool pea-green—leaves which are invaluable for creating a strong note among the foliage plants of summer. Having finished flowering and developed its seed, the huge green spadices flop over on to the ground and presently become immersed in a mass of glairy slime like frog's spawn. In this the seeds mature and if we forget to remove them masses of baby arums will appear, soon to be engaged in internecine strife.

The story has been told in another book of how we went out one spring day from Victoria, B.C., to hunt up not only *L. americanum* in its native lair but the lovely *Erythronium revolutum*, how half a day's tramp brought us to a swampy meadow which, from end to end, was an eruption of those glorious golden spathes, while in the drier coppices of oak hard by that exquisite dog's-tooth was filling the undergrowth with its ivory turkscaps, the air with its ineffable sweetness.

That was a good many years ago, but on our return home both plants were established in the garden where they have been ever since. But neither of these are as commonly seen in this country as they deserve to be, and the arum is still, it appears, so unfamiliar to the trade that you will find it listed under the unlovely name of skunk-cabbage. Wherefore, let the warning go forth to all who would avoid having as a substitute for the golden glory of their hopes the squalid turtle-headed, liver-coloured, carrion-haunted ogre, *Symplocarpus foetidus*, the aforementioned cabbage whose stench even a skunk might disdain to own.

Our first experience with the beautiful white-flowered species, *L. kamtschatkense*, the same as that over which Farrer became so rhapsodical when he beheld it in that 'stinking deep slough of the Hokkaido' (*The English Rock Garden*) was a curious one. For years we failed entirely to run to earth this waterside wonder, but at length secured some seed from a botanic garden. That seed was sown in a pan and put outside to winter and, behold! when spring came there appeared, instead of our long sought arum, a lusty crop of *Iris sibirica*!

Said I to the Lady of the Garden, 'An enemy hath done this thing, for are there not tares among the wheat?' And she answered me saying, 'I see no wheat, but suffer the whatever-it-is to carry on until autumn, when we may likely find some.'

This we did, and when the pan was turned out we discovered one very infantile arum, yet surely the very one we wanted for its leaves were bluer than those of the yellow fellow.

However, that little mite was tenderly brought up and after the course of years opened that strangely beautiful hood, marble-white like that of a calla but more finely wrought and sheltering with dramatic contrast the vividly green spadix—a pickling cucumber, *var. erectus.* How the iris seed got into the pan did not matter, nor did it occasion much surprise for these plants have a way of emptying a capsule where they happen to fancy. It was enough for us to know that we had at last got a long-desired treasure established. Nor has it ever looked back. It has borne us families of its own and is one of the most arresting objects of our early waterside garden.

Cardamine macrophylla is a lush and hearty thing with sappy green watercress growths which ramp about any moistish spot. Even in February it will put up its nine-inch sprays of bright rosy-lilac flowers, giving a splash of cheerful colour long before most of its neighbours are beginning to awake. Nor does it seem to mind if, later on, it is entirely covered by the ferns, rodgersias and senecios which share its territory. Indeed, one may perhaps regard this summer suppression as helpful in steadying-down the aspirations of a too ambitious nature, and that other pretty rogue, *Anchusa myosotidiflora,* to which I have already referred, offers a case for similar treatment. This is so lovely when its flights of wedgwood blue stars are hovering above the leafless crown, but so big and coarse is its summer foliage, so determined to ramble are its roots—and roots they are which defy extraction—that one has to put the plant under some sort of subjection or do without it.

To return to cardamine, there is no better plant in the spring garden than the double cuckoo-flower, *C. pratense fl. pl.* Yet this comely herb, with its sheaves of clear soft lilac, stock-like flowers, can be a very murrain of a weed. But it was not until one ill-guided day when we brought in from the hills some local double cuckoo-flowers that our troubles with this plant began. These wildings did not only rapidly deteriorate in blossom, but they commenced forthwith to propagate themselves by leaf-cuttings, as is their habit, and did so with such amazing fecundity that we very soon had myriads of their pestilential spawn, which dug themselves into other plants and exercised every imaginable cunning in eluding our efforts to eradicate them. And this we have not yet done. The wild double cuckoo-flower is still with us, a heart of vengeful fury lurking in its mild and innocent rosettes.

Now, there seems reason to believe that the double carda-mine which is vastly superior to our collected plants which brought woe into our garden world, is of exotic origin. It may not be a descendant of that double 'Cuckow Flower' which, so Parkinson tells us, was introduced and sent to him 'by my speciall good friend John Tradescante' some three hundred years ago. But it very probably came from the same Continental source, and is not only a plant of much greater merit than our native but it is well behaved. At the same time we would not give even this plant too moist a spot. It is quite content with rock-garden conditions and there is perfectly safe and decorous in manners. But who can say that there runs not in its veins that passion for water which, taken in excess, will let loose forces of anarchy in creatures which are, on normal rations, sober, law-abiding citizens?

For the same reason we keep that super celandine, *Ranun-culus Ficaria major*, well out of reach of temptation. This butter-cup, a sort of water-lily that a long time ago abandoned aquatic life for residence on land, still nurses a silent yearning for its old wet life. And one hardly dare contemplate the lapse of moral balance which might befall it were it to be given unrestrained freedom within reach of its favourite tap. So we have it segre-gated where no evil shall divert it from the paths of virtue, and, rather than fretting against this precaution, it amply rewards us throughout the early year with its suns of glistening gold which a half-crown piece will not cover.

Close to the waters of the rivulet dwells that liliaceous N. American, *Helonias bullata*, the stud-flower. Making a clumpy tuft of strap-shaped, pale green, glossy, evergreen leaves, and increasing, but very slowly, by offsets, this rather dismal look-ing object presents a brave show for a few weeks in early spring. Stout fifteen-inch stems rise stiffly from its flaccid rosettes, and each of these terminates in a cone-shaped inflorescence of coral pink. Not a first-class performer, perhaps, but one that is wel-come enough here in these early days.

The same plea might be made for *Orontium aquatica* which

trails ropy spadices of a shrill lemon-yellow over the mud. But the golden-club is not quite so early and is preceded by another more interesting member of the same household, *Rohdea japonica*. This oddity, with erect dark green leathery leaves, endures a life shadowed by the horrid fear that it might at any moment be mistaken for an aspidistra by some careless passer-by. So it does its best to look like a yucca, and shyly hides within its embracing green a shower of wee white bells, but it has not yet managed to follow on with any of its red fruits.

The earliest of the calthas to give us colour is the smaller form of the double native, *C. palustris*, and it is very early. These 'monstrosas' we devoutly abhor in most parts of the garden, but this little water-goggles is not boisterously aggressive in its monstrousness. It is, indeed, curiously attractive, possibly because it is ablaze six weeks before any of its friends have opened an eye, and it is usually the last to go over. But the best of the *C. palustris* section is undoubtedly Tyerman's Variety for which our water-garden is indebted to Mr. R. D. Trotter. This is finer in the flower, perhaps more bronzed in leaf, and generally more well-bred in tone than the wild one commonly is.

The noblest Roman of all the kingcups—

> ... *minted flower,*
> *Cup of a king in gold,*

is *C. polypetala*, which ought to have been *polysepala* since of petals it has none. The old romance about this plant having been filched from the Vatican gardens has rather lost its spice, for the species has, I believe, been not only found wild (by Mr. E. K. Balls among others) in Eastern Europe but introduced from there. However, the plant remains the chieftain of the clan, a splendid hearty thing which, flinging out red-bronze arms of a yard in length, will float them on the water and adorn them with a succession of golden goggles until summer is nigh.

Before we had our present choice of ground wherewith to indulge in such things a number of erythroniums were put on a well raised streamside bank. The soil being cool, yet free, these are not only still there but they have increased abundantly. Long before the willow gentians which entirely cover them in

THE GOLDEN-YELLOW CALLAS OF LYSICHITON AMERICANUM

ERYTHRONIUM HOWELLII
Part of a self-sown colony of this beautiful dog's-tooth violet

CARDAMINE PRATENSE FL. PL.
The double cuckoo-flower

summer have made an inch or two of growth these dog's-tooths are in full bloom. They are all so delightful with their dainty, lily-like grace and engaging refinement of line and poise that to make comparisons between them one can not. Perhaps *E. Howellii*, with bold mottled leaves and ivory-yellow flowers, several to a stem, standing at fifteen inches high, is the most robust, and it seeds with unusual freedom. Then there is the elegant and sweet *E. giganteum* already mentioned, the revolutums in both carmine and rose, the chrome-yellow *californicum* and *Hendersonii*, a most stately plant of at least a foot, bearing on each slender stem several gracefully hung, reflexed flowers in a pale lilac darkening to a maroon eye.

E. tuolumnensis we planted with some mistrust as to its permanence, but it has made good and for a number of years has put up its plain green leaves over which, at the height of a foot, swing the bright canary-yellow blooms. *Purdyi*, with flowers of ivory-cream aglow with yellow at the throat, also promises to be a stayer, while the familiar *dens-canis* varieties are naturalised in half-a-dozen places in the woodland and elsewhere.

There is a charm so attracting about these erythroniums, an appeal so undoing, that not even the cyclamen of autumn and winter have more completely won our affection. We plant a few every year, starting fresh colonies, enlarging old ones or trying new kinds. Most of them do their part by increasing on their own account, often popping up in unexpected places, and yet we have not enough of them. And I believe this riotous excess had its beginning on that copsy slope of British Columbia where we first saw these sylvan fairies in such rare perfection. It was there that we said in all sincerity that, once back in our home garden, we should make these beautiful things as the dust of the earth, so that if a man can number the dust of the earth, then shall they also be numbered.

One of the jobs which calls us to the waterside when the cuckoo is telling us its name from every brake, and the white-throat's gurgling reel accompanies the April treble of the river's song, is the overhauling of our creeping mimulus. Most of the more robust forms of *M. luteus* have had to make way for less troublesome things, but we are still faithful to our own namesake, which we found years ago on a Welsh moor. Though it shows an affinity with *luteus*, this fine plant, usually under two feet, does not ramp like that good American which seems to have made every brook and sheep-drain in Britain its home. It grows sturdily erect above its bronzy-green pads of leaves, and the unusually large and velvety flowers it bears so freely are a rich wallflower-red, or deep crimson-scarlet, each segment being evenly margined with gold. A very charming thing massed along the water when the stately *Iris sibirica* is belting the banks with blue.

This mimulus, which I feel sure is a hybrid and not a colour form of *luteus*, we dig up every spring, re-planting in the same site, from which it works its way into the shallow water on one side and into the irises on the other. Without this attention it is apt to decline, if not to disappear altogether, and the same applies to *M. Burnettii*, a handsome and not too lively creeper with flowers of a glowing burnt-orange, and to the charming *Langsdorffii*. The latter, by the way, has solved for us a little problem in garden upkeep by so completely carpeting with its close-set mat of small green rosettes a narrow pool-side border, which was always one of the weediest spots in the garden, that this now asks but little attention. If the mimulus is thinned down by winter, as it usually is, it also is dug up in April and re-planted in a little fresh loam and sorbex. After which it goes ahead at once, weaves its weed-proof fabric over the moist soil and for a long period in summer gives us a band of soft yellow flowers on stems of not more than six inches.

Curiously enough, *M. cardinalis* is one of the most permanent of our monkey-flowers, maintaining itself by self-sown seedlings which give us yellow and blush-white flowers as well as scarlet. The blue-violet *ringens* helps the nurserymen by asking for frequent replacement, but while *Lewisii*, the type, with rose flowers, soon miffs off, its lovely white variety usually keeps up its own stock by stray seedlings which always come true. *M.* (*Mazus*) *radicans* makes dense mats of its tough stems and rather dismal leaves which it cheers up with the bonniest of blossoms, almost stemless and milk-white with masterly touches of orange and royal purple, and the wee *M. primuloides* we grow among such dainties as *Calceolaria tenella* and Mr.

Millard's fine form of *Houstonia cœrulea* on rather higher, yet damp ground.

It is our principle, as the reader will observe, not to do much fussing over a plant that declines our attentions after reasonable civility. But there are some exceptions, some much too good to turn down because they happen to ignore our well-meant services. Among several mimulus which we deem worthy of annual restoration whensoever they may need it, is the beautiful *M. Bartonianus*, one of the finest of the family, consisting as it does of the best features of *cardinalis* and *Lewisii*. In a drier place than most of them get this grand plant is fairly permanent, often going several years without loss of vigour, but it comes so easily from cuttings that we generally keep a small reserve stock at hand.

M. Bartonianus we have had three feet high and four or five feet across from a single crown, a glorious object when covered with its rose-pink, yellow-throated flowers against a distinctly silvered green. And worthy of it is that remarkable branch-sport which Mr. G. N. Smith found on *M. Bartonianus* at Daisy Hill. Sunset, as it is called, has all the vigour and easy elegance of the parent, but the flowers, harking back to *cardinalis*, are a fiery scarlet of uncommon brilliance.

A waterside place elevated enough for the foregoing gives hospitality to the charming *Astilbe simplicifolia* and those later introductions of the *A. crispa* group. These latter are most fascinating little plants of six to ten inches which, above a crimped and close metallic foliage, all crispily frizzed, raise stiffly erect pyramids of blossom. The latter may be milk-white or some shade of pink, and the Lilliputs answer to the names of Gnome Perkoë, Daumlung and other fairy-like terms. Perfectly hardy, easy and immortal, these are extremely satisfying, pleasant little fellows. To propagate them we do not find a simple matter, but the Lady of the Garden, greatly daring, has been known to slice a piece off one of their thick and turnipy roots. This has grown away as would a budded chunk of potato or dahlia and the parent has not greatly resented the affront.

A. simplicifolia, its airy sprays scintillating like rose-tinted foam, is verily 'a gift of the gods', and I take it to be one of the parents of those dwarf astilbes usually listed as *A. s. hybrida*.

These are a singularly useful and beautiful group of hardy plants which do not often exceed a foot in height. From a central root-stock they put forth a sheaf of elegantly drooping flights of blossom in a variety of colours from white to ruby-carmine. The matchless elegance of *simplicifolia* is united with the brilliant hues of the larger hybrid astilbes in these delightful plants, and while they are extremely accommodating in the garden they do not 'run' or display any other evil ways. There is a troublesome imp called, I believe, *A. chinensis pumila*, with spikes of pucy magenta, which we would do much to avoid, and I am inclined to think this has crept into some of the *simplicifolia* hybrids, not to the improvement of their colours or their stay-at-home virtues. But, with that exception, we give the warmest welcome to this engaging race.

Lysimachias are so tempestuously invasive that one must place them with care or do without them. One of the best is *L. clethroides*, which is mentioned elsewhere, and *pseudo-Henryi* is a good yellow. We also like the treacle-gold *L. punctata* of two feet, a riotous weed but a beautiful thing properly used. I have seldom seen anything of the sort more impressive than a four-foot belt of this lysimachia running for some thirty yards between a laurel hedge and a lawn in dear old E. C. Buxton's garden. It seemed to be in flower nearly all summer and never failed to yield enough of its warm yellow to blend with the tints of autumn. Which, by the way, only goes to demonstrate that to condemn a plant off-hand as a ramper is not only wrong but may be an admission of failure on our part.

'That thing was an ungovernable scourge before I put it there,' E. C. B. once said to me, adding: 'Now it is one of my most satisfying delights, never asking a moment's attention.'

And that venerable gardener would not have claimed any more originality for that than he did for the way in which he controlled his enormous white beard. This appendage, whenever it got in the way, he would roll up into a bob and, securing it with a broad red elastic band, so that it suggested a white mare's tail done up for a show, he would set forth to garden or to pursue the grouse. So will the exercise of a little ingenuity, not forgetting the line of least resistance, ease one's way with unruly plants.

To come back to lysimachias, *L. Ephemerum* is a species which earns our affection for there is a refreshing coolth in its glaucous foliage and tall spires of pale lavender flowers in the hot summer days, but instead of erring on the robustious side it is none too easy to winter. A still more uncommon plant is *L. phyllocephala*. A lowly herb of some six inches here, with reddish stems and hairy evergreen leaves, this bears terminal clusters of blossom in a rich old gold with a flush of purple within. So far this species has not shown any great ambition to spread and it is apt to perish if not treated with care.

L. (Steironema) ciliata is also fairly willing to 'stay put', and there is a decided charm about this stately herb. A sound perennial anywhere in a moistish soil, it starts the season with crimson-bronze shoots and, rising to two feet or more, adorns its erect sheaf of leafy stems with nodding wide bells of clear yellow. Even when its willowy leaves are announcing autumn with brilliant shades of carmine and orange it will still be tossing out those yellow blooms.

The lythrums of the *L. Salicaria* set, which are so valuable along the waterside when the irises are streaked with the gold of approaching autumn, we have in variety from clear rose-pinks to rich purple-crimsons. The only precaution we exercise with these consists of the prompt removal of the spent flower-heads lest they sow the parish with their spurious offspring. *L. virgatum* and *alatum* do not offend in this way. These are much smaller plants, seldom over a couple of feet, and if their colour, a rosy-magenta, may trouble some people they have a rare and slender elegance of line and poise.

This lythrum colour is again, so it seems to me, largely a matter of placing. In any event, a group of *L. alatum* rising out of a carpet of the semi-aquatic fern, *Lastrea Thelypteris*, at the brink of our little pool, is exceedingly charming for it has at its back the silver-grey foliage of that beautiful dwarf willow *Salix lanata Stuartii*. Without that setting the loosestrife might be considerably less pleasing, but, so placed, even those who profess to be ultra colour-sensitive are at least tolerant in their attitude. For that willow, by the way, we have a sentimental regard, for it came to us from Farrer's old Yorkshire nursery. But, apart from that, it makes a delightful waterside shrub, with its lovely May catkins, its cool suede-grey of summer, and autumn tints. Although an old bush it is only some three feet high with a breadth of eight feet.

Mention of the seeding prolificacy of the purple loosestrifes recalls the same trouble we once had with *Spiraea Aruncus*. The native meadowsweet is bad enough, and I know of no weed more difficult to extricate than a meadowsweet seedling which has got itself anchored in the middle of an iris or trollius. But this plant at its worst is a mild affair compared with goatsbeard, whose fecundity is as amazing as its resourcefulness as a coloniser. However, a good many years have passed since we had the last of our anxiety over this stalwart, and the remedy was a simple one. It so happens that *S. Aruncus* believes in husbands and wives occupying separate establishments, and all you have to do is to eradicate the females and grow only the males. The latter are, in any case, very much handsomer in their plumes than the more drooping, tasselled ladies, and they are happy enough unconsciously waving their magnificent beards to an unresponding world.

With other plants which are determined to 'go native', to sow the seeds of anarchy in the peace of the garden, remedy may not be so easy nor so obvious. Most knotweeds go about with treachery and malevolence, but if some are beyond hope we still keep, on parole, that delightful creeping shrub *Polygonum vaccinifolium* and the highly ornamental *P. amplexicaule*. The latter, with leaves like a well dressed comfrey, and yard-long, branching arms crested in summer and autumn with heads of brilliant ruby blossoms, came here with a fairly clean record for a clan so nefarious. But it eventually broke out in reckless greed and hostility against all garden discipline and was about to be cast forth. But, being too good a plant for expulsion, we put this daughter of the horse-leech on a waterside bank densely backed by male-fern and there it has been for years. Not only do the ferns check its abounding ardour but their fronds make an admirable support and background for its wide-flung, graceful growths and flowers, not to mention the rich autumn tints in which the plant closes down in November.

All of which, need I point out, again goes to show that there are more ways of controlling a metaphorical dog than that of

MIMULUS
LEWISII ALBA

*A pure-white
monkey-flower
of rare charm*

THE CORAL PINK DRUMSTICKS OF HELONIAS BULLATA, THE
STUD-FLOWER

WAHLENBERGIA HEDERACEA, THE IVY-LEAVED CAMPANULA

ASTILBE CRISPA
Proud pigmy of a mighty race

choking it with butter. And what de Quincey said about the art of murder—'Design, gentlemen, design, grouping, light and shade . . . sentiment—' yea, and what a great king once said about keeping Scotsmen out of London by laying down poisoned porridge in Euston station—these illuminating suggestions all have an application of practical value in promoting the elasticity of the garden mind.

To return, for a moment, to those spring operations by the waterside, the 'doing-up' of a bed of that best of all wet-loving sedums, *S. pulchellum*, is an annual duty. This charming plant we treat as we do the mimulus, re-planting its separated bits in fresh soil, for only thus does it really prosper. We once had a great ambition to see *Gentiana pneumonanthe* raising its azure bugles above the broad rosy-blue-lilac of the stonecrop, but what suits the latter the marsh gentian would not have—not permanently at any rate. So we now grow the Styrian variety of the gentian elsewhere and are well content to leave the native beauties on the breezy marshes of Anglesey, where we one day found a lovely pure rose form of this extremely variable plant.

However, we have acquired our azure and bluey-rose accompaniment to the sedum with two other delectable morsels of the moorland, the ivy-leaved campanula, *Wahlenbergia hederacea*, and the bog pimpernel, *Anagallis tenella*. These, indeed, are more satisfying than the gentian would ever have been, for they give a longer season, and what is more enchanting than the pale clear blue and glistening shell-pink of these moorland companions? Bring in a touch of gold, if you will, with *Saxifraga aizoides* and *S. diversifolia*, which seems to be a rare curiosity, let the gentle bog violet ramble where it will and invite the elfin *V. lutea* to look down upon these (from a slightly drier spot) with its dainty blossoms, and you may visualise a little waterside slope which has given us endless pleasure.

Thence you might wander into the next flat in which dwell some queer, rather reserved and mysterious folk, flycatchers most of them—sarracenias, *darlingtonia* and droseras. With them is an oddity, *Dipidax triquetra*, which, masquerading in the garb of a rush, produces starry white and pink flowers from a kangaroo pouch worn about its waist-belt . . . but of these another day.

CHAPTER XI

A Woodland in a Garden

WHEN THE glade garden had been going for some five or six years, which means that it had begun to wear a furnished (hateful phrase) and settled appearance, an opportunity occurred of acquiring that latest extension to the premises referred to elsewhere. This was a plot of good kitchen-garden ground some one hundred yards to the south, an open stretch of first-rate soil which would please the more sun-loving plants, give us some sixty yards of westerly border backed by a lofty wall as well as a dampish place near the river. Incidentally, it offered to solve the very pressing problem as to what we were going to do with our ever-growing population, which in infant rhododendrons alone presented a considerable crowd.

Further, the possession of this annex meant that we could extend a riverside walk which had thus far come to a dead end. This walk, tree-shaded and high-banked on one side with the water on the other, would thus become a corridor between the old garden and the new. So the latter came into being, and the way to it, under the leaning sycamores and our dear old alders, retained the name of the dingle, by which it had been known long before we had come to own it. Happily that name was an appropriate one, for the place is a narrow little copsy glen. At its head our smaller stream, the old mill-race which intersects the main garden, blends the merry prattle of its pebble-song with the more impressive music of the boulder-strewn river, and from that 'watersmeet' both swing along together, with stickle, fall and pool, round the beautiful bend which they themselves and the centuries have made.

That in thus adding a further responsibility to the garden caravan we were going to embarrass our prospects was manifest in the opinion of prudent friends. Some of them even shadowed our future by prophesying a staff of gardeners and the loss of that 'personal touch' which, we had been led to believe, was one of the garden's primary charms. Ambition was to be a Will o' the Wisp luring us to destruction. We were going to fall between twenty stools.

But all these dreadful things have so far been averted. There may have been, and indeed were, moments of shadow when I discerned in the Lady of the Garden distinct symptoms of hesitancy as to the wisdom of further loading an already heavy pack, moments in which it would have been manifestly indiscreet of me to plead that while the dingle would provide a sweet pasture for sentiment, the island—of which we had a wee one off the new garden—might invite me of a summer evening to sport with Amaryllis in the shade and play with the tangles of Neæra's hair.

However, to L. G., who is one of those practical people to whom shredded lapin is plucked rabbit, is extended, I hope, an always respectful ear, for honest doubt is ever the mother of sane progress. And I felt that once she discovered what pleasant nooks the dingle offered to *Primula Winteri*, hepaticas and little ferns, once the tribes of infant rhododendrons had been liberated in the spacious freedom of the new garden, there would arise an enthusiasm that would, incidentally, ease the way to the fulfilment of my own dreams of further magnolias and the like, to which the new territory offered such inviting possibilities.

Time proved all this, proved what indeed needed no proof, that people who talk of plucked rabbit are not without sentiment and that it may be of a more useful kind than that which is always upon one's sleeve. The dingle appeared like a pink worm on the estate plan and even Prometheus, by whom most of the heavier work had to be done, fell to with heroic relish. Balbus never built a wall as he built that which was to support our river walk against the ravening torrents of winter—and the hill Welshman who cannot raise walls immortal as the pyramids, and that with round, waterworn stones—the 'sheep's heads' of local parlance—is yet to be born. Moreover—and this was of no less importance to us—he at once caught the tune of the place, exhibiting an anxiety to avoid injuring its minutest natural features that amounted to tenderness.

All of which preamble brings me to a point in this narrative in which the dingle may serve to show that it is something more to us than what one may term its face value, that it may be taken as the key-note to the garden itself. That key-note is perhaps the voice of our singing waters which ceases not to pervade the garden at all seasons like the music in a shell, its message and its melody expressing the spirit of those principles which it has been our joy to foster and pursue. And what are those principles? The most sacrosanct of them is that which has already been touched upon in speaking of autumn colour—the preservation of a garden atmosphere which shall be, as near as is humanly possible, in harmony with the wild's uncultured beauty. That beauty, those often nameless wonders which un-numbered years have gathered here, may be no more than the simple familiar things which mark the common round of our country's year:—

Green loops of dog's mercury breaking the mould of February beneath the alders' ruddy flush; the gladness that shakes the wind-flowers to ecstasy when they feel the touch of an April wind; milk-white stars of woodruff among unfolding ferns; the melting sweetness of a willow wren's refrain in the hush of high summer's noon; the rich, ripe, nutty scent of dew-wet leaves which tells of autumn's mood and story; frosty footprints jewelled on the mosses of a woodland walk. It is these and not the alien iris, mocking the numb of our northern winter with the cowslip breath of its southern spring, which are to such a garden as this, the fundamental things, these the silver chords which bind our kinship with the wild and from which the spirit of the garden must draw its inspiration.

To the tidy-minded much of this garden may be a perversion of all horticultural standards of discipline. To others, including ourselves, it might have been something worse, a negation of its own spiritual entity, a place so troubled by noisy discords that the little horns of elfland would be frightened into silence. In other words, had we not exercised the most patient care in the conservation of those natural features to which the garden, as a whole and in its setting, is subservient the garden never would have been. Incidentally, had we not pursued such a policy as this, inviting the garden to do its own gardening, so to speak, we should not have been able to run

THE MILK-WHITE PLUMES OF SPIRAEA ARUNCUS, THE GOAT'S-
BEARD MEADOWSWEET (MALE FORM), RISE TO SIX OR SEVEN
FEET IN THE SHADES OF WATERSIDE ALDERS

GALAX APHYLLA

THE DINGLE
'. . . *a corridor between the old garden and the new*' (p. 120)

such a place at all with our own, often intermittent, labour and that of one part-time man.

So, to come back to the dingle; it was not what trees to cut down, what boulders to heave about, that concerned us. Rather was it how far we dare go without offending the *status quo*. But here in this green river-hewn glen canopied by trees, its lofty banks draped by ivy and ferns, mosses and other woodland herbage, there was obviously but one course to follow and that was to keep it green. To the practical mind this would be taking the line of least resistance, but actually it would be something more: It would mean its conservation as a refuge for nature's oldest and most restful of colours, so that at all times it would do its part—as other green retreats in the garden have done for us—in harbouring the most comforting and abiding of those garden pleasures which are as old as Bacon—and ages older.

To put the matter in another way: Our main objective here was not a woodland garden but a woodland in a garden. There is a very essential difference between the two, as, happily, we discovered long ago, the one implying a certain amount of cultivation, the other little or none. At the same time, while conscious of the fact that a gardener can do as much harm as a slug of his own size, as Sir Arthur Hort used to say, we should be sorely lacking as gardeners were we to be entirely content with nature's management of our woodland. The use of sympathetic plants with judgment and feeling need not vex those nightingales of which I have spoken, yet in dealing with such a sylvan sanctum you must take thy shoes from off thy feet and tread with a wariness that touches the borders of reverence.

One can readily admit that it is sometimes difficult to discern those subtle differences which, to use a bad metaphor, separate the plants of the desert from those of the sown, but there is a difference and upon its observance the making or marring of a garden woodland largely depends. There is a difference as wide as that which lies between the sweet persuasion of primroses along some hedgerow bank, and the smug self-satisfied opulence of blowzy polyanthuses bedded in a hazel coppice; or, shall I say a difference as fine as at that which tells you that while one daffodil may look vulgar and so-much-a-dozen in a wood, another can be as pleasing as the hyacinths of May.

Not forgetting that we already had in the dingle an invaluable asset in creeping ivy, ferns and mosses upon which to go to work, we had only to get luzulas, or wood-rushes, started to have as pleasing a ground-work as one could desire. A better evergreen carpeter for woodland I do not know than *L. sylvatica*. Nor have I ever seen it display its manifold charms to better effect than on some of the rocky slopes of the beautiful Dell at Bodnant. It is a fine glossy green at all seasons, it colonises with great rapidity, yet is easily controlled, and *L. campestris*, *nivea* and others are equal to it in a smaller, less robust way. And there is no lowly shrub for naturalising with these that holds so high a place in our esteem as *Hypericum Androsaemum*. In leaf, flower, fruit and manners, this familiar native is entirely satisfying.

One of the first herbaceous plants to go into the dingle was *Ranunculus aconitifolius* in its *major* form, a stately herb of nearly a yard with much elegance of foliage over which white buttercups, more than an inch in width, dance and flicker in the dappled sunlight. This hearty old-fashioned thing is in perfect accord with the tone of the place and it possesses that other qualification so desirable in a woodlander—an ability to take care of itself. This we regard with the utmost commendation in such plants, not merely because it means economy in time and labour but because almost anything of the semblance of cultivation is directly inimical to that which is a woodland's most precious charm. And by cultivation I mean not only the raw soil which is the trail of the spade, but the obviously planted look which is hardly less disturbing. A woodland herb or shrub, if exotic, must not advertise the fact. It should seem as if it had blown in as care-free as a wildling. That is one reason why we have a particularly kindly affection for the self-sown, and an ability to naturalise with seemly restraint is a qualification that cannot be too warmly appreciated.

Foxgloves, of course, have their own way with us here, doing their own housekeeping with commendable thrift. But they are inclined sometimes to show too much zeal, and here I shall risk the disloyalty of expressing a greater love for the *Digitalis dubia + purpurea* hybrid, at all events for special positions. This is less lanky, more branched, larger in the flower and softer in tone and practically perennial, much longer-lived than *dubia* itself. *D. ambigua* is always charming with its ivory bells and *ferruginea* we also have, but it is not a stayer. Then, among others is the equally modest *D. lanata* which Mr. W. T. Stearn sent us from Bulgaria with the encouraging inscription 'the sort of weed you like to grow'—and it is.

Lamium Orvala album is one of our ideal woodland plants of the bigger sort. Some sub-alpine forms of the purple type are passable, if rather too free, but this white one which first saw the light in old E. C. B.'s garden is a really fine thing, full of quality and its behaviour is exemplary. A sound perennial which comes true from seed (also easily raised from cuttings). *L. O. album* makes a massive clump nearly two feet high of its pale green nettle-like leaves, and gives from about mid-spring a long succession of large flowers, hooded and fringed and all swaddled in a fine white down which gives a touch of snowy purity to their rich creamy hue: an easy winner among lamiums and the saving grace of woodland labiates.

Where it does well *Meconopsis cambrica* is a first-rate woodlander. It can be troublesome enough in the wrong place, so much so that we have had visitors who, seeing it scattered about our shady ways, have offered us condolences most touching. But surely that which may be a vice in one spot may be a virtue in another. One would not, by way of example, give helxine a loose rein among choice rock plants, yet we have expended no little time and patience in efforts to induce it to film some of our shady boulders with its cheerful lettuce-green. *Arenaria balearica* is so invasive with some that I have heard of rock-gardeners attacking it with scrubbing brush and pail, yet we have never so far had enough of it. And *Linaria aequitriloba* and *hepaticifolia*, which can be positively virulent when out of bounds, we coax and cosset by every possible means wheresoever there are woodland rocks, stumps or banks which suggest their dainty vestment.

Wherefore, if the Welsh poppy, rejecting with indignation the gentlest hint on the subject of birth control, will so pursue its passion for reproduction that it will cheerfully endure the meanest soil of the most sunless and drippiest corner your garden knows, it must command at least a decent measure of politeness. And further, so far as we are concerned, if we were to slam the door in the face of a native whose haunt is the self-same hill-born streams as ours, we should be false to those very principles which it is our desire to foster.

Then, the Welsh poppy merits our respect from another angle. It holds an ancient record in garden genealogy. It was known in 1640 to Parkinson who figured it, and this, said to be the first illustration ever made of a meconopsis, holds the distinction of occupying the frontispiece of that masterly monograph on the genus by Mr. George Taylor published only two years ago. Moreover, to *M. cambrica* belongs the honour of presiding in the halls of botany as the type species of the entire meconopsis family—exalted position, indeed, in the presence of the illustrious aristocrats of Asia we know to-day.

While the rather acidulous yellow of the Welsh poppy can be as pleasing along our shaded river banks as wild globeflowers in the sunnier places, the most beautiful of its household in this garden is an old strain with single flowers of that bright warm orange one sometimes sees in Iceland poppies. These blossoms are at least double the size of those of the type, they are held well erect on stout stems above the ample foliage, and well-established plants will often stand at twenty inches in height. Although not such a determined coloniser as the yellow, this delightful poppy gives us as many self-sown seedlings as we require for the satisfaction of begging friends and our own use, and it comes so true to colour that in over twenty years we have never known it to revert, even when growing along with the yellow. Its thorough reliability as a sound perennial need not be emphasised, but the fact that it will flower throughout the summer, and again in autumn if the seed capsules are promptly removed, is one that will bear repeating.

That mop-headed monstrosity, the double orange Welsh poppy, which vulgarly violates every grace which it is a poppy's privilege to wear, finds no favour here. One presumes that the plethoric creature has some mission to fulfil for every nursery stocks it, but it is not for us. True, a single clump lives a leper's life away between a water butt and a potting shed and does so with valorous complacency, but we have only two reasons for its continued survival. One of these is to satisfy a deplorable weakness of conscience which persuades us that to allow prejudice to exclude a variety of a genus which interests us is hardly cricket, and another is this: That object by the tub enables us to give a satisfying, if evasive, reply to the many visitors, who, whenever they see our single Welsh poppies, invariably make tender inquiries after the double one.

Another perennial poppywort which we find admirable in lightly shaded woodland is *M. villosa*, long known as *Cathcartia*. Making a clumpy plant of twenty inches or more with deeply lobed, pale green leaves which, with the stems, are covered with a tawny fur, *M. villosa* thrusts up a sheaf of stately stems yielding a long succession of salver-shaped flowers in a soft-toned yellow. These handsome blooms we have had close on three inches across, they yield seed in plenty which germinates readily and occasionally we find self-sown offspring. A very delightful plant which ought to be more widely grown, especially with *M. betonicifolia*.

Not quite so good as *M. villosa* is the allied *Stylophorum diphyllum*, a perennial of the same size with more glaucous leaves, crimped and silvered with white hairs when they crop up in snowdrop-time. The nodding, pale yellow flowers of May and June go very attractively with the bluish veneer of the leafage, and these, too, enjoy a long run, often re-appearing in autumn, long after the seeds of the earlier ones have ripened in their lolling grey-blue pods.

Although this poppywort and *M. villosa* are certainly perennials we have not found either of them long-lived. This may explain why they are still uncommon in gardens generally and why they have their periods of rarity in nurseries. It certainly is the reason why we cannot keep their cousin, *Dicranostigma Franchetianum* for more than a season or two; and the fact that this pretty blue-leaved poppywort is not more permanent and self-supporting, so to speak, practically rules it out of our woodland list. Moreover, I take it to be rather a sun-lover, and all this applies no less to *D. lactucoeides* which we treat as a biennial. Then one cannot pass by that amiable weed, *Chelidonium majus*, which would always find hospitality here if only on account of its foliage and happy contentment anywhere. *Hylomecon japonicum* we once had and its departure has left an empty place which no one has yet been able to fill for us.[1]

Eomecon chionantha, which also takes a part in the dingle, we planted with little hope of seeing very much of its beautiful white flowers, for in this garden it seems to need a generous ration of sunshine as well as a root restriction which means starvation, before it will perform really well. But its broad, heart-shaped leaves, cool emerald and with scalloped margins, are lovely throughout the summer (rather like those of *Sanguinaria*) and they lose nothing by having near them the strong, highly polished green of *Galax aphylla*, one of the staunchest of all our woodland friends. *Eomecon*, we are hoping, will run among a neighbour on the other side of it, the deep green leathery-fronded *Lomaria magellanica* which, since it will wander about in rather widely dispersed tufts, seems to ask a companionable bed-fellow.

Houttuynia cordata, a ramper in any moistish spot, is also segregated along a few yards of alder-shaded riverside, and it, too, has a fern, *Struthiopteris* (*Onoclea*) *pennsylvanica*, for company. We thought that this robust and stately fern might have the salutary effect of checking the overweening ardour of the Japanese plant, and to some extent this has come off. But it has done more than that, for the slender red stems with their blue-green, heart-shaped leaves and broad white flower bracts, never looked so delightful as they do when clambering half-way up the stiffly erect shuttlecocks of the ferns. *Houttuynia* has made a virtue of a necessity and done so with remarkable grace. Yet behind that unaffected refinement of manner there lurks a stench whose vehemence the prince of polecats might envy.

Epimediums we have always cherished among the choicer shade plants, for they lack few of those qualities which are demanded of woodland dwellers. They are extremely elegant in line and poise, there is an elfin daintiness in their fairy-lamp blossoms, artistry in the cut of their leaves and finely drawn

[1]Mr. G. N. Smith of the famous Irish nursery at Daisy Hill, Newry, has since come to our rescue, as he has a way of doing whenever a rare woodland plant is wanting, and we now have a little group of long-lost *Hylomecon*, dainty as a wood anemone with its five-leafletted leaves and rich butter-yellow flowers.

stems. We grow, or have grown, about a dozen of them, species and varieties, and if some would not excite the enthusiasm of people who look for pride of blossom, not one has been deemed unworthy.

One trouble with epimediums here is that voles and mice love them as much as we do, and, to make matters worse, the creatures seem to have a special liking for the very spots which we would choose for the epimediums. Even so, these plants are too delightful to abandon on that account, delightful at all times for many of them are evergreen, their spring leaf tints which follow the flowers are delicious, and in autumn they fall into tone with the season with rich hues of bronze, russet and gold. No less might be said of *Vancouveria hexandra*, raising its candelabra of wee waxen stars on hair-fine stems above a leafage of matchless delicacy, and this foliage we have all winter.

In days gone by when one was more ready to give credulous attention to hearsay, I imagined I knew a little about these barrenworts, at all events in so far as their names were concerned. Then there came along a breaker of idols in the shape of a botanist, Mr. W. T. Stearn. I had not been corresponding with him very long, nor talking to him for ten minutes, before I discovered that I had been living in a fool's paradise browsing on an ignorance which was none the less profound for being garnished with bliss.

But if old illusions totter and fond romances flee before the dictates of science, there is compensation in the fact that the revelations which take their place as the W. T. S.'s of the world lead us into the way of truth are sometimes an hundredfold more thrilling than those Peter Bell ever dreamed of. And further, it is good to feel that when the herbarium and the microscope have done their part, a nimbus of mystery which is their own secret clings to these woodland waifs. Truant fancy can still roam in idyllic isolation among the gentle influences of epimedium or anemone, to find them as inviolate as the melody which pervades a Beethoven sonata.

So when the lovely pink bells of *Oxalis Acetosella rosea* come to gem our woodland herbage it is not the physiological explanations, if there be any, which might tell us why this pretty thing has assumed a colour so beautiful and why it so faithfully reproduces itself by seed, which stirs one's imagination, but the simple charm of the thing itself and the exquisite perfection with which it adorns its self-chosen haunts. An admission of weakness and idleness, perhaps, but each one of us has his own 'fostering star', and to even the pottering ruminant chewing the cud of contentment there is a job to be done which is not without honour and reward in maintaining the fabric of gardening.

This bonny wee sorrel reminds me that the white form of the oxalis which we used to call *O. floribunda* (*O. rubra* St. Hilaire) presents a conundrum which, so far as I know, has not been explained. For whereas the type plant, which is easily one of the handsomest of the genus, is rather fastidious and not always long-lived, the smaller white variety—less than half the size in leaf and flower—will prosper anywhere like a weed, even in grass or woodland herbage, in sun or shade. Again, while the type flowers but once and that for a comparatively short period, but admittedly with great splendour, the other will yield a nonstop succession all summer and autumn, even into winter.

Among our indispensables in the bigger woodland plants the willow gentians (*G. asclepiadea*) will always be given high rank. This not only because these noble herbs yield a pleasing colour at a season when flowers are few, but they also possess those qualifications which visé the passport of admittance to the most exclusive of sylvan sanctuaries.

Not the least of these qualities, I repeat, is a willingness to naturalise by seed, and that these willow gentians do with a freedom governed by a decent restraint. Most of them, even the lovely early flowering white, come very fairly true from seed, and true not only to colour but to form. And this seems the more remarkable when it is realised that the plants range from sturdy, stiffly erect kinds of twelve or more inches to monsters with flexible arching wands of four feet, and there are intermediate sorts in plenty. So in the matter of blossom they may be anything between palest sky-blue or a thin azure to the deepest violet-purple. All of these are good and happy plants, but I think the hour of deepest satisfaction with them is when the big fellows by the waterside are adding their royal purple to October's gold. It is a masterly touch, the good wine of the year seasoned to a bountiful heartiness and served up with becoming dignity.

Those excellent woodlanders, the saxifrages of the *S. umbrosa* and *rotundifolia* sections, with which I shall deal later, soon found the route in the dingle with that casual way of theirs which is so gratifying. But those included under *S. Geum*, a numerous and confusing clan of easy-going, tufty plants which will make themselves at home anywhere, must be given a passing notice. In flower they may not be exciting, yet their delicate scintillating sprays of silvery whiteness are just what one wants in the green-filtered sunlight of such spots. Their evergreen leaves present much variety in shape and size, the older assuming tints which gather increasing brilliance from autumn to spring, and the plants ring the changes between wee dense pads which hug the soil and loose and leafy affairs of nearly a foot. The dentarias we encourage by every possible means for some of them come early, flowering with the forerunners of the anemones; they have much charm of leaf and a quiet beauty which does not disturb the demure serenity of a primrose. Then there is *Potentilla alba*, another trusty friend whose silver leaves are always attractive, while it flowers nearly the whole year round if it can be given a spot of sun.

Tollmiaea Menziesii we should probably never have had but for some dear old lady who had long cherished it as a pet in a town window and who asked a kind home for it. But this queer Californian, so feeble in blossom, has turned out to be a most agreeable inmate of our woodland ménage and quite hardy. Its tiarella leaves are cheerfully evergreen and few plants will more quickly colonise a square yard or so of any cool, well-drained soil. And in its methods of increase it displays resource as well as agility. Converting its long-stalked leaves into stolons these take root and, starting from the base of the mid-rib, a new little tolmiaea is born. This rosette of infantile foliage grows rapidly, the biggest leaves leap away from the parent lap and, digging themselves in, very soon have a family of their own; and so the compound multiplication goes on at a most exciting pace. Thus far we have only used this oddity as one would use its cousins, *Saxifraga sarmentosa* or *Tiarella cordifolia*, but it promises great scope as a carpeter for wide shady places and as a ground-work for bulbs.

Of some of our woodland under-shrubs, gaultherias and the like, mention has already been made. These, together with anemones, cyclamen, bulbs and other oddments, such as ramondias, *Primula Winteri*, hepaticas and linarias over which the Lady of the Garden does the shepherding, must be fitted in to this chapter with what imagination the patient reader cares to exercise. These are the *bric-à-brac*, the intimate close-ups which impart a friendly touch to the place. But I must wind up as I began by repeating that, on a broad view, the dominant feature of these wooded banks and watersides is the native herbage, more particularly ferns and ivy.

Of the ferns, to do them justice chapters might be written, for this is a ferny country and to the indigenous kinds which range from osmundas tall enough to conceal the old ferryman's daughter to such mites as *Woodsia ilvensis*, we have added most of the hardy exotics which travel and the nurseries have been able to supply. And these alien ferns, which present such an end-less variety that one may have anything from the noble *Polystichum munitum*, a dense mass four feet high and a dozen feet in circumference, to a fragment one might grow in a thimble, blend with the others and their surroundings with the utmost harmony.

Fern fans we may not be in the sense that we know something of pteridology, for we do not. Their microscopical diversities bewilder us, of their classification we are afraid. As to their names, no garden label yet conceived by man is long enough to hold them and no life long enough in which to learn them. And deeply as I respect the botanist and acknowledge his illuminating labours in the pursuit of knowledge, I must, in passing, again utter a voice of protest against that coining of impossible plant names which, though they may seem easy enough for him, raise an unsurmountable barrier between botany and horticulture.

I am not advocating English names. A reasonable moderation is my only plea, and I select this moment to tilt at the botanist since the names he gives to ferns seem to be peculiarly difficult, unnecessarily long, ugly and repellent. And if it is true, as I do believe it is, that the garden career of many a good plant has been checked and hampered by the atrocity of a name inflicted upon it by science, this fern nomenclature is surely enough to explain why gardeners in general know so little and grow so few of the loveliest and most useful classes of plant life on the globe.

As for ivy, our inestimable friend and ally, those who know it and realise its many admirable virtues in a woodland garden will need no eulogiums from us. The others, heaven help them! who regard it with suspicion and reproach, must be left with the discords of the botanist in the valley of despair.

CHAPTER XII

Primulas and other Streamside Plants

IT WAS Maurice Hewlett, if I remember aright, who said that a man who had a trout stream in his garden was an aristocrat. We have two trout streams, but if ever we had paused to consider what social distinction these possessions had bestowed upon us something much nearer the navvy than that exalted station would have occurred to us. This because a water garden, that is, cultivated ground near enough to stream or pool to be kept moist in summer, is of all gardens the most difficult to keep in order. The damp stickiness of the soil is itself an obstacle to culture, and wheresoever dampness is there will the weeds be gathered together.

Now, as our garden increased in area, it became more and more obvious that something would have to be done to meet the demands of upkeep. Labour we had been obliged to employ more or less regularly, but to go in for assistance adequate enough to cope with our growing responsibilities did not appeal to us. So we followed what seemed the only course to pursue if the garden was to remain our own. In brief, we set out to specialise in shrubs, not only heaths and the like, which cover the ground and ask no attention, but others, such as rhododendrons, which are almost as self-supporting. Herbaceous borders were gradually transformed into mixed borders, which involved less than one-half the usual maintenance. The woodland floor was encouraged to carry on much in its own old way with its creeping ivy, luzula, ferns, wild hypericum and other natural herbage, and the watersides, with their everlasting menace, were stocked with astilbes and spiraeas, senecios, rodgersias, *Iris sibirica*, osmundas, buphthalmums, the stronger primulas and other big-leaved, valorous herbs which would very effectually smother the weeds of the only troublesome seasons—summer and autumn.

In a word, we decided that the garden itself must do no small

HYBRID ASTILBES THRONG A SUNNY REACH OF THE MILL-STREAM

IRIS SIBIRICA BELTS THE STILL WATERS ABOVE AN OAKEN SLUICE

GENTIANA ASCLEPIADEA
VAR. ALBA

ASTILBES, SPIRAEAS AND LOOSESTRIFES

part of the gardening, that it must consume its own smoke, for, failing that, the smoke would assuredly consume us. Indeed, we should have fallen in the battle long ago had we not adopted the strategic principle of recruiting those brave co-operators mentioned. One particular bed near the pool was a constant drain upon our time, as well as a strain upon our penitential backs—and we are not afraid of a reasonable crop of weeds. And it was this plot, I think, which first decided us to take a leaf out of the enemy's book and attack him with his own weapons. Our prospects were further promoted by the Lady of the Garden who, with the subtlety of her sex, recalled the old story of the serpent who rose up and devoured all the other serpents. That settled the matter. We soon dug up and removed all those plants—myosotis, dodecatheons, mertensias and the smaller primulas—which had occupied this bed and installed in their place a battalion of those herbaceous stalwarts referred to. Like Caesar, these came, they saw, and they conquered. And that weedy place, instead of giving us further trouble has ever since rewarded us with an imposing array of healthy, hearty plants with much charm of foliage and flower and which ask next to nothing in labour. Not more than once or twice in spring does Prometheus bend his weeding back over ground thus fortified. For the whole of the remaining year the 'big stuff' is entirely independent of us. It prospers, it conquers.

There are people who doubt the practicability of such a method of control and, it may be admitted, our semi-wild arrangements would not suit some gardens and that they do sometimes disturb the ease of the tidy-minded. But our contention is that the policy has solved a problem which is seldom far from any gardener's mind, and that of all labour savers and weed killers it is the most economical and satisfactory.

Moreover, as a principle the idea is one of far wider application than is suggested by the foregoing and for it we claim no originality, for is it not plainly to be seen in any meadow, woodland or brake? What, for example, could be more effectual than the rich green carpet of *Lomaria alpina* which entirely covers the ground occupied by our colony of osmundas? The evergreen creeping fern keeps the roots of the osmundas cool. It is beautiful at all seasons, especially in autumn and winter as a setting for the orange, russet and cinnamon of the great fronds above it, and no weed can exist in its matted fabric. Then there is *Gunnera magellanica*, cloaking with its dense network of rhizome and leaf the soil about some waterside trees. *Polygonum vaccinifolium* is no less useful and much more beautiful, the water fern, *Lastrea Thelypteris*, we have massed in impenetrable luxuriance over what was once a dismal and hopeless bed of clay, while the lovely *Omphalodes cappadocica* drifts in an azure haze beneath the rhododendrons and other shrubs of a waterside bank with sufficient vigour to enable it entirely to fend for itself.

There are some plants of course—yes, many—which do not lend themselves to such treatment. (It would not be gardening if we had things all our own way.) Of these are the globe-flowers (*Trollius*) which, while they do not, with us at any rate, make sufficient foliage to smother weeds, are not much more successful naturalised among ferns and other herbage. Even *T. europaeus* and its varieties do not stand up to competition for very long, and for the same reason those very distinct dwarf species, *T. patulus* and *pumilus*, which forfeit all right to be called globe-flowers by crowning their stems with perfectly flat blossoms, are accorded preferential treatment. *T. pumilus yunnanensis* is a good deal taller than the type, often rising to fifteen inches or more, but it is distinct and well-looking and we have also a nice little thing about the size of a primrose which came here labelled *T. pumilus* Wargrave Variety.

One might think that those splendid globe-flower hybrids, which open first in March and prevail until *T. Ledebourii* and its offspring are invoking the spirit of autumn with tongues of flame in bowls of burning orange, would be able to hold their own with our waterside herbage. But if they do so for a while it soon becomes apparent that they need more individual attention, and we now have most of them parked together where the gleam of their gold will be within eyeshot of the irises' blue.

Magnificent as these trollius are, reflecting the greatest credit upon those who have created them, if they get much bigger and goldener they will lose our distinguished patronage. Already I have perceived symptoms of restiveness in the Lady of the Garden in the presence of some of these daring beacons when flaunting their massive globes of gold above the tender croziers of uprising fern. And the squadron that is given a place apart does not seem quite in accord with the gentle verdure of a swamp cypress (*Taxodium*) which stands near their reservation. Indeed, only last spring, when we were pulled up with a jerk by the commanding brilliance of an ultra-resplendent table of these gorgeous things at a Vincent Square show, the Lady of the Garden said, 'Yes, but they would annoy your nightingales.' And so we passed on.

To return to those good friends, our ornamental weed-killers, some of the waterside primulas can justly claim to be so regarded, especially the candelabras. We have these in fairly extensive groups, both in the open and following the stream where it flows beneath the old alders. These groups are, so far as it is possible, each of one kind, and if they involve a certain amount of attention in the way of 'rogueing', transplanting seedlings and firming-down all those which have a passion for suicide by indulging in crown rot, or by pushing out of the soil by the downward thrust of their new roots, they more than earn it.

But much of the trouble with these primulas has been avoided since we went to work on the understanding that, though they may be classed as 'bog-primulas', they will not be happy very long in sloppy ground. There are exceptions, of course, *Florindae* and *helodoxa* among them, and the latter is never so good or so perennial as when it has its roots actually in water. One colony of this fine species now in its fifth year has never been even partially replanted. It is as robust as ever it was and never asks anything of us beyond a passing nod of appreciation for its sturdy independence.

George Forrest gave us nothing better than *P. helodoxa*, and that is saying much for we have not even yet realised the full measure of the wealth of his introductions. And that good judge of such things, Mr. E. H. M. Cox, never wrote a truer word than where he says of *helodoxa*: 'This admirable and graceful plant must be placed among the best dozen primulas in cultivation.' (*Primulas for Garden and Greenhouse*: Cox and Taylor.) Nor is it only those beautiful spires, rising to three or even more feet, with tier upon tier of soft yellow flowers which are so characteristic of the 'Marsh Glory Primrose'. It keeps its silvery emerald leaves throughout the winter, which few others do. It does not hybridise with its neighbours, but always comes true to type. It is easy and accommodating and is, as I have suggested, one of the most permanent of all waterside primulas.

To the old *P. japonica* we are still loyal, though we have not the time to exercise the selective process it deserves. But the bright burgundy-crimson type at its best is here in reasonably pure companies, and for some years a large patch of Miller's Crimson—which has no blue in its red—has held its territory against any aggression in the way of weeds. This contingent, originally self-sown and only subjected to an occasional thinning, entirely covers the soil with its broad and luxuriant leafage, yet it flowers magnificently. It is distinctly pleasing in the dappled light of the alders and will be still better when we have worked into one of its flanks a squad of that best of all white japonicas, Postford White. This excellent variety was given to us by our friend Mr. G. H. Dalrymple of Bartley primula fame. It appears to come 100 per cent. true from seed, as Miller's Crimson does, but whether these will live up to that reputation when grown in adjacent groups has yet to be proved here.

P. pulverulenta, the type, is not commonly seen these days, possibly owing to the superiority of its pink forms. But it is a noble primula, even when something near magenta, for it will often soar to three feet, it is more perennial than most, and the mealiness of its stems imparts to it a tone which *japonica* even at its best does not possess. The powder-puff, we know, will rescue from social obloquy the shiny nose, but why its application to a shiny plant should render the latter more *distingué* one cannot guess. We only know that it does.

For those distinguished daughters of *pulverulenta* in pink I have nothing but the highest praise. They have all the good and reliable qualities of the original, but their colours range from the exquisite almond pink of the Lady Thursby strain through infinite shades of the same colour to a sort of ivory-chrome with a delicate rosy flush, while most of the plants seem to have that remarkably telling 'eye' of golden-brown velvet and yellow. These charming things will even seed remarkably true,

PRIMULA INVOLUCRATA

PRIMULA JAPONICA POSTFORD WHITE

PRIMULA
CHIONANTHA

*The Snow
Primula*

RHODODENDRON RACEMOSUM
A rose-pink Wilson form trailing down a woodland slope

and excellent as they are in bold drifts I am not sure that a single well-grown plant, or, say, about three in a group, in an isolated position against such a background as ferns, is not even more beautiful. If Mr. Dalrymple had never achieved anything else, gardeners the world over would ever be indebted to him for the fixing of the Bartley strains of this primula, an achievement in which selection only, rather than hybridising was employed.

The *Beesiana* and *Bulleyana* hybrids, the *Moerheimi* and the Raby strains, the Aileen Aroons, Lissadels and Red Hughs we run in massed ranks wheresoever there happens to be space. These are all thrifty and vigorous, quite capable under reasonable conditions of looking after their own interests. The only trouble with primulas of this class is their passion for intermarrying, and if one desires, as we do, to avoid a medley of mixed colours which leads to the dappling effect of a bed of polyanthuses, the several sorts must be herded apart, preferably in largish crowds and not too near one another.

P. Beesiana, if you get a good purple, is well worth growing as a species, and so is the rich orange-yellow *Bulleyana*. Then there is *chungensis*, a rather more slender plant with whorls of a warm yellow breaking from scarlet-vermilion buds, and this pretty thing has not as yet offended by cross-breeding. *P. burmanica*, one of Ward's Upper Burmah plants, raises its stout scapes along our stream banks, wreathes them with golden-eyed flowers in a rich crimson-purple and earns our gratitude for being a stayer. The fragrant *anisodora*, with its drooping bells of deep plum-purple velvet, obliges us by appearing here and there in odd little settlements of its own choosing, as does the brighter coloured *glycosma* which shows a marked affinity with *Poissonii*.

P. Poissonii seems to be a variable species, especially in colour, and if its slender, stately spires of two to three feet should present whorls of a thin, pucy magenta, it can be horrid. But as we first saw it (at Bodnant, in shade, with a background of some very broad-leaved hollies) and as we have it, *Poissonii* is a singularly fine plant. And we flatter ourselves that we have the true type—this being corroborated by Mr. F. C. Puddle, which is good enough for us—and our admiration of its elegant scapes, with their long succession of bright burgundy-crimson flowers after most of the other candelabras are over, is not affected by what others may think of them. But it may be well to add that placing and light make a vast difference with such a plant as this.

Thus, you may grow *Poissonii* in full sun, as you may grow *burmanica* or *anisodora*, but I do not think you will get the same tone in the flowers, nor so pleasing a general effect as when it is given light shade with plenty of green around it. Even the irrepressible Wanda of the *Juliae* swarm, often so blatant and commonplace, can be tamed by kindness. As for Morton (not Merton) Hybrid—still one of the best of the Juliaes and for whose coming out the thanks of all of us are due to Mr. John Stormonth—this rich and splendid variety is one of our delights when, thronging a bank of the stream beneath the willow-green and tossing white bouquets of an exochorda, it mirrors its glowing crimson in the water below it.

P. Cockburniana, the Benjamin of the candelabra tribe and a fiery little fellow, is in a class by itself. It is next thing to being an annual and should be treated as such when it will repay you an hundredfold. The old *denticulata* and the rest of its drumstick fraternity we honour for its trustful good nature. It is one of those plants which, if it were rare or difficult, would be applauded to the house-tops, but since it is familiar and easy it goes disregarded, so fickle are the fancies of gardeners.

Before going on from this all too brief discursion among the candelabras *P. aurantiaca* must be given a passing notice, for the mahogany wine-red of its flower scapes, leaf stems and veins impart a richness to the already rich orange of the whorled flowers. If stubborn with some we have found *aurantiaca* quite tractable and reasonably perennial if in a soil that is damp, yet rather to the dry side, with part shade.

Some remarkable hybrids have been raised from this fairly new species, these being anything in colour from yellow through a fiery orange to tangerine and something approaching a glowing brick-red. And, as Mr. Cox has pointed out (*The New Flora and Silva*, p. 259, vol. vii), the orange-yellow of *aurantiaca* is so dominant that it effectually expunges any blue that might occur in this hybrid offspring. Moreover, some of these handsome 'natural bastards' which have cropped up here are so extraordinarily robust that if *aurantiaca* itself may not be fitted to work out its own salvation as a naturalised plant, these newcomers show every promise of being able to do so. *P. aurantiaca*, by the way, makes full amends for any short-comings it may otherwise possess by indulging in the admirable habit of reproducing itself by rearing a nest of little plantlets, rooted and ready for transplanting, among its whorls of ripening seed capsules.

P. Littoniana, which is said to be a waterside plant, will have none of it with us, nor were the amazing specimens which we once saw in full parade at Castle Kennedy in wet ground. We are now finding that this gorgeously apparelled nabob does best if sown direct where it is to remain, and the seedlings which most emphatically suggest this are self-sowns in a gravel bed over a light sandy loam with considerable shade. This, indeed, is what most of the larger primulas enjoy, for they are never quite so happy as when allowed to grow right on without a shift, and we naturally encourage this commendable easing of the labour problem.

The beautiful *chionantha*, if expressing no decided views, is generally amenable here. The only one of the exclusive nivalis section most of us can hope to satisfy, it will prosper on a bank with its toes in the water, in rhododendron soil, in a stiffish adhesive loam, in shade or sun. Yet it is anything but steadfast, thriving under one of these conditions this year, but as likely as not merely enduring it on another occasion.

But the 'Snow Primula' is so very lovely with its cool emerald leaves and paper-white flowers (occasionally drifting into cool lavender) the calyces of which are boldly striped with ebony, with its dusting of lemon-yellow meal and dignified bearing, that we usually have a group in several places. And if none of these is ever a disappointment, one or two will always be distinctly better than the rest. *Chionantha* often yields its own seedlings, but seldom on wet, cold ground, and plants will sometimes go on for two or three years. *P. ingens*, with the same silvery leaves, seems to be much akin to *chionantha*, but the flowers are lavender-blue and this novelty we have not had for long.

P. Florindae seeds so abundantly, even on the swampiest soil, that its family business is said to become troublesome in some gardens. This giant, with a yard of scape topped by a mop of powdery yellow cowslip-scented bells, so enormous that once in an idle moment I counted nearly two hundred flowers and buds in a single head, is a most valuable plant. It has had all manner of ill names, 'cabbagy' and the rest, thrust upon it, but we shall always hold it in respect and regard. This, not so much for its ornamental attributes, which we do not overlook, but for its unchanging good temper under any conditions that have any pretence to wetness.

Then *Florindae* is one of the very latest to flower, giving blossom far into the autumn. It rarely asks any help from us and goes its own way, subduing its own weeds and never abusing the hospitality afforded it. Mr. Kingdon Ward only found this primula in 1924 and perhaps the fact that it is already as well known as the blue poppy (*Meconopsis betonicifolia*) which was discovered at about the same time, is sufficient evidence of its sterling merit as a garden plant.

Florindae, so far as I know, disdains illicit unions with other primulas of its section with the exception of *P. alpicola* (*microdonta*). This latter, a dainty plant, swinging wide and very mealy, fragrant bells in primrose or pale ivory-fawn from a stalk of about a foot, will join issue with *Florindae*, with the result that one gets plants much like the last-mentioned but with flowers of various shades of yellow, deepening to apricot and rosy-buff. Once we got one of a bright red, but it was too good for this world and passed hence. We do not find *alpicola* any too steadfast, and the sub-species, *violacea*, with flowers of a rich plum-purple with a white interior and heavily mealed, a beautiful plant if no longer lived, can easily be raised from seed like the rest.

P. sikkimensis—not forgetting the ivory *flexilipes*—one must always have for its tassel of citron-yellow, delicately scented, adorns with such a finished grace the finely-drawn stems. And there is no need for any fuss with this Himalayan so long as it gets a uniformly moist, free soil where it will not be exposed to hot sun. The only snag in the culture of *sikkimensis* is this: It is so late in starting into growth that adults and seedlings are liable to be dug up, and the same risk attends *alpicola*.

Along with the Sikkim primula in quality we would place that prince of primulas, *secundiflora*. There is an air of quality about this Forrest primula which at once arrests admiration. In height (15-18 in.) and in balance, in the moderate tuft of glossy leaves and the glowing claret-crimson of its pendulous flowers, so strikingly set off by the white meal which stripes the dark calyces, *secundiflora* has a distinction of its own. Nor has it any fads and fancies, being quite content with any well-drained, rather damp soil.

Even so, *secundiflora*, like the other smaller species just referred to, is not a plant for rough country wear. It is not one of our ramping weed chokers, but a species for a carefully chosen spot where its charms may be accorded the intimacy they deserve. So also do we treat the adorable *involucrata*, which, if it necessitates some care, thoroughly deserves it. *P. involucrata* is hardy and a sound perennial. It is willing and generous with its beautiful and fragrant pure white flowers on a six-inch scape. But with us at any rate it has a habit—even in the absence of frost—of working itself out of the soil in winter, this necessitating an annual re-planting in spring. In other soils it may behave better, but having defeated all other efforts to frustrate its suicidal ambitions, we are now trying it with a mat of some lowly creeper like *Veronica repens* and *Mentha Requienii*. This covering of turfy fabric is probably all the poor little mite needs by way of preventing it from tumbling out of bed, and the Lady of the Garden tells me she is applying a similar corrective to her beloved *Sisyrinchium grandiflorum*, which we are always losing in precisely the same way.

P. Wardii is a good plant that might be described as a purple *involucrata*, but the colour varies and asks for rigorous selection. *Conspersa* and *chrysopa*, though of the same section, are not for the rough and tumble of the waterside, nor is the beauful *capitata* and its still more attractive sister, *Mooreana*. These, with a number of others, are accorded special treatment elsewhere, but most of the cortusoides group, especially *Sieboldii* and *lichiangensis* are entirely satisfactory.

Planted in colonies in almost any good moist soil these will cover their allotted space with a mass of their broad, fresh green, beautifully-lobed leaves, which, from the later spring onwards for a long period, will be almost hidden beneath the wide and rosy-pink flowers. *Lichiangensis* may run to magenta but this does not offend our senses amid abundant green, and perhaps the best colours—clear rose and rose-carmine—may be found in, well, let us call them affinities of *Sieboldii*, *saxatilis* and *cortusoides*, for all hope of ever identifying them we abandoned long ago.

Some of our groups of the allied *Veitchii* are particularly even and firm in colour, while the flowers are of good shape and there are some delightful things under varietal names—presumably of the *Sieboldii* group. But practically all of this class of primula are such satisfactory and long-lived garden plants, and so bright and cheerful withal, that some day, one ventures to predict, they must come into their own.

CHAPTER XIII

Miniature Rhododendrons

To say that modern rhododendron culture has brought about one of the most striking changes the garden world has ever experienced already begins to sound rather commonplace. But the statement will bear repetition and, incidentally, it gives me an opening to some pages which I approach with a diffidence not remote from fear. Further, we in our own way, as units of the horticultural universe, have been so moved along with the rest by this rhododendron influence that the story of our own career in this sphere reflects in brief epitome the story of that which has so transfigured the trend of English gardening.

To put the matter in another way, it so happened that the great revival in rhododendron growing, which set in with the opening of China and Tibet to the plant hunter, synchronised with a period of our garden history which could not have been more auspicious. Old styles of horticulture were passing or already dead. The age of the informal and the naturally grown shrub was in the ascendancy. The soil was ripe for the argosies of Asia, and, moreover, a rapidly increasing array of alpine enthusiasts, looking around for the ideal rock-garden shrub, found it among the dwarf rhododendrons which were pouring in in even greater numbers than other additions to the genus.

So this rhododendron renaissance found us also with a field that had, it seemed, been providentially prepared for this exciting departure. Having just then come into possession of more land, and that of a kind admirably suited in its various aspects, soils and other conditions for rhododendrons, what was more inevitable than that we should join up and take what the gods were offering us of this engrossing diversion?

Even so, I do not face this chapter with courage. Had I the audacity of youth, or that with which I once drove the pen of a hard-bitten journalist who would write up all there was to know and a little more about everything from a squid to an archbishop (happy days!) I might plunge into the labyrinths of the greatest of all plant families with unshaken confidence. But 'he that increaseth knowledge . . .' well, one knows the rest.

So whensoever I get among rhododendrons, whether it be in the garden or on paper, I feel what Tristram's ass must have felt like when he was so loaded with panniers that he got stuck in the door through which he was to pass and, finding himself unable to proceed or retreat, fell to eating an artichoke. Albeit, I enjoy not only artichokes but macaroons come my way, as they came to 'Jack'.

Rhododendrons are the greatest fun in the world—always provided you have the philosophy of that ass and do not take too seriously the goblins which peer from every bush, taunting with flippant gibes your ignorance of their dark secrets. You will find these imps everywhere in a garden and to do so you need not possess an inferiority complex nor what the Prayer Book calls a notoriously evil liver. They are just part of one's pack, and if at times they do pin-prick your peace none of us was ever the worse of being reminded that 'half a proper gardener's work is done upon his knees'. And it is upon the knees of, I hope, a becoming humility that I offer an amateur's nibblings from the fringe of a mighty subject.

In rounding-up these alpines I must plead a certain brevity, confining these notes to our own favourites rather than attempting any more exhaustive plan. And when it is realised that our rhododendron family now numbers close upon 250 species, irrespective of varieties and introductions under number which, so far as I know, have not yet emerged from the baptismal font of Kew and Edinburgh, the tender hearted reader will understand my plea for limitation.

But I have one refuge: The Lady of the Garden possesses a sort of Domesday Book exclusively for these swarming minions of hers. In it are recorded their names and numbers, their origins or birth certificates, their sudden deaths, passing humours and other incidentals. As a matter of fact, these smaller rhododendrons are more hers than mine. And she has a way with them which I do not and never will possess, from teaching the

RHODODENDRON HANCEANUM, DWARF FORM

RHODODENDRON LEDOIDES

RHODODENDRON LEUCASPIS

microscopic seedlings how to grow up with becoming manners to coaxing the fractious cutting and comforting the homesick and infirm. If she harbours any regret, endures any anxiety, it is that she is no longer able to give the little fellows that individual attention which, easily possible when numbered by dozens, is beyond hope now that mass production threatens to invade our peace—a calamity, I am assured, that will never rear its ugly head in our garden!

So let me proceed with the delicate steps of Agag, the D. B. under one arm, the Rhododendron Association *Year Book* under the other, to a few of the pygmies, to *R. radicans* which, no taller than a couple of inches, promises soon to have covered nearly two square feet with its crisp little leaves and ground-clinging branches. This wee shrublet, which envelops its dark green mat with nodding rose-purple flowers, ridiculously large for so small a plant, is easily one of the best rock-garden shrubs ever introduced. But it is equally happy here on the flat where it is companioned by *Gaultheria tricophylla* and one or two of the *R. repens* and *Forrestii* group which latter, though they express every contentment, are shy to flower. These glorious creepers need, I rather think, not only time but a sunny rock face to lean against—this being suggested by the noble old specimen at Bodnant which does so well.

A year or so before he introduced *R. radicans* Forrest sent in *keleticum* of the same series (Saluenense). A charming semi-prostrate bush, seldom much above six inches and neatly rounded, *keleticum* is also a splendid bloomer, the big flowers being much nearer crimson than those of most of this series which makes a speciality of purples. *R. prostratum* has not yet entered the fold, the nearest thing to it here being *prostigiatum* (what a name!), a hybrid between it and *fastigiatum*. Shortly after it came to us one autumn day from Lochinch, Prostig. opened some of its lavender-mauve blossoms which are singularly lovely just after sundown or in thin shade. This luminous blue effect we also get in a few of the *R. Augustinii + fastigiatum* and *impeditum* crosses, and exquisitely beautiful some of them are, while on a larger scale one may induce *ponticum* or other 'blues' to fill the shade beneath forest trees with a woodsmoke haze.

R. calostrotum, rarely up to one foot, and the taller *riparium* we have in goodly groups. Some of the latter (K.W. 7061 and 5828) have soared to well over two feet, which is much taller than they seem to reach on their own lofty mountain tops. But if both species, being seed-raised, show some variability in size, leaf and flower, not one of them is unworthy. In winter the frosty-emerald, ruddy with a cinnamon reverse, of the aromatic leaves and the nut-brown twigs are delightful in massed plants. And then when spring brings the wide and generous flowers in lavish abundance, the cool green of the foliage makes an admirable setting for the very vivid rose-purple which these plants carry with such pronounced dignity nearly all summer and often again in autumn. Both of them, and the other saluenenses mentioned, are hardy and easy. We have most of them in full sun, the soil being a sandy loam which holds summer moisture fairly well, but we help to conserve this by a free use of sorbex moss peat and on this regime practically all these alpine rhododendrons thrive remarkably well.

As a series the lapponicum rhododendrons could put up a strong claim to a foremost place among these miniatures. I have an impression that this, one of the largest of all the alpine clans, is already being regarded with no more than an amiable tolerance in many gardens where more uncommon and individually more striking rhododendrons are sought. There never was a greater error committed in the name of gardening, for the most ordinary of these lapps., with their ease of increase, willing good temper and perfect adaptability for community life, are all that is desirable for anyone who aims at those broad effects one associates with heaths.

The heaths of Eastern Asia they, in truth, are, and if you would bring into the garden the grace of harebell-blue melting into the blue-purple of our own heaths, these lapps. will achieve that end if anything will. In that way, at any rate, do we glean a satisfaction which never loses its zest. And if some broad drifts of *R. intricatum* or *hippophaeoides*, running their gentle azure like pools of moor water under an August sky between the bell heathers, or even the later ones of the *Erica ciliaris* class, do not touch your garden soul with a rhythm of colour melody too spiritual for words, then you must renounce the subtler pleasures of modern gardening and go back to your dear old Paul Crampels in a scarf of lobelia blue.

For *R. intricatum* at its best, when its blue is very clean and soft, we shall ever have an unchanging affection, and it will often be as full of flower in August as it is in March. But *scintillans* runs it close, and exalted among the choicest of these taller growers is that beautiful form of *R. hippophaeoides* which bears the label, 'Habo Shan'. There are few weeks in the year in which we cannot find some of the fine lavender-blue flowers of this form expanded, and the foliage, as in so many other lapponicums, is dusted with that silveriness which makes as delightful a background for blossoms of that colour as it does for the plum-purples. That one might name better blues than 'Habo Shan' may be admitted, but there are moments when a group of this bonny shrub with the clear yellow *Keiskii* in attendance is bewitching in its loveliness.

R. fastigiatum is yet another outstanding species, dense and bushy and abundantly free with its wide and flat lavender or purple blooms, and *impeditum*, rather more lowly and rock-hugging, may be bracketed with it as a lapp. of princely rank. The lavender-mauve *orthocladum*, a twiggy, dense little bush, the pale purple *Edgarianum*, *drumonium* presenting a flattish rusty cushion which it hides beneath a cloak of mauve, and the thyme-leaved *telmateium* with small white-throated stars of rosy lilac, all these and others come between the lavender shades and the deep blue purples in a bewildering gradation of tones.

This inconsistency in colour and other features is so general among alpine rhododendrons that one has to resort to propagation by cuttings if it is desired to increase any particular form. In fact, life to these carefree children of the hills is still a great game. Some day they may decide upon definite careers, fix the colours of their flowers, their shapes and their sizes and settle down to the dull business of like producing like. But that is not yet. Playthings of chance in a world of flux, they revel to-day in such a wanton disregard of anything approaching uniformity, anything in the nature of individual characterisation, that the botanist is confounded in his efforts to decide what shall be regarded as a species.

Yet who would have it otherwise, who forego the sporting zest inspired by raising these rhododendrons from seed in the absence of any certainty as to what the results will yield? Gardening would become a very matter-of-fact business if it were all to be worked out beforehand with mathematical accuracy. It is sometimes, and that is one reason why one delights in the waywardness of these little shrubs, why one cherishes them and a hundred other wildlings as sanctuaries precious to the name of romance.

In deep violets, or royal blues, the lapponicums attain a perfection no less striking than they do in lavender and wine-purples, *R. cantabile* and the taller *russatum* being a pair of indispensable beauties. We have nothing better than these in their own colour in this series—and nothing better in the way of companions for them than the bright yellow *R. muliense* and *chryseum*. All of these make neat and bushy little shrubs, charming in leaf as well as flower and of the easiest temperament. Even in pinks the lapponicums are not wanting though there is a good helping of blue in most of them. Thus the large-leaved, well-dressed *R. ravum*, which will make four feet, is rose-pink of a deep, clean tone. *R. tapetiforme* is another and *stictophyllum* will often stray from a persistent mauve to a fresh and silvery rose.

Other pinks come to mind and the one incomparable beauty in that colour among these diminutives is *R. crebreflorum*— ours being K.W. 6967. An almost prostrate bushling of a few inches, with a leathery foliage of bay green, this dear little plant raises above that sombre leafage, in May, clusters of flowers in an exquisite shell-pink warmed by the faintest infusion of cream. There is not a hint of blue in these lovely blooms, they are firm and waxen in texture, as prettily crimped as a shell, and delicately fragrant. Perhaps the lemon-yellow *R. Sargentianum*, with puckered corollas, suggesting when half opened a chalky yellow alpine auricula, may claim as rare a perfection in its own colour as *crebreflorum*.

But there is a peculiar and irresistible attraction about many of this Cephalanthum Series. *R. ledoides* and *sphaeranthum*, loosely built, yet graceful, narrow-leaved shrubs, are beyond praise when gracing a sunny stream-bank with their coral buds and bunches of rose and white flowers which might be those of *Viburnum Carlesii* reduced by half. *R. radinum* always looks fresh and dainty when decked with her white, rose-tipped blooms, while *chamaetortum*, lowly and almost a creeper, with pink flowers, and the yellow *gymnomiscum*, are also among our special friends in this fascinating clan. But even these are not to have the field to themselves for the Lady of the Garden has approaching maturity a crowd of G. F. cephalanthums many of which have great promise.

R. pubescens dwells by the well-drained waterside with *ledoides*. It is a rather ambitious, withal untidy fellow, waving slender, straggly wands of three feet or more, but it is easily forgiven when its twigs become thronged with axillary clusters in a shrill pink and white, and this in early spring. But it is not so early as *R. scabrifolium*, which bears the name of the group, for this species, which has much the same loose, ungainly manner, will often open its flowers in February. But although these blossoms look so delicate in their snowy whiteness, sometimes flushing to a virginal pink, we have many a time seen them escape a frost that has reduced other earlies to ashes. In the bud stage, even to the point of opening, they are surprisingly resistant.

Other scabrifoliums are coming along, and it has just occurred to me that I was about to do an injustice to one of the fairest daughters of the household by forgetting all about her. This is *R. hemitrichotum*, K.W. 4994, the flowers of which, widely funnel-shaped and borne in twos or threes at the leaf axils, are a silvery blush chastely margined with rose and they break from buds which are a warm yet bright brick-red.

The Lepidotum Series will not excite the admiration of those who look for a big noise in colour for they are, for the most part, unassuming shrubs of low growth with starry, often reflexed, bell-shaped flowers of almost shrinking modesty. Yet, we have no light affection for the little chaps, whose foliage is spicily aromatic and whose blooms come in full summer to drift on into late autumn. And they have a charm of their own, these nodding bells, which gleam like melting wax and whose colours, running from yellow to a honey-tinted red, purple, vermilion and ruby are peppered with gold, silver or red specks. Most of this troupe are seed raised from a K.W. 7229 packet, and to Ward also belongs the credit for having introduced the one 'star' performer of the series, *R. imperator*. And he is, every little inch of him, an emperor among his kind when, in May, the squat crisp cushion of fragrant leaves becomes hidden beneath a galaxy of flowers in a lively blue-pink. Usually borne singly, these crimson-stalked blooms are well over an inch across and they throw back their segments as if the better to show off their bright purple stamens and the even tone of their generous pink.

For general garden use, that is, for massing where few others of their character would do so well—in sun or shade, dry soil or moist—for use as fill-ups or as a background for smaller and choicer kinds, for making hedges if you will, we have no two opinions about the excellent *R. racemosum*. In the woodland some of the older forms of this variable shrub are among the earliest to give their apple-blossom pink and white. These are soon joined by some of Wilson's with a broad, rich green foliage, keen rose-pink blossoms and, not infrequently, a low trailing manner, and there are one or two really good whites— a colour, if one can use the word, that is wanting in most dwarf rhododendrons.

Then we have another colony of racemosums under the label R. 03989. These are a remarkably level and delightful lot with their olive-green leaves, crimson branches and copious crop of glowing pink flowers in April and May. There is a suggestion of that celebrity, F. 19404 in these Rock introductions, but they will get much taller, probably four feet at least. *R. virgatum*, K.W. 6279 (now *oleifolium*), I was going to say was a faultless beauty, but it has one failing here and that is its branches do not always support their heavily-flowered tips. This, however, may be due to our growing it near the sheltering arms of some conifers which ward off spring frosts. However, that is a minor matter, as is the plant's susceptibility to frost (what rhododendron is not?) and this *virgatum* will always have a place among the most treasured for the loveliness of those funnel-shaped flowers, which are well over an inch across and an exquisite pink without a thought of mauve to tarnish its purity.

Close up to the racemosums in garden usefulness are the glaucums, and *R. glaucum* itself, a Hooker introduction of 1850, is among the oldest inhabitants of this garden. Our first plant, now four or five feet across and half as high, is not so fresh in the pink of its ample bells as some which have come in since, notably from Daisy Hill and Mr. Harry White's Sunningdale nursery, but they are all pleasant, easy-going shrubs which take care of themselves in open woodland and flower unfailingly between the frost-traps of spring. But, loyal as we are to *glaucum*, I would not be doing this select series justice were I to omit giving *R. charitopes* a foremost place in loveliness. This discovery of Farrer's is about eighteen inches high here with a distinct look of *glaucum* in its foliage and lowly bushiness.   But the beautiful big bells, borne in twos or threes, entirely eclipse the older shrub in the delicious clarity of their rose-pink which flushes to a deeper tone with dim carmine freckles on an upper lobe. And this admirable sweet-tempered rhododendron flowers abundantly not only in spring, for we can always trust it to put up a good autumn show when its colour is even more enchanting.

R. tsangpoense rivals *charitopes* to which it is obviously closely allied, but the flowers tend to something near cerise. A first-rate shrub which should have a merry future when better known —it was only found (by Ward) some eleven years ago. *R. hypolepidotum*, one of the tallest of the glaucums, we grow and like for it has struck out a line for itself in its pretty yellow bells, and yellow is too valuable a colour in rhododendrons to be treated without decent respect, even when it is not a good yellow. Then there is *pruniflorum* to which the Rhododendron Association's *Year Book* grants three stars.

A number of this species all look much alike to my untutored eye, healthy, bright and bushy little shrubs with plenty of broad, glaucous-green leaves, which express their resentment to being interfered with by firing off at the offender a surprisingly potent stench. But whether it was this which induced some botanist who seems to have come to grips with it to hurl the infamous name of *sordidum* upon one of these plants, or whether it was the displeasure he experienced on first seeing the colour of the flowers that moved him to reproach so bitter, I do not know. However, in so far as this colour is concerned, the squeamish may mutter 'stewed plums' and indulge in other gibes, we find the normal crimson-purple of *pruniflorum* by no means unattractive, especially with the hue of its leafage. It may drift into a passable crimson in one direction and to parma violet in another, and why, O why, do people who delight in that violet affect to squiggle when they see the same tint in a rhododendron?

Some of our visitors express similar symptoms when confronted by *R. myrtilloides* of the Campylogynum Series, an almost flat, stubby little shrub with hard, glossy leaves, commonly bronzed in winter, and the quaintest of waxen bells. These, held perkily aloft, each on its own red stem, are a gloomy plum-purple set in a calyx of beetle-green and delicately powdered with a fairy's tinsel. The purple may be changed for mahogany-red or maroon, for *myrtilloides* is variable in colour as well as in size of bloom, but in its most sullen moments it can, when seen against a lowering sun, glow with those same wonderful ruby flashes which are emitted at times by the equally sombre leps. to which it is not distantly related.

Now for a final paragraph on one or two special favourites, and among these I have no hesitation in giving *R. leucaspis* and *R. deleiense* a distinguished place. That they carry the warning banner of the Boothii household, which suggests that they are not above suspicion in garden reliability, matters not. The voice of trial is the deciding factor, and they have come through our winters with sufficient distinction to give us every confidence in their future.

R. leucaspis, broad, blunt and bristly of leaf, with gnarled and twisty branches, is almost prostrate in growth, though it delights to lean up against a convenient rock. In early spring the fat round buds which terminate almost every twig awaken in response to the first mild period, each yielding a pair of blossoms, or perhaps three. These blooms, which open flat, are a good two inches wide. The richly-textured corollas are a warm milk-white with chocolate anthers, and they cling back to back, these 'silver shields', as if each, delicately sensible of its twin-sister's loveliness (and possibly its own!) were anxious to avoid anything likely to embarrass so exquisite a charm. Or, it may be, that they grow thus the better to display that subtle flush of violet which often clouds the reverse of the flower and which imparts to the face of the latter a more pearl-like purity.

The refinement of good taste, with quality and breeding in every line, *R. leucaspis* would melt the stony heart of a cynic with its quiet, gentle beauty. To frost the flowers may be as sensitive as those of others, but it is absolutely hardy in itself, not at all difficult, and may be flowered in three years from seed. But, even though we do sometimes lose its blossoms, we should regard ourselves amply rewarded if they were enjoyed three seasons out of five. And we get more than that, for our oldest bush, now covering two feet by three feet and less than half as much in height, is one of the few plants in the garden which is honoured by having a light covering thrown over it should frost threaten at flowering time—that is, if we don't forget.

R. deleiense, reared, so I learn in the Domesday Book, from seed packet, K.W. 8165, is now rather more than a foot high. It flowered when about six inches and has done so every year with great abundance, usually in April. An erect little bush with cinnamon bark and narrowly oblong, glossy green, sombre, drooping leaves three or four inches long, *deleiense* is not a strikingly cheerful object. But when its rusty buds break into wide-mouthed bells of the softest and purest wild-rose pink, with slightly reflexed segments, not even those of *Williamsianum* are more arresting in their fascination. *R. deleiense*, the type, has, I believe, darker flowers which tend dangerously near magenta, but whether Ward's 8165 is always as superior as the form we grow I cannot say. It is, in any event, a gem of the first pan, and it has so far proved hardy—much hardier than *R. tephropeplum* which shares its bed.

The saviour of the Maddenii Series is, of course, the old and well-tried *ciliatum* which, coming from Sikkim in 1850, is still easily one of the most beautiful of all the larger flowered early dwarf rhododendrons of anything near its colour—a really clear, pale rose-pink. Grown hard in a high and breezy situation, with all possible exposure, *ciliatum* makes a much denser, more compact bush than it does in our tree-filled glade, and this also so retards its flowering that it is the more likely to escape spring frosts. But, one way or another, this charming

Himalayan will be cherished by all who love a choice rhododendron. And we owe *ciliatum* no small debt for having taken a hand in giving us, among others, such excellent and hardy hybrids as *cilpinense*, raised nine years ago at Bodnant from a cross with *R. moupinense*, and the adorable *praecox*.

CHAPTER XIV

The Larger Rhododendrons

A NUMBER of our larger rhododendrons are still so immature I can pass them over with an easy conscience, while several others—*scyphocalyx*, sanguineums, aperantums, Stewartianums—are hardly through their reliability trials, and it is possible they never will be, excepting the Stewartianums. Of these, some half-a-dozen bushes are turning out so well and giving such fascinating colours in flat trusses of the rarest beauty that they promise to uphold all that Farrer wrote of his 'gleaming trumpets'—and more.

The noble *R. Falconeri*, although only eight feet high, has flowered freely since that first effort of which I have spoken, and a *fictolacteum* is making a start. But all other big-leaved fellows must remain for some time as foliage plants only, and to their distinguished services as such respectful recognition has already been offered.

R. dauricum is usually the first of our rhododendrons to anticipate the spring, its flowers, like rosy butterflies, being poised on the tips of its slender, leafless twigs before the year is many weeks old. It is soon followed by its pretty hybrid daughter, *praecox*. I shall not be unkind to the dainty and adorable *praecox* and say that *emasculum*, which may have had a similar origin, is better. The latter is larger and rounder in the truss, but where it shines is as a successor to the sister hybrid. We grow both in groups of half-a-dozen or so under the branches of our riverside trees, which help to ward off frost, but the ground is dry and stony. Underneath them the Lady of the Garden has laid a carpet of *Primula Juliae* and another of blue primroses raised from a stray seedling blue that was deemed worthy of increase. The effect is bright and harmonious without being garish, and if the rhododendron blooms are destroyed by frost the primroses carry on until another set of buds open to play with the perils of winter.

But if *dauricum* is good *R. mucronulatum*, now apparently ranked as a species, is better, being more robust in growth, with larger flowers and these are a more pleasing colour. Often coming into bloom in January, a group gives such a cheerful mass of vivid rosy-mauve that there are few winter flowering shrubs to compare with this hardy Korean. Although held erect on leafless twigs the blossoms are singularly weatherproof, even withstanding more frost than those of most earlies.

A philosopher once said that without error there would be no progress, and one of our errors is this: We should have planted years ago more *R. mucronulatum* than its allies and grouped them within eye-range of *Hamamelis mollis* which flames into spicy golden tassels at the same time. But these discoveries are the salt of gardening, and the realisation of them the stimulus which spurs one to further effort. And when we do stake a claim for *mucronulatum* we shall not omit to run in a few of its variety *acuminatum*, which is distinctly later by some weeks and equally good.

R. moupinense is another early bloomer, but so very beautiful that no one who aspires to the choicest of rhododendrons can resist it. A little, loosely built, straggling shrub with ovate leaves and broad, wide-open, scented flowers suggesting an indian azalea, it needs thoughtful placing if it is to escape frost. We find it tolerably safe on the north side of a woodland holly bush, where it is somewhat retarded as well as protected, and in that shaded site the exquistie white blossoms are inexpressibly lovely on a fine February day. There is a rose-pink form of *moupinense* which is even more bewitching, if one dare indulge in comparisons. *R. moupinense* is perfectly hardy in itself and its flowers are probably no more susceptible to frost-bite than those of most rhododendrons. Its very early start is the weak point in its armour. For the north and east Mr. Cox suggests growing it hard, as I have suggested for *ciliatum*, this tending to later flowering and a firmer, closer growth, and I am inclined to think that this exposure treatment would serve equally well in many other quarters.

The Triflorum Series is not far behind the Dauricum in precocity, and *R. yunnanense* has given us such unqualified satisfaction that we regard it among the most valued of spring

RHODODENDRON WIGHTII

RHODODENDRON FALCONERI

RHODODENDRON SOULIEI

RHODODENDRON ORBICULARE

shrubs. Whether it is on the dry slopes of the woodland, in the alluvial soil of the glade, in sun or shade, it is always healthy, happy and extraordinarily prolific, while its flowers may be anything from an almost pure white to a good firm pink. One sound white we have is particularly gay, for in it the freckling which adorns the upper segment of the *yunnanense* shield is a flare of carmine—a most spectacular touch.

R. oreotrephes, with trusses of silvery-lavender to rosy-mauve, is another of our friends, and its broad and leathery, oblong, glaucous leaves have a cut of their own as well as an aromatic scent. In some forms introduced later the leaves of *oreotrephes* are still more beautifully blued, these making a perfect setting for the flowers when they happen to be pure pink, as in Rock 59591 (*R. timeteum*). But *oreotrephes* is always well-bred and in some of our specimens the flowers are distinctly fragrant. Even should the winter be hard enough to strip off most of the leaves—when the Lady of the Garden reproaches her for being undressed yet unashamed—there is no denying that the mountain dweller has tone.

A really blue rhododendron we shall probably never see, but *R. Augustinii* at its best is perhaps nearer that elusive tint than any other, but I am not at all sure that some of the hybrids raised from it, such as *Augustinii + impeditum* (Blue Tit) are not better. A cross between *Augustinii* and *fastigiatum* shown by Lord Stair at the Rhododendron Association's show in 1935 we thought the bluest thing in rhododendrons we had ever seen— a most enthralling beauty—but the lovely Blue Diamond which, if I may trust a memory that needs re-conditioning, is of the same parentage with a dash of *intricatum* thrown in, is held to be even better by some.

To return to safer ground we have *R. Augustinii*, singly and in groups, in various parts of the garden, hoping that soil, light and other mysterious factors may induce some of them to give us that clean and luminous blue which is doubtless decided nearly as much by local influences as by strain. One of the most prized of this collection is a stripling raised from cuttings kindly given to us by the distinguished owner of Monreith and taken from his best colour forms. As this has only just commenced flowering one cannot say more than that it promises to be worthy of the famous garden whence it came.

But if it should not do so, if we in our light shaley soil do not attain the colour in these rhododendrons which one may see at Monreith or Bodnant, I am confident that we shall not thereby suffer any evil complex. After all, if we had never seen a 'real blue' *Augustinii* we would probably have cherished the paler and the rosy-lavender forms, for few of these are other than very beautiful in light woodland shade. Even *R. polylepis* and *concinnum* and the magenta *villosum*, which horrify some people, are not hastily to be turned down when in the right place, always provided you keep the mischievous imp of comparison well under control.

R. charianthum, which might be described as a rose-pink *yunnanense*, runs the latter close in quality, a better shrub here than *Davidsonianum*, which varies from almost white to rose. *R. chartophyllum* is again close to *yunnanense*, but our representative has flowers of a full-toned rose close upon two inches across. The lavender *R. sycnanthum* is another we grow and then there is *eriandrum* in mauve, with a beautiful white form, the excellent *Searsiae*, again in white or mauve, and the ever useful *lutescens*—useful because it is one of the few decent yellows among the triflorums.[1] And further, *lutescens* carries a simple grace in the elegant and lightly diffused foliage, which latter is very persistent in winter, while the red-bronze of the young shoots is delightful. Most of the triflorums seem to need rather more moisture than the average rhododendron, *lutescens* in particular, and it we are using along with waterside primulas and lilies.

Comparatively dull when out of bloom, many of these triflorums may not be big drums even in their best and brightest spring uniforms. But there is this to be said for them: Their gentle tones and studied restraint will never vex the nightingales of our woodland garden, and their modest, slender foliage blends very happily with natural surroundings. For these reasons and others—hardiness and ease of culture—we grow as many triflorums as we can fit in, even K.W.'s quaint

[1] A pygmy form of *R. Hanceanum*, which has only just flowered, is even better, the blooms being like those of *oreotrephes* in a bright daffodil-yellow.

'mahoganys' not being amiss among the bronzy-gold of up-rising ferns.

To turn for a moment from Puritan modesty to triumphant splendour—who was it who, having taken up a quill pluckt from an angel's wing, cast it aside for a pen dipt in hot and noble blood?—let me introduce a few of our Series Neriiflorum and its subs., begging meanwhile the patience of the reader who may be irritated by these names and terms, for of other names they have none. It may be poor comfort to those who do me the honour of enduring these pages unskipped, incidentally to re-mind them that such beautiful and familiar words as *chrysan-themum* and *delphinium* were once no less foreign to our ears than those of later coinage, and that getting accustomed to such cacophonics as *hirsuticostatum* or *Mlokosewitchii* is only a matter of digestion and time.

The neriiflorums, specialising in blood-reds as I have sug-gested, have as yet given us nothing quite so moving in its magnificence as *R. neriiflorum* itself, which began flowering when a foot or so in height. Its drooping, loosely disposed bells are a scarlet, generous and warm; they are very freely yielded and seem to be more lasting than those of most rhododendrons. Yet, there is an entire absence of gorgeous sumptuousness in these rather small and neat, open trusses. *Neriiflorum* understands the inestimable merit of moderation and therein lies much of its charm. The taller and closely allied *R. euchaites*, which we have not yet flowered, is regarded by some as even more beautiful and a better garden plant, and *haematodes*, almost a rock-garden shrub and also among our novitiates, excels even *Forrestii* and *repens* in the astounding brilliance of its big crimson scarlet corollas.

None of these neriiflorums—and I can include *floccigerum* and *pocophorum*, of which we have some good scarlets under Forrest and Rock numbers which bloomed when quite little bushes—are any too hardy, though they get no coddling here. But a more troublesome fault is their passion for flowering themselves to death. *Neriiflorum* itself is not exempt from this pleasant form of suicide and we have not found disbudding the salutary antidote it is supposed to be. Rhododendrons are very like daphnes in one respect: If they make up their minds to go to a better land, go they will.

R. dichroanthum, so well-favoured in its rosy-yellow or orange, also has a reputation for 'going off' just when looking its finest. But as our old specimen, a rounded thick-set bush, nearly six feet across and half as high, has not yet shown a single truss we have at least been spared that dramatic end. Meanwhile, its ever spreading skirts are enveloping a group of *Lilium Szovitzianum* whose blazing suns divert one's thoughts from the barren fig-tree beneath them. *R. didymum*, on the other hand, so old-maidishly prudent in deferring its flowering until June, so excessively respectable in the sombre, almost black-crimson she wears, flowers with seemly discretion year after year and lives for ever.

The chief lions, however, of the rhododendrons of this caste, omitting all those not yet come to flowering, consist here of a colony of *R. chaetomallum* raised from the cradle, their seed packet being K.W. 6805. Jacob did not wait longer for Rachel than we waited for this leisurely little family to grow up, but our reward was more gratifying than his. For, instead of our being hoaxed like that ingenuous lover, the first flower that opened exceeded in beauty our most sanguine expectations and its successors have been worthy of it. Wide and ample, rich in texture and a glorious blood-crimson of arresting intensity, these are blooms of so deep and glowing a hue that to compare them with others—even *haematodes* itself—would seem ungenerous. And they are a hardy, sturdy lot, these chaetomallums, with a stature of one, two, three, or four feet, with a stout, erect carriage and comparatively large and leathery olive-green leaves and swaddlings of red-brown wool—good and hearty fellows to look upon at any season.

Unwillingly, the rest of our neriiflorums[1] must be passed over, for the April days which bring most of them to colour bring others not less appealing, and of these the Thomsonii Series and its attachments is more weighty in numbers, perhaps even more generally admirable, than any already mentioned. *R. Thomsonii* itself, one of the finest rhododendrons ever introduced (and one of the oldest, for it is of Hooker's 1849 Himal-

[1] *R. sperabile* (F. 26434) just concluding a 4-5 weeks' run (April) has been excellent; flowers a warm bright scarlet (not a trace of blue) against a glossy deep green foliage. Buds more frost-hardy than in most others.

ayans), may vary a little but it is always good. Still, we were fortunate in our oldest plant, now some eight feet high, for its leaves are more than usually glaucous and the flowers a strikingly vivid, yet full-toned blood-red with that remarkable calyx in conspicuous prominence. We try to place our Thomsoniis so that the lowering sun will light up the splendid blossoms with that gleam of ruby-crimson one sometimes sees in old stained glass. But it is a shrub that will invariably assert its supreme merit. It is, moreover, as willing and easy in cultivation as the faithful *Fortunei* or, shall I say, the old and well-tried Ascot Brilliant, still one of the best hybrids of its class and colour, flowering early in life as well as early in the season.

That peerless jewel of the series, *Williamsianum*, we have found a little touchy about making a start, especially in the rather low-lying alluvial soil of the glade beds. But having an unshaken belief in the theory that, in the majority of cases, it is only a matter of discovering the right spot if we are to satisfy an unhappy plant, our Williamsianums you would come across in half-a-dozen odd places. It may be true that Providence eases the way of babes and sucklings, for the first plant we put in of this precious shrub is also among those which have never looked back. That was in the early days when we only had the red, shaley soil of our woodland slopes to play with. Nevertheless, *Williamsianum*, planted with abounding faith and little experience (but what giants we were in the days when it was rare!) on one of those unpromising slopes, is, as I have said, still there. And more, it covers a space over four feet wide; it is robustly healthy and the oak boughs high above it help to screen its exquisitely beautiful flowers and almost as beautiful foliage from the frosts of spring.

Believing that it is a good and joyful thing for brethren to dwell together in unity, the Lady of the Garden is convinced that this *Williamsianum* owes its long life and well-being to the fact that it is crowded up by others. Thus the pretty *R. serpyllifolium*, two or three feet across, jostles it from one side, an old *glaucum* elbows it from another, *Vaccinium Mortinia* invades the rear, *Cyathodes robustus* and *Leiophyllum buxifolium* are allied in a frontal attack. And each one of these, I am assured, derives mutual aid and comfort from the other. It may be so.

There are some sound reasons why it should. In any event the plants themselves certainly have a ready answer for those who hold what they term overcrowding to be one of the seven sins of gardening—people who are ill at ease unless they have an earth space around each individual, which is just what most plants heartily abhor.

R.R. callimorphum, caloxanthum, Souliei and *campylocarpum* make a quartette of shrubs which, gracing one of our alder-shaded lawn-beds with *orbiculare*, are alone enough to raise this class of rhododendron high among the most treasured of the genus. The first three all flowered freely before they were three feet in height, and if the rose-pink of callimorphum's umbels, breaking from vivid carmine buds, touches a note of purity which is rare, the fat and tubby bells of *caloxanthum* are not less entrancing as they emerge from orange-scarlet to a clear sulphur-yellow. As for the delectable *Souliei*, with its wide bowl-shaped blossoms so daintily poised on their long red stalks, so masterly in elegance of line and in the subtle rosy flush which pervades the silvery whiteness of their exquisite tissue, lyrics of praise would leave its gracious loveliness unsung.

Yellow rhododendrons of merit are still few. We have our share of those bitter, misanthropic yellows which wear the disillusioned look of those who feel they have been deprived of their rightful measure of life's colour. But to the more favoured minority, of which some have been mentioned, one must add the worthy *campylocarpum*. Of this we appear to have got the typical early style, for it is a compact and neatly-rounded bush of no more than about three feet. We had to wait an unconscionable time for it to show a blossom, but since making a start a few years ago it has performed with entire satisfaction every spring. The orange-tinted buds expand to a truss of medium size in a clear canary-yellow, with that telling well of crimson at the base of each corolla which *callimorphum* and a few others display with such *chic*.

The excellent *R. croceum* and *Wardii*, and that prince of scarlets, *Hookeri* the magnificent, must be passed by with the few barbatums and lacteums we possess, for their coming out is not yet. But *R. Wightii*, one of our prides only to be presented to the best people, is a shrub of great merit with a massive and beautiful foliage and it annually gives us its bold trusses of clear yellow, and again crimson-eyed, blossoms—an eminently satisfying, well-looking bush.

R. orbiculare lays a trap for the unwary, for while the average gardener's eye at once associates it with *Williamsianum* and others of the Thomsonii clan—to which I believe it once officially belonged—it now seems to occupy a position of its own as an appendage of *Fortunei*. However, if this merely adds another complexity to an already difficult world, *orbiculare* remains where it was, a rhododendron that is distinguished even among the most *élite* of the genus, one to be honoured and adored along with such superlative species as *Fargesii* and *Thomsonii*.

With *orbiculare* we again had the good fates on our side, for the first plant to get away and do well in this garden was one of the low-growing, spreading forms which have so much to recommend them. This specimen, now four or five feet across and barely half as high, could hold its own, and that easily, in much larger collections than our's when, in May or earlier, the long-petioled bells, full and round and a lovely rose, of the loose corollas nod above the soft, seductive green of the handsome leaves. Dignity and elegance, blue-blooded quality and an indefinable charm of its own belong to this aristocrat of China, and we find it neither difficult nor tender. One hesitates to question the opinion of the R. A. *Year Book*, but that inestimable volume is surely unjust in damning by faint praise this species as a flowering shrub by stating that its 'chief beauty' is in its foliage and rounded symmetrical shape. However, the book does accord *orbiculare* three stars and that moves one to forgive it.

R.R. decorum and *discolor* are both first-rate species, handsome in leaf and flower, and their late blooming gives them a special value. With us *discolor* has been much the more vigorous, but its growth has been made at the expense of its flowering. On the other hand, its ally, *decorum* (of Forrest's and Wilson's introductions) has gone to the opposite extreme, blossoming with such imprudent prolificacy that every season it threatens to flower itself into another world. The Lady of the Garden, who is made of sterner stuff than I am, disbuds with unflinching severity, but the plant takes not the slightest notice of the snubbing.

The long and large trumpet shaped corollas of these rhododendrons, borne in a loose corymb, not too big, are white or pale rose, waxen in texture and deliciously scented. Against the fresh pea-green leafage these are extremely lovely, and at their season they have the field pretty much to themselves.

Of the Arboreum Series the only species growing here that is worthy of mention at the moment is *R. Delavayi* (F. 27718) 'the Chinese *R. arboreum*' which surprised us by flowering when only two feet high. Moreover, the richly textured blooms of this plant are a really fine crimson-scarlet, warm and glowing in tone and an even colour all through without so much as a freckle. A good as well as beautiful shrub for it seems quite hardy on our warmer slopes, if it is rather to the precocious side with its mid-April, or earlier, blossoms.

R Smirnowi, of the Pontic household, is often treated with scant courtesy, but there is no denying the fact that its large bright green leaves with the white felt which is so conspicuous upon them and the younger wood, make an attractive show with the carmine-pink buds and clear rose of the wide flowers. Further, *Smirnowi* is so indestructible that it will grow anywhere and make a useful shield for tenderer kinds. Then we have in *R. Makinoi* another ponticum which does us equally good service, asking little if it does not give a great deal. This, a thick-set bushling of less than two feet with little ambition to mount much higher, has extremely narrow deep green leaves whose margins are incurled upon a dense nap of rusty fur. And over all this in May *Makinoi* spreads so lavish a crop of blossom that it becomes enveloped in a mass of rose-pink, clean and fresh in tone.

Although a Boothii, *R. auritum* promises to be quite hardy here. It is not a spectacular species, but we have a friendly eye for it because the ivory-yellow flowers, slightly flushed with rose on the lobes, strike just the right note along our woodland margin. For the old *cinnabarinum* in all its forms we shall ever have a hospitable welcome. Its glaucous foliage and lapageria trumpets of cinnabar-red, orange or crimson overlaid with a bluish bloom are unreservedly 'the quality'—even brilliant

RHODODENDRON
CALOXANTHUM

*The sulphur bells break from
orange-scarlet buds*

ODODENDRON
MPYLOCARPUM

*ose canary-yellow flowers have
a basal spot of ruby-crimson*

RHODODENDRON WILLIAMSIANUM

AZALEA HINE-MAYO
Bright pink and typical of much that is best in Japanese azaleas

when seen against a low sun; the plant is thrifty and willing almost anywhere, the flowering season is not too early, often not beginning until the end of May, and the slender, erect growth has obvious advantages in a small garden.

Forrest never introduced a better shrub than *R. Grierson-ianum*. That may be a bold statement, but who would deny this magnificent species an honoured place among the most eminent of this vast family? Whether its well-balanced, moderate trusses of wide corollas are 'geranium-scarlet', brick-red vermilion brightened with an infusion of rose or pimpernel scarlet—for plants vary somewhat from seed—the colour is always attractive, always distinct in its own ardent splendour. One might think that such gorgeous blossoms would be a little over-whelming, perhaps disturbing, in the natural environment of a woodland garden. But they are not. We grow *Griersonianum* along the dryish parts of our lightly tree-shaded slopes, with creeping ivy, wood-rush and fern for company, and have not found it anything but desirable and pleasant. If the plant blazoned its glorious fires with the redundancy of one of the hybrids it might offend against the tenets of good taste. But this is a comparatively small shrub, its branches few and the trusses distinctly moderate in size and number. It has made of restraint a fine art and knows just how to express it.

Only a severe frost in spring has had any really ill effect upon our Griersonianums, this causing a certain amount of bark-splitting. But, grown in rather poor, sharply drained soil with a little overhead shelter and happed around with natural vegetation, the plants rarely suffer. In any event the species is such a valuable one that it is worth any amount of risk. And this value is something much more than skin deep. It includes not only a remarkable beauty but the habit of flowering so late that the shrub does not break bud until most others have closed down. Then there are those wonderful hybrids which have been raised by crossing this species with other rhododendrons— F. C. Puddle, Fabia, Vanessa, Tally Ho, May Day and others —plants which afford the most emphatic proof of Grierson-ianum's potency as a factor in hybridisation and which are un-doubtedly the forerunners of a race of late blooming rhodo-dendrons of superlative merit.

CHAPTER XV

Azaleas and Azaleodendrons

IT IS not without some diffidence that I use the name azalea here. But custom dies hard, very hard in a garden—and so long as most of us, including the nurserymen, hold the word in common usage the inclination to retain that word in such a book as this will remain stronger than one's conscientious desire to heed the voice of authority.

To anyone who can grow azaleas at all these shrubs will ever command a place of honour high among the choicest and most useful of all spring bloomers. This not merely because of their abounding generosity in bloom, their amazing wealth of colour, but because they are so thrifty and content. With us at all events azaleas have given these good things in brimming measure, whether they are the old yellow pontics, now big bushes even on some of the dry woodland slopes, the squat little Japs which adorn still hotter and drier, sun-baked places with their brilliant colour, or those who dwell in clover along the glade and waterside. Whether in sun or shade, dry soil or moist, lean or fat, there is scarcely an azalea in our garden which is not satisfied and satisfying.

And further, where will you find a group of shrubs that will cater so admirably for anything in the way of colour to which taste or ambition may aspire? The swarming hosts of *mollis*, *sinensis* and Ghent present a splendour so opulent, a pageant of colour so extravagant in its reckless wealth that anyone who wishes to do so may aspire to creating a miniature Chelsea Show in his back-garden for an outlay of a few pounds, and count upon an autumn bonus in the way of leaf tints as well. Then, at the other end of the scale, should your inclinations lean to more delectable fare, to hues which are the essence of refinement coupled with a grace of unexampled daintiness, there are azaleas which will fulfil these demands to the letter.

In writing of our azaleas, picking out a favourite plum here and there, and omitting, without prejudice, many a good and worthy plant, the first few that come to mind are all among the older ones. Is there lurking deeply in our veins some diehard relic of a crusty conservatism that we should still regard these friends of long ago with so much favour? I think not, since it is fairly obvious that azaleas like *A. Vaseyi, canadensis (Rhodora)* and *mucronata*, not to mention *pontica*, have not been equalled, certainly not excelled in their own way.

There are few azaleas more lovely than *A. Vaseyi* when its naked twigs are clustered with those beautifully clear pink or white flowers which in line and poise suggest some magnolia in miniature, and none gives us a more glorious leaf colour in autumn which, developing early, is retained for many weeks. As for little *canadensis*, whose lilac butterflies hover so jauntily over its slender twigs even in March, it is the very stuff of the youthful spring. But to enjoy *Rhodora* at her best, one should have in a group half-a-dozen plants at least, and if these are near the waterside with some *Primula rosea* and kingcups in the offing, so much the more charmingly will the little lady in the may-flower frock whisper the shy secrets of spring.

Before leaving the select Subseries Canadensis, to which *Vaseyi* and *Rhodora* belong, the famous *Albrechtii* must be mentioned. I do not like to think how long we waited before securing plants of this rare Japanese, but we have at last a small group of it in one of the glade beds. The two-inch flowers, widely bell-shaped, which we are expecting this year should appear just before the bright green leaves in early May. This colour will be either a vivid rose with an infusion of strangely luminous purple, an unstained rose of the purest dye, or some intermediate shade. But whatsoever the colour may be *Albrechtii* is always so fiercely brilliant that our plants have been carefully segregated lest they quarrel with others. I notice, however, that the Lady of the Garden has invited the white-belled *A. nipponica* to join this flambent company, doubtless convinced by her perennial optimism that this will tend to allay the fevered passion of *Albrechtii*, whereas I rather think the result will be a burnt offering with that innocent lamb in the flames.

A. mucronata, the nearest approach we have to a hardy *A. indica*, is one of those shrubs over which one might spend the most lavish of praise, only to feel as Solomon felt before the Queen of Sheba. Yet that metaphor does not sound quite right, for there is more of the madonna lily's immaculate chastity than eastern regalia in this azalea. The first plant of *A. mucronata* we put in years ago beneath the light shade of some old alders is now nearly ten feet across, yet little more than three feet high. Its low-spread branches, dense with evergreen leaves, are sheeted in early May with cup-shaped, snow-white flowers, over two inches across, whose fragrance is ineffably sweet. You may get plants of this beautiful azalea whose flowers are narrower and smaller, as you may in the charming silvery rose-lavender form—another adorable shrub—but *A. mucronata* is never other than distinguished and well-bred, standing out from the common run, secure in the detachment of her perfect beauty.

A. rosaeflora, another hardy relation of the florist's *A. indica*, is also a semi-prostrate, wide-spreading shrub, and very winsome it is with its double salmon-red camellias which anyone who has ever been to Chelsea Show will know full well. For nearly twenty years this has made a slowly widening, cushiony mass at the foot of a streamside eucryphia, and it now topples down the bank, thrusting its most adventurous posies through the golden-brown croziers of youthful ferns until they dip into the dancing water.

For many a season *A. yodogawa* (*yedoënse*) was treated rather shabbily in this garden. It was suffered, but not gladly. There was a something about its spindly, straggly manner which displeased us. The double blue-lilac flowers were so double that they hung their heads in languid indolence. But one bright day something was wanted to inter-plant a few new rhododendrons on a riverside bank, already carpeted with self-sown *Omphalodes cappadocica*. The opportunity suggesting a refuge for our yodogawas, half-a-dozen of these Cinderellas were rounded-up from the various parts of the garden in which they had been tried without success and put in, with little civility, to companion the rhododendrons.

The result was astonishing. The slightly elevated position the river bank afforded gave the flowers a dignity and elegance they had never before possessed, the shelter and possibly the

CIMICIFUGA
CORDIFOLIA

RHODODENDRON (AZALEA) MUCRONATUM
A silvery-rose variety

GERANIUM WALLICHIANUM, BUXTON'S VARIETY

GERANIUM ARMENUM

smell of the water increased them in number as well as in size. But the master stroke of this purely accidental bit of planting, which incidentally raised poor *yodogawa* from the slums to the higher planes of garden society, was the blending of those blue-lilac blossoms with the clear blue and rosy azure of the Cappadocian forget-me-not, with a backing of rhododendron and ivy green. From which story a very pretty moral might be gleaned.

We had been growing *yodogawa* for a long while before the arrival of the type, or species, *yedoënse var. poukanense*, and so, I take it, had everyone else, for the former, a Japanese garden form, was the first to appear in cultivation. Wherefore, since *yodogawa* was also the first to be recognised by the botanists, we are here presented with the anomaly of having for ever to live with the cart before the horse. But so long as the Rule of Priority remains unalterable, for so long must we suffer this contradiction in terms. And this is the more unfortunate when it is realised that *yedoënse var. poukanense*, the species, is a much better garden plant than *yodogawa*, the usurper, being taller and of good habit while the single flowers are large and a bright rosy-mauve.

Into the bewildering mazes of the Japanese azaleas I decline to be drawn, for in number these are as the stars of heaven, while among the difficulties their names and origins present better men than I am have been bogged. But this does not prevent our growing them singly and in colonies in all sorts of places, and if we should lose their labels, as we often do, our peace is not disturbed.

They are such easy going, easily contented little plants, especially all those of the Hinomanyo and Hinodegeri description, the splendid *Kæmpferi* and *malvatica* classes, with their homely names—Mary, Alice and Anny (which we do lose when we can) and the cheerful small-flowered amœnas of the lists. In prodigality of blossom, as in their amazing range of colour and form, and their pretty evergreen foliage, these Japs are among our gilt-edged investments. Depressions and conversions never affect their bountiful dividends, the black shadow of the tax collector never darkens the brightness of their ever accumulating wealth. We plant them in increasing numbers and have at this moment on its way from Japan a little cargo including that mighty atom, Gumpo, and some of his illustrious brethren.

No less, perhaps even more, might be said of the bigger hybrids, those flamboyant wonders to which I have alluded. But in a garden such as ours, limited in area with an essentially natural atmosphere predominating, one has to keep a careful check on the overbearing influence which these hybrids are apt to exert. There is such a thing as being unable to see the garden for the flowers.

So we can sometimes turn from these with a sense of relief to the delicate loveliness of *A. rosea*, a better plant and later (May) than *nudiflora*, with trusses of fragrant clear rose flowers of rare refinement. Then, along by the waterside, when *Spiraea bracteata* is spending the last of its white wreaths, when *Neillia longiracemosa* is hanging ruby-tinted tassels among its bronzy green, we have *A. viscosa* which, again, is a decided and charming pink, if you select a good form, and the sticky honeysuckle blossoms are deliciously scented. Add to these the beautiful rose and white *arborescens*, so much taller, so balanced and bosky, so excellent and lasting in its autumn colour that we have given it a 'specimen' place on the long lawn, and you have a trio of azaleas which would not startle the dryads of Arcady.

A. occidentalis, through whose fragrant thickets we once pushed shoulder high on the far side of America, must also come in here for it, too, seems to understand the precious value of restraint in woodland planting, its late summer flowers being comparatively small but exceedingly dainty. From the famous Knap Hill Nursery, and possibly some Continental sources, have come a series of occidentalis hybrids which inherit in part both the lateness of this species and the modest charm of their warm white, pale mauve, or soft pink blossoms.

To most of these our woodland sanctuary is open, and in the same category may be placed another older and remarkable hybrid of Knap Hill, *A. viscosepala*. I always thought this had some *occidentalis* 'blood' in it, but the authorities do not admit this, though the parentage is still a matter of conjecture. However, this a really first-rate azalea for June flowering, yielding every season an astonishing crop of blossoms which are pure white with a yellow throat, and I know no other azalea which pours forth its lily-like scent so copiously.

Our brightest and best performer of that group of azaleas presided over by the peerless *Schlippenbachii* is *A. reticulata*. Now about five feet high this is a most striking shrub when its leafless hazel-brown twigs are tipped with their ruby-crimson goblets, two inches wide, which have just enough—the merest hint—of blue in their pigment to give them a vehemence of tone which is so brilliant, yet not in any degree strident, that one never gets quite used to it. *A. reticulata,* moreover, is as hardy as it is easy, and it will come from seed like mustard and cress.

Also of this exclusive little company is *A. Weyrichtii,* and again one has something of the same daring style of colouring in large flowers on naked twigs. But in this species, of which our group is now just opening its blooming career, the blossoms are distinctly warmer in hue, with a glow of fiery scarlet lighting up their brick-red when seen against the evening sun. As with *Albrechtii,* this is an azalea for which it is not easy to select suitable colour companions, but we have avoided any difficulty of that sort by giving our plants a setting of late flowering heaths.

The *première,* however, of this select little troupe is *Schlippenbachii* itself. Extolled by the voice of authority, acclaimed by Mr. Lionel de Rothschild in the R. A. *Year Book* (1934) as 'one of the most beautiful azaleas that has ever come from Asia', and granted four stars, hall-mark of high merit, in the same volume, *A. Schlippenbachii* is a triumph of loveliness. The flowers which appear in May or earlier, just as the large and somewhat pear-shaped leaves are breaking, are about three inches across, most delicate in texture and a soft, medium rose of exquisite tone. Although said to be rather difficult to please in regard to soil, and susceptible to frost owing to its precocity in spring, our Schlippens., now coming to maturity, seem happy enough. But they have the light shelter of overhanging alders and the free loam, which is never dry, was and is generously treated with leaf mould and sorbex.

Of *A. quinquefolia* there is a stripling down in the woodland which is hopeful and happy, but it does not get away with the vigour of *pentaphylla*. However, the five-leaved azalea is, as we once saw it at Vincent Square, a white-flowered azalea of such enchanting beauty that one might wait half a lifetime for it to bloom and yet feel rewarded.

Of the azaleodendrons, that isolated group of sub-evergreens which forms a garden link between the deciduous azalea and the rhododendron, we have collected about a dozen, and would secure others did we know where to cast the net. This not only because the old things when they are good appeal to us, but because there is about many of these hybrids just that quality or tone which seems to be in sympathetic accord with our often hoary natural wildness.

Let those who are able to do so look up Vol. II of *Flora and Sylva*—that noble tome which will be one of the most abiding monuments to William Robinson's status as a book-making gardener—and he will find opposite page 152 a coloured plate by the excellent H. G. Moon of *Rhododendron Smithii-aureum*. This beautiful plate gives one at least a guide to that colour note which, ranging between softest ivory and creamy primrose to orange-buff, is common to the more important of these hybrids—with one notable exception—and which goes remarkably well with a prevailing glaucousness of leaf. *R. Smithii-aureum*, excelling in this blueness of foliage, is said to be the result of a cross between a yellow *Azalea sinensis* and *R. caucasicum*, the genius who sponsored this mating being one, Smith, who had a nursery at Norbiton well over a hundred years ago.

The flowers and trusses of this shrub are about the size and form of a *mollis + sinensis* azalea, and the colour might be described as primrose over an old ivory ground with orange blotches. But, good plant that it is, flowering freely from an early age and very distinct in foliage, *R. Broughtonii-aureum* is better. This shrub, which seems to have had a somewhat similar origin, has a more compact and shapely habit and the blossoms, in a nice average truss, not overcrowded, are a creamy yellow which suggests to the Lady of the Garden's practical mind, not a filtering of September sunshine on primrose banks of spring, but that Broughton, whoever he was, had more eggs in his custard than poor Smith was allowed. *R.*

Broughtonii-aureum won the Award of Merit a little while ago, a recognition which, one may hope, will do something towards advertising its undoubted merits.

Glory of Littleworth is another of these old stagers, and the difficulty we experienced in getting a specimen—rather a seedy one for a long price—testifies to its rarity. Here again one has that blue-green foliage, and the wide flowers, thick of texture, in a rich and mellow ivory with a bold flare of orange-brown, are so exceedingly quaint that one of our visitors suggested they would not be amiss among the old roses did they bloom at the same time.

More familiar is *R. azaleoides*, the *fragrans* of Paxton's time. This is the exception I refer to, and while *azaleoides* is quite a different colour to those mentioned it must be numbered among the best garden kinds. Indeed, so far as I can gather, it seems to have been the most popular of the azaleodendrons during the last fifty years, and it is still stocked by most nurseries. That its parentage is *R. maximum + A. viscosa* (*Flora and Sylva*: Bean's *Trees and Shrubs*) seems fairly certain. It is particularly valuable on account of its late flowering season (June-July), and flower it does with such prodigality that bushes of two or three feet will be canopied by an unbroken mass of blossom year after year and that under almost any conditions. These flowers are white, more or less flushed with rosy-lilac, and so sweetly scented that their fragrance will often pervade the garden air of a summer evening.

Mr. W. J. Bean, to whose masterly volumes we always turn for guidance and inspiration in these matters, is enthusiastic in his praise of this delightful little shrub which has near allies in the fragrant *Gowenianum* and *Cartoni*, all having been raised about 1820. The former of these we grow, but it is not more than a poor relation of *azaleoides* and *Cartoni* I have never seen. Then we have in *Torlonianum* a dear old thing whose pucy-rose, quietly relieved by a ribbon of faded gold, might have come direct from one's great-aunt's second-best tea-time cap.

That set of triplets, two girls and a boy, which Mr. Harry White says are fairly new, and which are for ever doomed to endure the names of Katie, Nellie and Jack, are quite pleasant little people. They give their rose or yellow flowers at an early age and give them with both hands. They are nicely mannered, in no hurry to grow up, bless them! and ask of the cultivator next to nothing. Along with these, in an open part of the woodland, is yet another azaleodendron, which looks like remaining the midget of the family. This is *gemmiferum,* but the kittenish look of the wee bush is merely one of its tricks for it will grow to five feet if it does outlive an oak in doing so. However, like other diminutives, this amusing little creature which here you might cover with one of Mr. Churchill's hats, carries an air of tremendous importance, holding aloft the funniest of tight little bunches of flowers stained with a carmine-purple of provocative pungency.

Whether she did not know what else to do with the imp, or whether she did it in one of those moments of whimsical perversity which sometimes sways the mind of woman, has never been divulged. But the Lady of the Garden placed this oddity at the feet of none other than a large bush of R. Loder's White! Notwithstanding, the dauntless mite of Impudence stares up at the peerless Dignity above it without a wince of humility, though one of its podgy doll's-house posies would easily go inside a single corolla of its magnificent neighbour, the Great White Queen of all white rhododendrons.

CHAPTER XVI

Hardy Geraniums and other Woodland Herbs

FOR THE hardy cranesbills we have always had an affection, and this may be explained, in part at any rate, by the fact that a number of them are really good woodlanders. That is to say, they are able to stand up to the rough of a semi-wild life, most of them are long-lived, they ask little or no cultural attention, they look and do well in light shade and, above all, they fit in with their surroundings with that subtle sympathy which weds the harebell to the heath.

Being a native and one of the most beautiful of our wild flowers, *Geranium pratense*, with its rosy ally, *Londesii*, can be sure of an open door with us. Inviting selection, we have worked up a strain of this species which gives us plants of three or four feet with larger flowers of better form and a clearer blue than those of the lane. The white variety has been no less responsive and both come fairly true from seed. But, even so, for planting in colonies in part shade, I think we prefer something nearer the type, which may not exceed a foot or so and whose blue-lavender has a luminous quality in subdued light. The old doubles of the *pratense* group we grow in their proper place—among the equally old roses—but *G. sylvaticum* comes into the woodland where it is happy enough in a not too sunless spot. A variable plant, good forms of this cranesbill of the north should be looked for, these having a large and clear white eye within a zone of bright plum-purple.

The dusky cranesbill, *G. phaeum*, is another of these wayside weeds which we encourage, not that the Mourning Widow is a particularly cheerful person, but because her engaging gentleness of manner suits the woodland mood, and there is no denying that her flights of dart-like flowers, which may be anything from a black-purple to a slate-mauve (*lividum*) possess a dainty elegance of poise. Indeed, most of the geraniums of the *reflexum* school possess this grace, as well as a charm elusive as a sleeping smile. Even the modest *punctatum*, if that be its name, is not to be hastily passed by, for the broad palmate leaves, a lively primrose-green in spring, are blotched with the stain of her sloe-black flowers, and these adornments the dusky widow also flaunts upon her leaves with gay splashes of carmine and cream whenever she feels like a breakaway from the drab of everyday wear. Yet another of this set is one which, with leaves like a hollyhock that colour well in autumn and a stature of over two feet, crests this massive pyramid with down-turned blooms the size of a shilling in cool violet. Coming in as *G. sinense*, which I think it is not, this stalwart awaits the verdict of botany as to its name.

But the most charming of the reflexums here is *G. Delavayi* Franchet (*G. platypetalum* of some), a plant introduced by Delavay in 1886, and also by Forrest. Making a shapely fifteen-inch clump of dark green, deeply-lobed leaves, *Delavayi* waits until mid-July before its branching stems put forth the sharply reflexed flowers whose petals, a rich port-wine purple with a velvety gloss, are centred by a bold wisp of bright ruby stamens set in a circlet of coral and gold. A most brilliant performer, this, yet so far from being garish and noisy that it will not disturb the serenity of a wood violet. And the plant is hardy and long-lived and has the pleasantest of manners.

There is no better carpeting plant for light shade than *G. grandiflorum*, which only makes about a foot, yielding in long succession its fine lavender-blue bowls and flourishing abundantly in ever widening colonies. But, while we should never turn down this old friend, the plant listed as *G. g.* Gravetye Variety (*alpinum*) has still bigger blooms whose wonderful prussian blue is accentuated by a white eye. That these fine plants have any right to the name, *grandiflorum*, has been doubted. But this much seems clear: The one which was introduced from Sikkim by Max Leichtlin and first flowered in Miss Willmott's garden (forty years ago) and which was (by Leichtlin) given the name, *grandiflorum*, was not what we gardeners now regard as the old type but the so-called var. *alpinum*, or Gravetye Variety. The superb coloured plate in Robinson's *Flora and Sylva*, Vol. I, No. 2, together with the Rev. Wolley Dod's description, is conclusive evidence as to

KIRENGESHOMA PALMATA

This Japanese aristocrat announces Autumn with flights of ivory shuttlecocks

ORCHIS FOLIOSA

Noblest of all hardy orchids with massive spikes of imperial purple

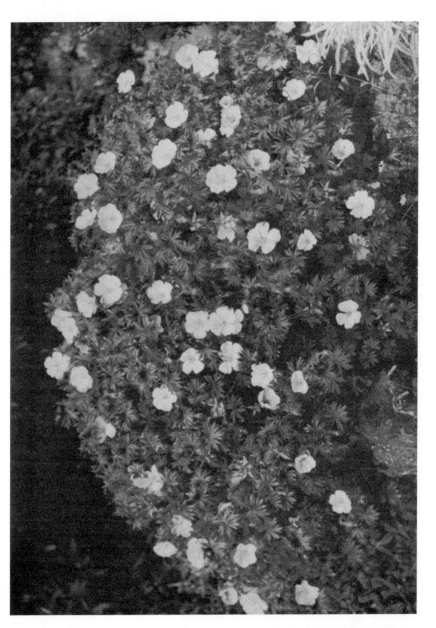

GERANIUM NEPALENSE

that. However, I know of nothing in the entire range of woodland plants more inspiring than a drift of this geranium, its
big rich blue bells illumined by the low rays of an early morning or evening light—nothing, one may add, more easy to
attain, even in the rootiest of soil.

G. Endressii, a Pyrenean growing to a foot or so above a
tangled mass of rhizomes, must be included with these woodland cranesbills. It seems fairly constant in the colour of its
flowers, a chalky raspberry-ice pink, and, uniting on its own
with the rather bloodless *striatum*, it has given us and others a
number of delightful hybrids. Of these we have three more or
less distinct types, a tall lady in a brilliant cerise, one less ambitious in silver-pink while the third is warmed by a tint of
salmon.

All these are of the utmost value, for they seed true or nearly
so, they crop up anywhere, in sun or shade, even in grass, and
they flower throughout the season, occasionally even in winter.
Only one other cranesbill known to me blooms so persistently
and that is the hybrid, Russell Prichard, an admirable thing for
the border but a trifle garish for wilder places. One of its
parents, *G. sanguineum* (the other is *G. Traversii*) of our limestone cliffs is as free as the *Endressii* hybrids, almost a weed,
and its flowers are near enough to magenta to offend some people. But the plant has a pleasant way of occurring fortuitously
even in the most arid of spots, it varies widely in colour and
gives a tall white of such purity and distinction I should not be
surprised to hear it proclaimed as a species.

The best of the *sanguineum* household here—always excepting the delectable *lancastriense* of rock-gardens—is that commonly called *G. nepalense*. A foot in height, with a broad and
copious, deep-cut downy leafage and crimson flowers as round
as a crown-piece, this is a fine thing for any dryish spot, preferably in sun. But, good as this is, we hope some day to dis-
tribute an even better one which we found one day in a thicket
of blackthorn on a cliff near Glenluce. A robust plant of twenty
inches with silky leaves, this carries from May to August large
blooms of an exquisite wild-rose pink, quite free from that
arrogant purple which is the insignia of the bluggy geranium.

G. ibericum and its ally usually listed as '*var. platypetalum*' are both a little borderish for our woodland. The former is brilliant in its autumn leaf colour, yet not so brilliant as *Lowei*, a biennial, which in broad leaf and sturdy branch dies off in wonderful shades of orange and blood-red, and in this garb it will often remain until mid-winter. There are folk base enough to list *G. anemonefolium* as a synonym of *Lowei*. But whereas the latter might be described as no more than a magnified *Robertianum, anemonefolium* is undoubtedly the handsomest and most distinct of hardy geraniums in cultivation. We have had this noble species a yard in height with a spread of five feet, its glossy hemlock leaves nine inches across and the branching stems, gleaming with viscous iridescent hairs, an inch thick at the base. Such a plant will carry an enormous yield of blossom from early June to mid-August, and these at their best (for there are inferior forms) are a delicious peach-blossom pink, rich and satiny, with a glow of ruby at the base. Hardy this excellent plant may not be everywhere, nor is it reliably perennial, but it seeds freely and enough seedlings will generally escape even a hard winter to keep one's stock going.

G. armenum may seem a trifle near the gorgeous for sylvan surroundings, but being too good a plant to exclude we run it along the fringe of the woodland with the gladwin iris (a form with ivory-white flowers) and ferns, solomon's seal, libertias and actaeas, so that an abundant green may cool the passion of its splendid crimson and jet. *G. Grevilleanum* (a name I do not guarantee) a trailer after the fashion of *Wallichianum*, but with much larger blossoms in a lovely pink, is a first-rate part-shade plant which deserves a wider public. As for Wallich's cranesbill, both the purple and the rare nemophila-blue Buxton's Variety, these enjoy the fullest shade and a stony soil, but even with sharp drainage we find them none too permanent. Yet another trailer of quality is *albanum*, which will spread over a square yard its clear pink saucers lined with carmine, and with this and a friendly nod for dear little *G. celticum*, pleasantest of our weeds, I must cut short this cranesbill story for the bellflowers are all a-jangle for a passing word.

Campanulas and aquilegias ought to play a prominent rôle in our woodland undercrop, but they suffer one setback in common and that is they are the favourite prey of mouse and vole.

This means we have abandoned many kinds and now grow only those which the enemy does not consider caviare. Among these one of the best is *C. latiloba.* The blue or white pillars of this old-timer look delightful in self-sown colonies, especially in shady retreats giving shelter from wind, they yield several months of bloom and the plants will hold their own with the things of the wild.

C. lactiflora is to the big side for us, but it responds to a timely snubbing by growing bushier, and the delicate azure of its shower of bells is so lovely we should miss it with the gold of early autumn days. A dwarf form of this would be an invaluable acquisition and it is reported, as I write, that Mr. A. K. Bulley, sponsor of so many good plants, has got one. *C. latifolia,* in all its forms, is a precious woodlander of erect and stately bearing, with a handsome foliage and splendid spires of violet or white flowers which never look gross in spite of their size. *C. Trachelium* must take second place where *latifolia* is concerned, but it is nevertheless a graceful plant, its finely-tapered spires of bells being violet-blue, white or a pale slatey-azure, and we should be wanting in principle did we not offer so distinguished a native a spare room on the first floor.

No columbine seems to be mouse-proof, and of those which haunt our wooded places with any show of endurance the most persisting of the species is the charming little *Aquilegia formosa,* with a tenderly beautiful foliage over which hover flowers of scarlet and gold. This takes care of itself, seeds about with reasonable freedom and it is the only aquilegia I have ever met which can resist inter-marrying with its neighbours. As for the rest of the tribe which fringe our ferny woodland walks, most of them are mongrels with a strong infusion of the best of *A. vulgaris* which, at one time, we made gallant efforts to 'improve'. And there is, after all, nothing much better for the semi-wild than a good strain of these Old English Columbines with their rigid and erect stems and broad, short-spurred flowers in purple, violet, rosy-amaranth, amethyst or white—especially the excellent Munstead White with its copious foliage a cool frosty emerald.

The deep moist soil beneath some waterside alders is enjoyed by the funkias, some of which, notably *F. Fortunei,* also have leaves of that attractive glaucous hue. But *Sieboldiana* (*glauca*) is still better and bluer. Both of these put up spikes of white, pale lavender or lilac blossoms, towards the 'back-end' and, like the hellebores, *Trillium grandiflorum* and the mighty *Saxifraga peltata*, which is segregated still nearer the water, they are plants which live for ever on a cultural attention that amounts to nothing.

And no less can be said of *Kirengeshoma palmata*, a massive clump of which, six feet across and half as high, is threatening to smother the said funkias—which I suppose one ought to call hostas, Mr. Funk having been deposed by the umpires of the plant-naming league. *K. palmata* is a Japanese dignitary with ebony stems and vine-like leaves in a hearty green. Though it starts early, early enough to be cut by a May frost, it does not get beyond being a foliage plant, albeit a remarkably fine one, until autumn is on the way. Then, when days are rapidly shortening, when the irises are slashed with yellow and most things closing down, *K. p.* tosses forth all over its leafy mound loose airy flights of ivory shuttlecocks about two inches long. These, perhaps, have little attraction in a showy way, but decorative they certainly are and in harmony with that dignity of line and deportment which pervades the entire plant. By way of companions for them we want nothing better than our deep violet-blue willow gentians.

At the gentlest touch of frost kirengeshoma surrenders with dramatic suddenness. There is a momentary flare of yellow, and down come leaves and stems like a house of cards. That same yellow, pale as moonlight, comes to another good woodland herb, solomon's seal, which, by the way, is in no such haste to relinquish its autumn rights. The chief lion among our solomon's seals (*Polygonatum*) is a tall fellow of over three feet with almond-scented flowers which was started years ago in a position elevated to eye level so that one can appreciate to the full its matchless grace of foliage. The entire genus might well be more generously used in woodland, but the one referred to is the finest of our little collection and it is enchanting when (seen from below) its plum-black fruits are hanging in the wan yellow radiance which filters through its autumn leaves.

Disporum (*Prosartes*) *Hookeri* is another liliaceous herb in the way of a solomon's seal, with drooping ivory bugles an inch or so in length. It crops up before most of its neighbours are awake, a pleasing, graceful creature in its own quiet way that will carry on until those neighbours—astrantias, vancouverias, uvularias, poppyworts and the rest—are bringing in the later spring, and in autumn it gives fine coral fruits.

Those uvularias are admirable and easy-going in any moist-ish soil, *U. grandiflora* being the troupe leader with a stature of two or three feet and creamy bells in spring. *U. perfoliata* is another pretty rambler of the daintiest modesty, which here haunts those places in which lily-of-the-valley and little *Maianthemum bifolia*, with her grown up Canadian sister, love to dwell. And in the cool humoid soil enjoyed by these wood-land folk you would find the soaring bugbanes whose Lin-naean name, *Cimicifuga*, sounds less indelicate if it means the same thing. These noble ranunculads may seem rather a fade-out compared with the spiraeas and astilbes which, during the former's season, belt some reaches of our streamsides with so magnificent a splendour. But the folly of such comparison could hardly go further, for while the latter (with the excep-tion of *S. Aruncus* which is much earlier) are plants of the sunny open, the bugbanes have a preference for shade. Moreover, whereas most of the gay spiraeas and astilbes would strike one as an anomaly in woodland, the others, with their neutral tones and gentle grace, are here in perfect accord with their environment.

All the cimicifugas are well worth growing and, being tall and slender and not overweening in foliage, they take little room. The latest of all, *C. simplex*, with bottle-brushes of white is one of the most charming, but *racemosa* is also good and we have the fullest admiration for the milk white plumes of *cordifolia* (four or five feet high) surging upwards beneath the glowing lanterns of *Lilium superbum*. And not less touching in quiet beauty are some astrantias (*major* and *helleborifolia*) whose stars of green and silver mosaic stare coldly up to the swinging orange and yellow bells of *L. canadense*. But these masterworts would be curiously appealing in any company. We like them among ferns as much as anywhere, but I think the most beau-tiful of them, the chalky shell-pink, *A. carniolica*, needs rather more sun than others, and it is worth the best one has to offer.

The common wood-sorrel ceases not to insist upon our recognising that the woodland is its own, which, verily, it is. The Lady of the Garden is constrained to punish it when it threatens to overrun her shortias or to be pushful in the presence of pyrolas, but no wilding is more readily forgiven its trespasses. It ramps pretty much where it will, it is cherished no less warmly than the mosses of the paths, which also so enjoy their ancient prerogatives that even of the hoe of Prometheus they are unafraid. And *Oxalis Acetosella rosea,* an adorable little thing, is even more lovely than the type, more intimately fascinating and more progressive than its bolder American sister *O. oregana.* A troublesome creature in other parts of the garden, *O. obliqua* is pleasant enough in woodland colonies. Prospering even in sunless spots and successfully contending with any lowly undergrowth, its enormous blue-green trefoils, three inches wide and adorned with chevrons of purple, colour well in autumn and the bright violet-mauve flowers on nine-inch stems are decidedly well turned out.

So I might proceed to a eulogy upon the evening primroses which, as strays from the borders, are naturalised here, to the useful *Verbascum nigrum,* in both white and yellow, which follows the foxgloves, to prevail until November. Then there are drifts of honesty which, entirely white beneath a copper beech, are on another slope entirely purple—not the watery purple commonly seen but a deep burgundy colour which is now as constant as the white. But *Orchis foliosa* begs a concluding paragraph, and to omit a mention of this admirable plant would be unpardonable. Whether this noble Madeiran is naturally a woodlander I know not, but it has expressed its satisfaction with the light shade and cool vegetable soil of our wood bottoms by spreading into ever widening clumps. In height it reaches close upon three feet while the splendid heads of imperial purple are eight or nine inches long. So hearty and robust is it that one colony thrusts its way through a thicket of *Onoclea sensibilis,* and those richly apparelled spires are, I think, even more striking against the steely emerald of the fern than those of another group which have as a background the warm orange-yellow of *Primula Bulleyana.*

CHAPTER XVII

Lilies: Of Glade and Woodland

FOR ANYONE who goes forth to garden carrying the high stomach of a good conceit let me recommend a short course of lily culture. Those who are not beyond hope may doubtless get relief from that affliction against which the gods of all good gardens raise so reproachful a finger by taking in decent humility doses from any other bottle of the horticultural dispensary. But, as a group, lilies are, I think, the acid test, for few things will so effectually checkmate your best laid plans, few are so contradictious, so utterly baffling in their behaviour, and that is one reason why we like them so much. For after all, is there not something refreshing in discovering that there are still some mysteries left in a science-ridden world, that there are some children of caprice still at large, still ready to make bright mischief with the exactitudes of science which would rob them of their secrets and waywardness and label them with the cold, hard truths of the laboratory?

I once knew an old gardener who so cherished the problems which every hour his plants presented him that he would often go out of his way to avoid any results of research which promised to steal from him the mystery he loved. He was like the little dog who, having found too soon the golf ball he was hunting, would pretend not to see it and go on prancing about with every show of being in hot pursuit, just so that the joy of the chase might be prolonged. And there is something in the attitude. No matter how deeply we may be indebted to the discoveries of science there is a felicity in doubt; a salt-lick of romance garnishes the unknown. Were it otherwise, then in truth might we repeat those lovely lines of Mr. Yeats:

> *The woods of Arcady are dead,*
> *And over is their antique joy.*
> *Of old the world on dreaming fed,*
> *Grey truth is now her painted toy.*
> *Yet still she turns her restless head. . . .*

So, to come down to more practical politics, it will be obvious to the discerning that I am not going to offer any guidance as to how to grow lilies. Indeed, I am not at all sure that it is wise to speak of our lilies at all, for you are never quite sure where you are with these ladies of many moods who will to-day lead you along an avenue of fairest hope and to-morrow turn those hopes to ashes. Why, we have been growing *Lilium candidum* for three or four hundred years and I honestly think we are as much in the dark regarding the ways of this old-timer as ever we were. She is often amazingly responsive to what some of us hold to be the misguided efforts of the fool, and she will reject the attentions of the skilful cultivator with her tongue in her marble cheek.

Many years ago, when I was anything but a gardener, *L. candidum* did so well for me that when I left the cottage the congested masses of bulbs were two feet across and so heavy that it was all a man could do to lift one of them. And when we first came to this garden, then quite a little place, the wanton beauty throve astonishingly under conditions which one would now regard as utterly impossible. Yet with a wider scope and, I hope, more intelligent cultivation, I cannot say our madonnas are much of a success.

Ah! but you have no lime, no chalk, says the liliaceous visitor—quite essential, you know, for *candidum*. But the latter statement I might contend with abundant argument. The madonnas of the old garden of my blundering youth probably got, not lime, but a generous ration from the farmyard midden, and I know of some wonderful old plants to-day which prosper amazingly round about some cottage doors of our own parish where they seldom see much sun and doubtless know all about the ministrations of the slop-pail, the dregs of the family tea-pot and the carefully swept up offerings of passing horses applied hot and strong.

Why *L. candidum* prospered so happily in the raw yellow-brown, acid and irony soil of this garden when gorse and bramble began to make way for it and other plants, and why it slowly but surely declined in that same soil under precisely the same conditions we do not know. Again, at that time, in the freshly exposed soil, that lovely little thing, *Linaria alpina*, used to abound, sowing itself freely, but it, too, eventually went back and we have never been able to enjoy it to anything like the old extent. Confronted with problems of this sort the gardener is baffled and science is dumb.

Talking about manure just now reminds me of another diverting incident in lily culture. It concerns *L. Martagon album*, one of the most beautiful of lilies. We do not find this any too responsive, yet in a neighbour's garden the plant, laid out in rows like jerusalem artichokes by the garden man, flourishes with abounding vigour—and it is given, every year in spring, a heavy dressing of fresh cow-cum-pig manure, rich, raw and fragrant, straight from the farmyard buffet. 'Grrand stuff, yon!' exclaims Giles, as he shakes if off his sticky fork beneath an appreciative nose, and it would be idle to pretend the lilies do not share that view, for every year they reach five feet and carry splendid campaniles of flower. Moreover, instead of being left in their established positions according to lawful practice, the bulbs are frequently dug up by the complacent Giles and laid out, again in drills well laced with the excellent manure.

I am aware that the use—with reservations—of old farm manure for lilies is not so emphatically denounced as once it was. (It is warmly advocated by Messrs. Woodcock and Coutts in their admirable volume, *Lilies, Their Culture and Management*) but such evidence as the above suggests that we have still some way to go before we can indulge in anything like conclusive ideas on the treatment of lilies.

Was it not Sir Herbert Maxwell who used to feed his *L. giganteum* on the rotting carcases of superfluous pike fished out of his lake at Monreith? Pretty stout fare, that, and if it agreed with *giganteum* why not with some others? In any event, I am trying it on the dog and giving some of our more anaemic lilies a tolerably stiff manure tonic. And if anyone should come along and, in horror-struck accents, tell me that I am a rebel defying the canons of gardening, I shall retort by repeating what I have already said—that if nearly everything we did were not very largely empirical our gardens would not be what they are. I might also add—in special reference to manure for lilies—that even as some of the most delectably fragrant preparations of the beauty parlour are extracted from rotten fish, so out of the strong shall come forth sweetness, yea, even the sweetness of lilies.

To come back to our candidums, we get fairish results by planting so near the surface that the bulbs are eventually not covered at all. I also have sufficient confidence in the aid of lime, which, incidentally, bothers the slugs, to apply this—usually in the form of basic slag—to them in autumn and spring, as well as to some recognised lime lovers. But that lime *per se* is not the philosopher's stone it is held to be by some, I am convinced.

Not long ago we went into one of the limiest localities in England where *L. candidum* is grown by every cottager. We saw literally thousands of these lilies in bloom, hedges of them in some gardens, yet I cannot say that these were very encouraging for, though all carried good heads, the stems in most cases were as utterly devoid of green leaves as a walking stick. *Botrytis?* It may have been, but whatever it was it did not seriously affect the lilies, except in appearance, and the people who grew them would tell you that they were always like that in summer and that there would be plenty of leaves about Christmas!

The authorities mentioned seem inclined to discredit the virulence of the bogie, *Botrytis*, quoting Mr. Cotton of Kew as one who believes that 80 per cent. of the supposed cases of this disease are not this affliction but something else. Our experiences of such visitations have happily been rare, *L. candidum*, *testaceum* and *chalcedonicum* occasionally showing ugly symptoms but getting no worse. Half-a-dozen bulbs of *candidum* which were planted in the autumn of 1934 and grew away splendidly suddenly collapsed the following May when two or three feet high. This was diagnosed as *Botrytis*, but instead of destroying the lot, as is our way with most diseased things, we decided to try a little experiment. The semi corpses were carefully lifted, the tops were cut off close to the bulb and put on the fire and the bulbs re-planted in the new garden where there were no other lilies. To our surprise they put up magnificent leafage, clean and robust, the following autumn, and at this moment they are presenting fine leafy stems crowned with abundant blossom!

The beautiful Salonika form of *L. candidum* which we first saw at Abbotswood in perfect health—Mr. Mark Fenwick assuring us he had found it entirely immune to the troubles that beset the old sort—has not yet flowered here, but it is very promising. *L. testaceum*, whose slightly rose-tinted nankeen turkscaps are so bewitching in their charm, does reasonably well, and the glorious sealing wax red *chalcedonicum* also thrives. But I feel sure that *L. c. var. maculatum*, which is more vigorous and equally handsome, is going to prove a still more satisfying garden plant. The burnished scarlet of these lilies is not the easiest colour to place in a garden like ours, even yellows in association give a little too flamboyant an effect. We like our chalcedonicums better against the cool slate-green and white of *Senecio Monroi*, just as we have that superb hybrid, *L. Maxwill*, with the soft glaucous green of one of the old *Rosa alba* varieties behind it. Surely this hybrid is one of the greatest triumphs of modern lily culture. With its slender, yet rigid, stems of six to eight feet, its finely-drawn, healthy looking leaves and heads of widely and elegantly disposed turkscaps in an intensely fiery tangerine orange-red—we have had thirty-eight on a single spike—this lily is the last word in the refinement of splendour. And, blest be the gods, it has a first-rate constitution, demanding no fuss, arousing no anxiety.

To not many gardens is given the privilege of growing just what lilies your fancy may favour. Wherefore, the wise will discover, or hope to, what kinds will prosper in their particular conditions and concentrate upon them. At the same time, we have been gardening long enough to learn that one must not discard a plant should it not respond to one's first effort, for it may thrive with abounding success only a few yards away from the spot which it wholly disdained. That, at least, has been, and still is, our policy, not only with lilies but most things. And it is a policy calculated to bring in not only the fattest dividends of pleasure in the way of success, but one likely to save a deal of that trouble and disappointment which arise from unhealthy plants or those which simply exist owing to the fact that they are in the wrong place. So, as I have said elsewhere, you have some valid reasons why we focus our limited supply of energy and time largely on rhododendrons, lilies and other semi-woodland things which enjoy our humid, tree-filled valley rather than upon alpines, most of which loathe it.

I often think that this matter of healthiness in plants is not given the attention it merits, not merely because one smilingly robust specimen is worth an acre of the not quite so well, but because one feels confident that the surest means to the avoidance of many of the plant ailments which vex the gardener's peace is not by way of the chemist's prescription, preventive or remedial, but by maintaining a high state of vitality by what one may call natural means.

It would be going too far, perhaps, to aver that vigorous health will alone shield a plant against such a disease as *Botrytis*, but there is more in the suggestion than is generally supposed. Is there, by the way, a physiological reason to explain why the Salonika form of *L. candidum* will remain immune from *Botrytis* in the midst of infection, or are we to understand that this variety, being seed-raised and fresh to cultivation and therefore vastly more robust, is able naturally to resist the evil to which the older lily, constitutionally weakened by centuries of garden life and vegetative procreation, falls such an easy prey?

However that may be there is testimony in plenty to prove that it is, nine times out of ten, the least strong plant which is the first victim to disease. Even the prowling slug will attack the feeble with more voracity than it displays towards the lusty. Why, no one has ever explained, but that is a matter of common observation, and I have a fairly firm belief that these things are governed by what are vaguely called the laws of nature. Nature abhors disease and creates weapons in the form of disease whereby to destroy it, and she is no less severe in her punishment of the effete and weakly.

And this creation, or infliction, of disease it would seem has not merely for its object the elimination of the unfit, but it suggests a resentment on the part of the governing principles of life towards anything which, being contrary to those principles, tends to be detrimental to racial well-being. Thus we have only to go in for intensive cultivation of any crop, be it apples or potatoes, conifers in forest blocks, clover, rhodo-

THE MARBLE-WHITE
TRUMPETS OF THE
PEERLESS
LILIUM BROWNII

THE BURNISHED
BRASSY-YELLOW
TURKSCAPS OF
LILIUM
MONADELPHUM

LILIUM
AURATUM
VAR. PLATY-
PHYLLUM

WITH
A PRETTY
CAPRICE IN
COLOUR
AND RARE
ELEGANCE
OF POISE
LILIUM
SPECIOSUM
TELLS OF
AUTUMN'S
APPROACH

dendrons, wheat or lilies, we have only to grow any of these in large pure colonies to find that sooner or later Nemesis lifts its forbidding hand in the ugly shape of disease. The history of cultivation is one long story in evidence of all this, and as to which will win the battle, the research station plus the allied forces of science, or the steadfast purpose of nature's mysterious way none can tell, but I have little doubt as to which side will be ultimately victorious.

Evolution ever climbing after some ideal good . . .

Even so, and the virile fecundity of the grey squirrel—to give a familiar instance—is sustained, not directly by the solicitous nursing of the species but indirectly by the decimating hand of a periodical epidemic, relentless and thorough in its unflinching purpose—the fostering of the A1 individual and the extermination of the rest. The moral of which discourse may be boiled down to this: Keep your lilies fit and you will avoid a deal of trouble, anxiety and expense and be rewarded by the fullest measure of satisfaction. We still experiment, as I have inferred, mainly with the object of discovering how far this or that species will respond to our conditions—remembering that those conditions may vary enormously within quite a small area. But cultivation means much in the maintenance of health, as does the raising of your own stock from seed, and while we do not do much fussing over foods and feeding, a well-worked sub-soil and a drainage that is as perfect as possible are regarded as of first importance.

Along both sides of the glade garden the ground flanking its streams has an exceedingly stony sub-soil. Two feet and more down it is practically the base of an ancient embankment. In it all lilies so far planted have done splendidly and we attribute this success mainly to the sharp drainage effected by the underlying boulders together with the uniformity of moisture ever rising into the free, sandy loam of the top-soil.

Starting with the lilies which march with the smaller river you would find a lusty clump of *L. pardalinum giganteum* thrusting through the light leafage of *Rhododendron lutescens*. *L. pardalinum*, the type, is a little further on raising its fiery orange above the grey-green of *R. canadense*, while hard by is the fine *L. Roezlu* which, for some obscure reason, is freer with its speckled orange-red flowers than the more common panther lily itself. *L. canadense* is also here, and if our plants have not yet aspired to rival those one may see at Wisley, they are good enough to encourage one to indulge still further with this beautiful lily. It does not matter what shade of yellow or orange the flowers happen to be, *canadense* carries an elegance, poise and balance which give it a distinction even among the choicest of its exalted family.

The trustworthy old *Hansonii* prospers in various places, both along these raised watersides and in drier soils, but its hybrid, *Dalhansoni*, has thus far shown a hesitancy about settling down, perhaps inheriting some of that shyness which possesses our martagons, many of which rather look as if they were yearning for a taste of that pig-sty cordial of which I have spoken. Very different is the response made by *L. superbum* and some auratums, which, planted with scant ceremony some six years ago over the buried rocks that bank the mill-race, have shown increasing vigour with each passing season. During 1935, in spite of the drought, the American turkscap reached 9 ft. 3 in. with a sheaf of stems only a foot or so lower, each of them bearing a magnificent spire of thirty to forty golden-orange-crimson blossoms above their handsomely leaf-whorled stems. One of the oldest of our lilies, none ever merited a more fitting name than that of *superbum* which Linnaeus bestowed upon it, for superb indeed it is in every feature.

The auratums in this part of the garden were bought as a 'job lot' with some other things. They were merely labelled 'lilies' and miserable dried-up things the bulbs were. However, they were put in along the mill-race and gave a very presentable show the following year. But every subsequent season they have shown steady improvement in stamina as well as stature and blossoming, every summer standing six or seven feet high and each stem carrying about thirty of the enormous and very lovely flowers of this magnificent lily.

Moreover, the success of this colony is the more surprising on account of the fact that a ramping battalion of *Lysimachia clethroides* has so completely usurped the original site of the lilies that these are now in the midst of that ambitious loosestrife. Bad gardening, perhaps, putting top-dressing and all that out of the question, but the lilies are perfectly happy, their white-spired companion is a charming thing, and it stirs one's garden pulse to see the great plum-bronze fists of the auratums bursting through the matted strangle-hold of the creeper in daffodil days.

L. auratum var. pictum dwells on the other side of the glade, thrusting its lovely blooms, which are not so arrogant in their splendour as the others, through the skirting branches of that stately beech, *Nothofagus obliqua*, which, by the way, has shot up at the rate of four or five feet a year. The rare *L. auratum var. virginale*, so exquisitely pure in its almost unspotted crystal whiteness, we had a difficulty in getting, in spite of Mr Constable's best efforts, but the lovely creature is, we believe, in residence at last.

L. auratum, the Queen of Lilies, is peerless in her majesty, richly apparelled, a prodigious bloomer and extraordinarily fragrant. She is endowed with all the attributes a monarch among lilies should have, and her habit of flowering late, even well into autumn, is a valuable one. But, remembering what Thoreau said about a double-coach-house to the cottage, we have to admit that there are many less magnificent lilies which suit our garden better. There are degrees of ornateness which, while being all very well in some surroundings, touch a note of incongruity here, and auratums we find more difficult to assimilate with our surroundings and mode of gardening than most lilies. That we shall continue to grow them I have no doubt, but with reservation.

There are places, indeed, where *L. auratum* seems all wrong, yet where the grand old tiger lily, *Davidii* (especially *macranthum*) and the graceful *Willmottiae* blend quite amicably. In such a matter we find this a fairly safe test: If a lily will go harmoniously with dwarf rhododendrons it will go almost any-where—and we have seen auratums in such company which looked everything that was ill-placed and uncomfortable.

Alpine rhododendrons and many heaths make especially good associates for most of the more slender lilies, notably the dainty *cernuum* and *concolor* class, the bewitching *L. Duchartrei var. Farreri, lankongense*, Ward's 'Pink Martagon' (*Wardii*) *formosanum*, (not any too permanent here) and nomocharis. To all these and others the Lady of the Garden grants a share of her rhodo. preserves, but we are not at all sure that it is a wise policy to do very much in this way with the larger sorts, which if they do happen to suit their environment are apt to interfere with the culture of the shrubs. As a matter of fact, we have for some time rather gone off mixtures of this description. Primulas in particular, which need almost annual attention and which obstruct the top-dressing of the rhododendrons, we have for the most part segregated elsewhere. For it comes to something like this: If I invade the precincts of 'her' rhododendrons with my lilies or primulas we sooner or later find ourselves involved in that domestic tangle summed up in the words, 'Your children are quarrelling with my children and ours are joining in.'

L. maritimum we ought to be able to grow along our elevated watersides, but it is still shy and uneasy. And since I am dealing here only with those lilies which we have flowered successfully for three or more years, this Californian lady remains among the doubtfuls. *L. amabile* is also in that category, and *lankongense* is the only one of the trio mentioned above which is going ahead with real promise. We shall be disappointed if ultimate success does not reward our efforts with the 'Marbled Martagon', which is so easy under similar conditions in many gardens, and so very, very delightful. But if *Wardii* should turn down our attentions, which I hardly think she will, the beautiful *lankongense*, now raised to specific rank, is so like her and so willing that we shall not grieve over possible failure with the former introduction.

While *L. regale*, prince of lilies, and that aristocratic beauty, *Sargentiae* (not so easy-going as yet) which is a few weeks later, enthrall us with their charms; while those of the *dauricum* household may blazon their appeals (not always successfully) to our admiration and *Henryi* give sufficiently of its glowing wheat-field yellow to encourage us to do it better and still better, the matchless *Brownii* still holds the field—the one lily we should have no hesitation about choosing were we ever doomed to grow but a single kind.

Happily, this peerless, deliciously fragrant lily, with its massively wrought, marble-white trumpets, so faultless in line and balance, so spiritual in their inscrutable serenity, yet so infinitely gracious, is numbered among our successes—numbered, too, among the most fascinating of all those marvels that have come to us out of the Orient, not excepting the great Kaempferi irises which mirror the unwritten secrets of their loveliness in the still waters. Nearly a century has passed since *Brownii*, the 'mystery lily', was first flowered in England, but its origin, I believe, has not yet been revealed and it has never been other than rare in gardens. And so may it ever remain.

L. giganteum is still more or less on its trial with us, for not yet has it done quite so well as we think it ought to do. Of the three or four colonies put in as many different spots with the hope of finding one to the handsome creature's liking, some have given us pillars of six feet which is not good enough, beautiful as they are. Its Chinese half-sister, *L. g. yunnanense*, which some say is easier, is still in the seedling stage here. All those lilies of the *dauricum* class, with the upturned goblets, are easy-going, but they are not, as I have suggested, among our favourites for, although there are some charming tints among them, there are also many which are florid and beefy or wanting in distinction of tone. The erect flowers, too, are often somehow ill-balanced and awkward and we like better, among the easies, the good-natured *croceum*, one of the oldest lilies in cultivation, and one that will always give a good account of itself in thin woodland, looking well and living forever under the grossest neglect.

And no less can be said of *L. pyrenaicum* which is one of the few lilies to naturalise in this garden, a splendidly hearty thing, with speckled turkscaps of indian gold and scarlet anthers. The scarlet variety of this is also good, perhaps a trifle dull in the dye and it has not yet decided to flourish as freely as the type. The rich scent of *L. pyrenaicum* is not, it may be granted, the essence of *auratum* or *Brownii*. The elegant noses of the Smell Society might even be seriously offended by it, but we find the drifting perfume very pleasant with the sultry sweetness of wild hyacinths in the woodlands of May.

Of the dainty little *L. pumilum* I would not speak with any more certainty just yet than I would of *rubellum*, *rubescens* and a few others, for these are still on trial. But the gay *pomponium* of the Maritime Alps, a diminutive of *pyrenaicum*, with shorter stems and flowers, proportionately larger, of a vehement pillar-box red, is well established, both from wild bulbs and seed. We have some groups of this sunlover at the feet of the exquisite *testaceum*, not because they flower at the same time, for that they do not always carry out, but because both like much the same, rather dry, stony soil, and lime in some form, including old mortar. Whether this last is of any value in a limy sense I do not know. Gardeners have been using it for generations with the profoundest faith, but I should not be at all surprised to hear from some chemist fellow that the thing is a hoax, that old mortar, being insoluble, is just about as efficacious as the obviously insoluble lump of sulphur which people have been putting in the dog's water with the same devout faith for as many generations.

Oddly enough, the old tiger-lily, although practically naturalised, we do not find so robust as it used to be. We are beginning to think it is one of those lilies which eventually become soil-tired, so 'fresh blood' is being infused for this is, after all, one of the best of all late lilies. Happily, that brace of beauties, *L. monadelphum* and *Szovitzianum* are not only sturdy and vigorous, but look like remaining so. I notice that Dr. Fred Stoker, upon whom the mantle of Linnaeus has fallen with so much distinction (*The Lily Year Book*, 1935) refers to these magnificent lilies as distinct species. There is always gratification to be derived from the news that some favourite plant, once held to be a variety, has been raised to the peerage and *Szovitzianum* is a case in point. It is not that it is a better lily than *monadelphum*, for both are of the elect, and there is really little garden difference between them.

Rather early lilies, these have been in flower at the end of May here, and, making a height of some four or five feet, the stout, leafy stems carry splendid heads of massive, campanulate, reflexed flowers in a decided yellow with a peppering of black in the throat. There is doubtless some variability in the tone of each, but of those we have *monadelphum* is clearly a richer, more burnished chinese-yellow than the other. But both are in the very first class. They take a while to settle down but, asking nothing more, go ahead with admirable vigour, and content-ment under any reasonable conditions.

So I might proceed with this rather sketchy lily story to commend the grace and prolificacy of the stately *Willmottiae*, and the estimable qualities of the even better *Davidii*—better because it is strong enough to support without staking its great head of blossoms, in which its ally often fails. But there is not a deal of room for comparison in these excellent plants whose orange-cinnabar-red blooms cause even the tigers, burning bright in the beacons of autumn, to 'pale their ineffectual fires'. However, some specimens of *L. Davidii macranthum* promise to carry out the reputation that came with them and to eclipse even the type in both size and brilliance. But these rambling notes must be brought to an end with a brief reference to *L. speciosum*, than which no lily more richly deserved its specific name.

Almost the earliest of all our lilies to push up in spring, what time the festive slug setteth forth, *speciosum* is the latest to flower, so late that we have often cut blooms to save them from November frost. Not a tall grower, seldom exceeding four feet with us, the woody stems require no crutches, and the sharply reflexed, waxen flowers, whose segments are beautifully waved at the margins, stand out with a rare elegance of port. And so variable are these finely modelled blossoms that they may be anything from an almost snowy purity to a crimson or carmine, with many intermediate forms, and the petals will be streaked, margined or spotted with gay little tufts of papillae in tints vividly in contrast with the ground colour.

L. speciosum is popular enough among florists, but unless our experience is exceptional it is surely a mistake to regard it with suspicion as an outdoor lily. No species has had less attention in our garden than this one, yet it prospered from the start. The oldest clumps, put in ten years ago, are still full of vitality and subsequent plantings of named varieties have all done well. They are given full sun with lowly ground shade, and the sandy loam is merely enriched to a depth of some two feet with decayed leaves and vegetable refuse—our general stand-by that is always on tap. Like most other stem-rooters these speciosums are planted some six or eight inches deep on a bottom well-firmed after preparation, but we do not indulge in much foot rule fussing over such matters, feeling convinced that any lily, almost any bulb, will regulate its own depth in its own way if given a fair chance.

Do we grow nomocharis? 'M, yes, that is to say, we are treading with, I hope, decent modesty the unknown tracks which we trust may some day reward us with a glimpse of the promised land of these ineffably charming things, even if we do not aspire to Mr. Harley's enviable heights. Most of them are in the infant stage, being brought up from seed, but we have every reason to believe that all the better known kinds are going to like us and our ways.

Indeed, we had no little encouragement from the start—a pod or two of seed (*N. pardanthina*) given to us by Mr. Kenneth McDouall when visiting his inspiring garden at Logan a few years ago. Some of this seed was scattered in autumn in a gravel-topped bed in which *Iris tenax* was flourishing, the rest put in pots. All germinated the following spring, yet the open ground seedlings were the first to flower and exquisitely beautiful they were, their wide bells of delicatest shell-pink trembling in transcendent loveliness above the silvered irises. Other pardanthinas and *N. Mairiei*, with their varieties, are coming along, all in the open, but, if they could not be more promising at the moment, time only will show what they will ultimately do.

This much I think one may safely say regarding nomocharis in our garden: They seem to enjoy more sun than they are supposed to like (those among the californian irises suggest that) and we have not found in them that objection to root disturbance which they are reputed to have. Nor, for that matter, have we discovered any ill effects, beyond a slight check, from moving lilies when in active growth. Infants and anything up to half-growns seldom utter a word of protest at being spring shifted, but the number of little bulbs we have moved in the dormant state never to be seen again has put us off that for ever. But I must wind up as I began by saying that, in dealing with lilies or nomocharis one can do no more than give the results of one's own experience for what it is worth. Dogmatism in anything appertaining to the garden is the garb of ignorance, with lilies and other things after their kind it is puppyism grown up, as the Victorian wit would have said.

EPIGAEA REPENS ($\frac{1}{3}$ NAT. SIZE)

EPIGAEA ASIATICA (NAT. SIZE)

LINNAEA BOREALIS

'. . . *rambles about with charming abandon*' (p. 200)

NOMOCHARIS
PARDANTHINA
AND
IRIS TENAX

CHAPTER XVIII

Among some of the Lesser Woodland Plants

MUCH WATER has flowed under the bridge since *Tiarella unifoliata* came into a garden which was then a mere strip of half-tamed woodland. I was doing an hour or so's cleaning up during the war-time for E. C. Buxton—once such a splendid specimen of physical manhood, then aged and infirm.

'Put anything interesting you find on the path,' he had said, as he toddled away, leaning over his two sticks.

During his absence I came upon a rhizome of a plant showing one small ivy-shaped leaf in a pale amber-green which I had not seen before. It was expiring beneath the shade of some overgrown shrubs.

On his return E.C.B. turned over the object on the path with the rubber 'foot' of one of his sticks—a part of his equipment he was ever losing—and exclaimed, 'How very odd! It must be ten years since I last saw that! . . . The best woodland plant in the garden, I used to think, *Tiarella unifoliata*. . . . If you can make it into two, half of it is yours.'

Since that date this beautiful foam-flower whose rose-flushed spires rise in an erect sheaf to a couple of feet above the solid clump of big, vine-like leaves, which never puts forth stolons like the familiar *T. cordifolia*, has been one of the most cherished of our woodland treasures. Many have had snippets of it, but it still seems as uncommon as ever it was, and it has just been joined by a mauve flowered British Columbian, probably *T. laciniata lilacina*.

Another curiosity which we first saw in that Bettws y Coed garden, and which we still foster, is the parsley-leaved form of the common wood sage, *Teucrium Scorodonia*. Canon Ellacombe had a friendly regard for this plant, and none of our visitors who has a quick eye for the unusual fails to notice the goffering and elaborate 'perm' of its downy sea-green leaves.

A plant that is very much at home in our hot, dry and stony slopes upon which the winter flowering *Lithospermum rosmarinifolium* loves to dwell.

To one side of the shadier end of the glade garden are two beds. These the Lady of the Garden, with less regard for descriptive elegance than she has for a getting-there brevity, calls respectively the lozenge and the kidney. Gallant efforts on my part to refer to the one bed as an oblique angled parallelogram, and to the other as a reniformed bean, being shadowed from the first by failure, the names have stuck with an indelibility not given to all garden labels.

However, the lozenge gives temporary habitation—for they are moved on as they outgrow their cots—to a family of seed-raised baby rhododendrons, tucked in with a self-sown colony of that bluest and brightest of navelworts, *Omphalodes nitida*, which is rarely out of flower the year round. The much more extensive kidney, a monstrously enlarged organ, is also mainly occupied by rhododendrons, but of a more permanent kind, and round about these is found congenial quarters for a number of little things which delight in coolish, leaf-mouldy conditions.

Here the pretty *Linnaea borealis* rambles about with charming abandon, including its super form, *americana*, and the lovely white one. We rather suspected this last would be one of those rosy albas which pass for white, but it is a really sound white, and in this garb the dainty twin bells seem to possess an even more elfin sweetness than the coloured. A most engaging woodland gem, for which we have to thank Mr. Ingwersen, and which is as hearty and content with us as the others.

An old tumble-down mossy wall flanking one side of this bed has provided us with a long-sought solution of the problem as to what to do with that microscopic version of Kenilworth ivy, *Linaria aequitriloba*, which comes from Mediterranean islands. It would never have anything to do with what we considered suitable spots, yet its mischievous desire to thread its way into a mossy saxifrage or some other forbidden ground knew no limits. It sulked, or died, where it was invited to prosper. It indulged in reckless transgression wheresoever it encountered discipline. But now, on these moss-clad boulders, it is perfectly satisfied, creeping with more tenacity than its compatriot, *Arenaria balearica*, challenging even the slightly stronger *L. hepaticifolia*, and adding in summer to its closely woven fabric of verdure a dappling of lavender flowers. Moreover, both of these reformed midgets, having an upward tendency in growth, have not yet shown any inclination to give trouble in the beds below them.

They do, it is true, threaten to envelop the ramondias, *Primula Winteri* and haberleas which fill many of the lower crevices, and I perceive signs and portent of coming strife between them and the nerteras who, though supposed to occupy the flat, persist in invading the vertical territory of the linarias. But the Lady of the Garden regards such acts of aggression with imperturbable complacency, interfering only in cases of obvious bullying which do seem to be remarkably rare. Comber's nertera, for example, which might be taken for a lusty chickweed, would swiftly overwhelm the old one with its bolder growth were it not occasionally submitted to a scissor snubbing, and this lively stranger, being thus far less liberal with its orange beads, disciplinary measures are more severe than they might otherwise be.

The white *Primula Winteri*, a *protégé* of Mr. Clarence Elliott, and easily one of the best half-dozen plants we owe to his *flair* for the new when it is good, is one of several other white-flowered forms of coloured plants we have along this shaded retreat. One of these, the linnaea, has been mentioned; another is the white *Schizocodon soldanelloides*, a nugget from that mine of rarities which Mr. Marchant runs with such conspicuous success. There are one or two ramondias which do not blush apologies for pretending to be white, a choice haberlea aptly labelled *virginale*, which is lovely against the moss-greened rocks, some white cyclamen and at least half-a-dozen violas which have all renounced the world of colour.

The best woodlander, by the way, among our white violas is *V. Riviniana*, which we had always been taught to regard as a development of *V. sylvestris*. But it has been elevated to specific rank by Kew and deserves that distinction. Its snow-white flowers, which we first saw dappling the woodland floor at Wisley, are larger and of better substance than those of the finest of our wood violets and it increases by seed with never a trace of departure from its own model. Even so, there are other violas in plenty which run *Riviniana* close in their steadfast independence and engaging comeliness, the sweet and confiding *V. odorata* itself being among the most treasured. Not 'florist-fed in fatness' but grown in a rather lean soil, these do not get too lush and leafy, yet flower abundantly, and the white, the pink and the delightful little nankeen-yellow one—*pallida* or *sulphurea* it is sometimes called—are among the most precious and abundant. But we have also the winsome St. Helena violet whose flowers, 'cool as water, soft as sleep', in the tenderness of their bog-violet blue, are ineffably sweet, and for this there is no happier playmate than *blanda* with, if you will, a sprinkling of *biflora's* gold about her skirts. Other good 'stayers' are the dusky eyed white *canadensis*, *cucullata*, a bonny, bouncing wench in white or blue, *septentrionalis*, especially pleasing in white with purple rays, the dainty *arenaria rosea*, all those of the *sylvestris* and *canina* tribes who reveal with such finished grace what every violet knows about the winning charm of modesty, the yellow *V. glabella* and *Nuttallii praemorsa*, the deep blue, big-flowered *adunca* and *striata*.

Here I might be tempted to tarry a while further among some of our more uncommon pets, but as I am dealing mainly with those of the semi-wild a brief reference to *V. lutea* must satisfy. There is a curious fascination about this moorland waif which has the puckish daintiness of *V. gracilis* combined with so freakish a fancy for variation that it diverts from the ancestral yellow into a bewildering range of colours. Making low, dense mats of bright green, some cuttings of this pansy gathered on a Scottish roadside are gay with blossom the summer long. With every day a fair day and life a toy, these wayward children of the hills play with colours with such a pretty caprice that their sprightly faces may be a self-toned purple, mauve, claret, plum-red, slate-grey, yellow or ivory, with the most fantastic diversions in streaks, mottlings and bi-colors. But they are always winsome and pleasant, always amusing and happy enough in any soil that is not too arid and hot.

Mitchella repens, like a wee emerald ivy with crimson fruits, and the twin-flowered *Mitella diphylla*, with other sylvan

SHORTIA UNIFLORA (NAT. SIZE—PERHAPS THE ORIGINAL TYPE)

SEDUM TRIFIDUM

RAMONDIA PYRENAICA

CORNUS CANADENSIS

dainties, dwell in amiable unity with the schizocodons. Here, too, are the shortias, or rather some of them, for one or two of our older colonies are away in the woodland proper, and *Epigaea repens.* This last will test the average gardener's skill if anything will, and it has tested ours and found it wanting more than once. But it might be nearer the truth to say that *epigaea* will test your conditions for you and, finding them agreeable, respond to decent civility. But, finding them disagreeable, all the king's horses will not make it grow.

Schizocodon we are doing better in an annex to the kidney bed than we have ever done, not only the pink and the white *soldanelloides,* but *alpinus, illicifolius* and *macrophyllus.* All of them have that look of smiling content which is one's great reward, and they flower, off and on, the season through. Why they are prospering here, why *Epigaea repens,* as well as *asiatica,* have found life less boring in this particular spot, why *Shortia galacifolia*—a more temperamental plant than *uniflora*—is so robust and hearty, and why some of the smaller and most sensitive of gaultherias, such as little *G. myrsinites,* have not turned their face to the wall as is their wont, I know not.

The ground which these things have found more than tolerably agreeable is anything but what one would prescribe. It is rather sandy, distinctly on the dry side at most seasons, and soon after it was made it was threaded by battalions of elm roots which rendered it drier than it would otherwise have been.

Now the Lady of the Garden, who has the care of these inmates, tells me that she is beginning to believe in roots, even the roots of a wych elm, that they drain and aerate the soil and that roots enjoy the company of roots. It may be so. I have been in a garden long enough to realise that one need not be surprised at anything. Let wisdom cry aloud in the street, let her utter her voice in the broad places. I only know that the more one deals with such living things as these the deeper one becomes involved in 'learning more and more about less and less.'

You may toy with theories and indulge in diversions of practice and it is all great fun. It keeps your garden soul alive. But only the fool says in his heart there is no god, only the audacity of ignorance will venture to dogmatise over a dandelion.

Go to *Epigaea*, thou lord of creation, learn her ways (if you can) and be humbled. We went—to Mr. A. K. Bulley's garden in Cheshire, to Mr. Millard's in Sussex, and saw the wanton flourishing with abounding ardour in the full noonday sun. We went to America where it was pushing its way through the planks of an urban sidewalk and looking up at us with derisive smiles. We tried it in half-a-dozen spots in this garden, and while in one it would be happy enough in another it immediately languished, though conditions in both seemed to us to be precisely the same. Agricultural chemistry and the accumulated knowledge of generations of gardeners are impotent to explain these problems.

Wherefore, am I prepared to take the philosophic view, even in the presence of an elm's tentacles, to regard root association as a more than probable means towards the welfare of many things—and it saves a great deal of trouble. There are limits, of course, and not only in one's tolerance of roots. It is possible to become a fanatic, to develop an ungovernable horror of these component parts of almost all fertile soils. And the Lady of the Garden will go even farther than I do in these matters. As I have suggested, hers is a spirit so indulgent that the way of the transgressor is easy in her sight, even the way of that pretty rascal, *Veronica filiformis*. At which the hairs of Prometheus have been known to stand on end like the quills of the fretful porcupine, when he might have muttered, 'I told you so', but did not before falling upon the culprit in secret.

People brought up beneath the shadow of the Shorter Catechism are like that. No sooner have they escaped from its restraining coils than they become the most tolerant beings in the world, with a peculiar, almost sympathetic generosity of heart towards the treachery of the garden's most abandoned libertines.

Mossy saxifrages may not be considered good company for such plants as those dealt with in this chapter, but since they enjoy the cool conditions and the part shade in which many of our so-called peat plants live they are invited to spread their mats of green, which are so pleasant in winter, along the margins of these rhododendrons and mixed beds. But the mossies used thus are mostly mongrels of the close and compact *moschata* type of which a selection kindly sent to us by Mrs. Lloyd Edwards, and known here as the Pixie Sisters, are among our best friends. This not only because they resist winter wet more successfully than those with looser rosettes, but their little short-stemmed flowers, bright as they are, do not blazon 'garden origin' at you with so gorgeous an aggression as many do, and, what is still more important, inquisitive birds rarely pull to pieces their densely woven rosettes.

However, at the other end of the scale there are some which are to us no less admissible to similar company and conditions. The white James Bremner and Miss Willmott, both tall and large-flowered, can be as charming with, shall we say, *Galax aphylla* as *S. granulata* which, in its best single form, is so supremely beautiful. Then there is another tall one, the tallest indeed of all mossy saxifrages, Monreith Seedling. This chieftain of the mossies appeared as a stray seedling in that sanctuary of choice plants which bears its name, and from its distinguished owner it came to us with many other precious things. We have had this stalwart twenty inches in height. Its fine broad petalled, substantial flowers, glossy as satin, open a rich plum-red and fade to a silvery rose with a ruby eye and rays. A plant of quality and distinction which never fails to arouse the interest even of visitors who affect a coldness towards mossy saxifrages.

But is it not a fine line which would divide one set of saxifrages from another, venturing to say which shall be associated with sylvan plants and which shall be barred? Thus, while that charming little London Pride, *S. primuloides* Elliott's Variety, is undoubtedly one of the best of rock-garden plants, I would give it a high place among the smaller woodlanders. Mr. Elliott tells us (*Rock Garden Plants*) the story of his finding this delectable mite which, from the two or three rosettes he collected in the Pyrenees, must now be gracing pretty nearly every rock-garden of the gardening world.

S. cuneifolia is also admirable in woodland where a lowly green carpeter that will take care of itself is desired, and there is nothing of the sort more attractive than it is when allowed to ramp over stump and boulder with the native wood sorrel, or, better still, the latter's lovely rose-pink variety. *S. rotundifolia* is yet another delight. Its mounds of foliage are handsome, its tall spires and showers of white, red-speckled bells in perfect accord with any tree shaded environment. The glitter of its shimmering sprays accompanies the matchless elegance of the harebell poppy (*Meconopsis quintuplinervia*) with a harmony of rarest grace, and it will naturalise so successfully that we have had the same strain going for many, many years. *S. Geum*, whether one has the type species (or something as near it as is horticulturally possible) *crenata*, *dentata* or any of its numerous forms, is never out of tone with such retreats, and of its clumpy masses, big and little, of spoon shaped or round toothed leaves, something has already been said. Then there is, of course, the late flowering *Fortunei*, the stoloniferous *sarmentosa* which usually winters safely here about the ancient wall mentioned and along sheltered wood banks, and the still hardier *Veitchii*, an ally of *sarmentosa* to be trusted almost anywhere.

And so I might proceed to a dozen more saxifrages with which selected representatives of the mossies have every right to fraternise on equal terms. Even if they did not we are at least not forbidden by any canons of gardening to grow what we will and where we will. We garden to please ourselves, to suit our own conditions and circumstances, and if our efforts also please others then is our reward the greater. Thus, to allow some self-sown mossy saxifrages to drape the rocks in the splash of the little waterfall which topples over an oaken sluice in our smaller stream, may suggest a plant in the wrong place, a subversion of the proprieties of good gardening. But we like those evergreen rugs, they thoroughly enjoy the water even in winter and all is well in a perfect world.

To return to a few more inmates of this partly tree-shaded spot, *Cornus canadensis* must be applauded as it has been so often for the gentle beauty of its white stars, its fine autumn colour and unchanging amiability. It is everything a woodland carpeter should be. But I cannot be so enthusiastic over *C. suecica* which we brought with us from the Sow of Atholl by way of some compensation for failing to find *Phyllodoce cœrulea* upon that monster's flanks. It lives and it flowers, this highland wean, but does not prosper. And the same disappointment has been ours with that exquisite gem of the northern pine-woods, *Trientalis europaea.* There is no lovelier wildling in our flora than this, as one sees it in those silent forests, a thousand pearl-white, diamond-point stars, each hovering on its hair-fine stem, all gazing heavenwards into the whispering green darkness above them.

That keen gardener, Sir Oscar Warburg, was good enough to send us a few years ago a large square of turf containing the roots of this engaging nymph, that undoubtedly being the best way to get it established. For some seasons after that we had a goodly number of flowers, but eventually they declined and the place knows them no more. Since then further efforts have been made, and being among those who believe that discovering the right spot is four-fifths of the battle with most of these shy little things, we are at last being heartened by prospects of real success. *T. arctica* and the rosy *T. latifolia* are also here, being sent us by that keen grower of good plants and most skilful of exporters, Mr. Lohbrunner of Victoria, B.C.

Whether there is any special virtue in pine needles and the leaves of other coniferous trees for such plants as trientalis I do not know. But I do know that you may walk through northern woods and find the plant beneath or around conifers. We know also that the shortias are found naturally under similar conditions, both in America and Japan, and the most extensive and most robust colony of *S. galacifolia* that I have seen in this country was in the Bettws y Coed garden referred to, and the plants were at all times littered with pine needles and never got anything else. And the same may be said of *Epigaea repens* in the wild, of pyrolas and others of like temperaments.

In this garden we certainly never had *S. galacifolia* so vigorous until it was 'fed' with pine needles, both the natural fall and applied partly decayed. Even so, one prefers to keep an open mind on such topics, but there is this much to be said for the natural fall of coniferous leaves: This fall is very gradual and gentle. It does not envelop the plants and smother them as broad leaves do, and everyone must have noticed that the mould from long decayed needles is always extremely friable, light and airy.

Spiraea (Eriogyna) pectinata, now referred to as *Luetkea* (Kew *Hand List,* 1934), a trailer from the Northern Pacific

Slope of America, so easily tricks the unwary into the belief that they have discovered a mossy saxifrage obviously in happy unity with woodland ferns, that I might have used it to strengthen my argument in favour of using certain mossies in such places. A creeping, prostrate herb of the rose family, this gentle haunter of cool shades does not yield up its secret until summer comes along when, for a brief period, it waves aloft fluffs of white flowers on three-inch stems.

The Japanese *Tanakea radicans* on the other hand, though of the Saxifrage order, looks like anything but that. Yet there is to the most casual eye some resemblance to an astilbe in the pointed, toothed leaves, deep green and leathery, which make a tidy tuft of two or three inches. And the similarity is still further emphasised when summer crowns the plant with plumes of white on six-inch stems. After which the astilbe suggestions vanish, for the leaves grow more leathery and a grey-green, and from the heart of the plant leap red, hair-like stolons which bend over like strawberry runners to grow little tanakeas at their tips. Yet another masquerader here is *Clintonia (Smilacina) trifolia*, a frail little thing which hides its affinity with the lilies and its solomon's seal big brothers by growing no more than four inches and greeting the spring with a tinkle of wee white bells.

That splendid ranunculad, *Glaucidium palmatum*, with which nurserymen so assiduously draw our half-crowns, lives and languishes and that is about all. It has been accorded all the ceremony its price and persuasion merits, yet it likes us not. But convinced that perseverance and the discovery of the right spot, which has at length satisfied the once equally stubborn *Anemonoposis macrophylla* and which is working wonders with *Ranunculus Lyallii*, will some day bring it what it desires, *G. p.* has not been written off as impossible.

A. macrophylla, with leaves like a bugbane and waxen white flowers backed by lavender-white, rises to some 18 inches. A slender, well-bred looking plant with a general likeness to *Anemone rivularis*, it seems fairly easy and content—once you have satisfied its rather exacting fancies in the way of a coolish vegetable soil, faultless drainage and uniform moisture. Like treatment appears to suit its relation *Anemone patula obtusifolia*, the romantic blue buttercup. This we had on our 'wants' list for many a year until a noble six-inch potful came along from Mr. Slinger of the Donard Nursery Co., who seems to have discovered the secret of propagating the rarity, its resentfulness to all efforts towards increase being the main cause of its continued rarity.

The blue buttercup came from a high altitude in Burmah, having been introduced by Lady Wheeler Cuffe (*The New Flora and Silva*, Vol. I, p. 257). In leaf it bears a dangerous resemblance to a common buttercup, but the flowers are a real blue, cool and clear in tone, while in the centre of the bowl nestles a wreath of golden anthers—a masterly touch. Moreover, these beautiful blossoms are borne from April onwards into autumn and we have had a few still showing colour in December. How it is propagated I do not know. Mr. Millard, in the note referred to, tells us he has entirely failed with seed, which is not encouraging since he has a wizard's way with most difficults. It is said, with what truth I know not, that the seed must be sown green.[1] We are trying this and shall see—more out of curiosity than necessity, for the plant itself, once you have got it, is obviously hardy and long-lived, and, growing in girth year by year, makes a massive tussock.

That a plant which shows a partiality for shade when hot weather comes along thereby expresses a natural desire for a moister root-run than it has got is, I think, obvious. At any rate that beautiful little myrtle, *Myrtus nummularia*, when first we had it, was given a warm, rather dry spot, since the prospect of a myrtle being hardy was a doubtful one. But it soon showed us by threading its way into any bit of shade within reach that it wanted, if not less sun, certainly more to drink. To put the matter in another way, provide unfailing moisture and it will revel in full sun, but where the soil is liable to dry out, then a modicum of shade will serve as a compensating factor.

Our largest patches of *M. nummularia*, a yard wide, are in the open, the bed being permanently moist, but other plants are scattered about the shadier places with which I am dealing, and a bonnier prostrate evergreen than this I do not know. In its wee round leaves, dark green, glossy and leathery, and red stems it

[1]Mr. Knight, of Knap Hill, tells me he has just raised it by this means.

bears a striking similarity to *Leiophyllum buxifolium*, especially the prostrate form, but there its likeness ends. The myrtle, with its very slender and angular fish-bone branches, weaves a dense, flat mat and, rooting as it goes, quickly covers several square feet. In May, and often again later, the wonderful green of its springy fabric is studded all over with pure white powder-puff flowers and these are followed by snow-white, rosy-cheeked berries as big as marrowfat peas, all sitting on the upper sides of the branches, the better to be seen by the passing blackbird.

Since this delightful carpeter has come through 25 degrees of frost without a wince it must be the hardiest myrtle in cultivation. It is the easiest of plants in our free soil and will be cheerful anywhere—provided the spot is not too dry and hot. *M. nummularia*, being a native of the extreme south of S. America, notably the Magellan region, it should be able to put up with almost anything weather can do. But in spite of its hardiness and adaptability and singular attractiveness it is still quite uncommon, and this is the more remarkable when one realises that it was discovered and described so long ago as 1796, and that the great Darwin collected it on Tierra del Fuego just over 100 years ago (Bean: *Trees and Shrubs*, Vol. III, p. 243).

Sedum trifidum was so rare a few years ago (but it had not even then escaped the discerning eye of Mr. Smith of Daisy Hill who sent us our first plant) that a note and photograph which I sent to the garden Press brought in urgent appeals for seed from remote parts of Europe and America—the appeals being eventually appeased. This oddity lives against the mossy wall referred to, its buniony root-stock, like a Magnum Bonum potato, bulging out of its bed of sandy loam and leaf mould. In late spring the lazy creature puts forth a sheaf of eight-inch growths which, naked until near the top, are there loosely draped with a few flaccid, eccentrically jagged leaves. Come harvest time, with the rippling music of the reaper drifting over the stream from the fields beyond, trifidum crests its leafy tips with broad cymes of rosy-amethyst flowers which prevail until October when, as a thrifty plant should, it sees to the ripening of its seeds.

OURISIA
MACROCARPA

*Shares a waterside
bank with Cornus
canadensis*

PRIMULA WINTERI
In the Dingle on a January day

THE ORANGE AND SCARLET FRUITS OF ROSA HOLODONTA

WOODLAND COMPANIONS
Harebell Poppy (Meconopsis quintuplinervia) and Saxifraga rotundifolia

For neighbour this Himalayan has *Deinanthe cœrulea* who is Chinese and looks it. A strangely beautiful creature this, with its bristly horse-chestnut leaves, standing at about a foot, over which nod clusters of flowers which are like nothing else the eye of man hath beheld, though they suggest, now an anemone, now a hydrangea and anon 'some monstrous, waxier pyrola that has known sorrow both wisely and well' (Farrer). Enthralling is the only word one can use for those massively graven salvers of gleaming nacre painted with that subtle violet which shadows the cleft of a glacier or stains the fleece of an autumn mist; a reverent humility the only attitude with which one can approach the unfathomable serenity which invests the mystic fascination of this Oriental.

Deinanthe cœrulea is one of the many good plants we owe to E. H. Wilson. Dr. Henry seems to have found it earlier, but it was Wilson who sent us the seed from Hupeh, and Elwes first raised it at Coleborne. That was in 1909, but until recent years the plant has been rare and costly. Yet there seems nothing difficult about its culture. Here it does very creditably in any decent rhododendron soil with part shade, but at Bodnant I have seen it prospering with splendid vigour in a much stiffer, almost clayey, medium.

Companioning the above is one more plant which must not go unnoticed and that is *Ourisia macrocarpa*, one of the few New Zealanders which are reliably hardy. From a thongy rootstock this puts up dull green, ribbed and hairy leaves, rather suggestive of a plantain's. Not an inspiring creature at this stage, but when early summer calls up the stout flowering stems, when these break out into bold whorls of snow-white blossoms with a yellow eye with the likeness of a streptocarpus or a pentstemon, we have a really handsome plant of dignity and breeding.

Closely akin to *O. macrocarpa* is *O. macrophylla* with longer, but narrower leaves and comparatively squinny flowers of the same style and colour. But this is not so satisfied with us as *macrocarpa* which has carried on for many years with scant attention. These scrophulariads submit to division of the rhizomes and this, we think, is rather good for them, tending to further their permanence. They also yield their dust-like seed in quantity, but though others have germinated this we have utterly failed to do so.

O. coccinea (of gardens, for its name has been usurped by another) is prolific enough now that we are able to give it a good moist loam with what Prometheus calls 'body' in it, and a garnishing of sorbex. In this it makes lush and generous mats and swings over them the season through its spires of scarlet bugles. But we do not yet seem to have struck the happy medium with this Chilean, for though it flowers over a long period it does not put up a really generous performance at any one time. It certainly does better in the moist soil with 'body' in it than it did with leaner fare, but its excessive leafiness suggests that it has not escaped the demoralization which comes of ease and luxury to many plants.

EUCRYPHIA (PINNATIFOLIA) GLUTINOSA

THE COBALT-BLU
TRUSSES OF TH
SUMMER-AUTUM
CEANOTHU
AUTUMNAL BLU

CYTISUS SUPRANUBIUS

*The rosy-white sweet-scented
Teneriffe Broom*

CHAPTER XIX

Shrubs and Trees: Concluding Notes

IT WAS an old bush of Darwin's berberis which finally settled the matter. I had been wondering how these concluding pages could best be filled, with the fullest possible justice to the garden—and the book—and with the least offence to the hosts of good plants which must be left unnoticed. But that veteran barberry, rising to a dozen feet with a spread almost equal to its height, every branch aflame with the red and orange blossoms which it has yielded with such prodigal wealth every spring for nearly thirty years, seemed to give me the decision I wanted.

Yes, it is to our shrubs and trees more than to any other planted things that we are most deeply indebted for the making of this garden, and that grand berberis which, by the way, was discovered by the illustrious Darwin just 100 years ago, is a beacon for all time blazoning to a not always responsive world the fact that first-class shrubs are the very warp and woof of the fabric of gardening—and I might well couple with Darwin's berberis the splendid *B. stenophylla*. These may be common and we may not be exempt from the taint of snobbery. But a common thing is not necessarily vulgar. Even old Gerard in his day had a dig at our 'inconstancie and sudden mutabilitie' in 'esteeming no longer anything, however precious soever it be, the whilst it is not strange and rare.' How very, very true!

That red-hot splendour, *B. linearifolia*, may rival Darwin's, even eclipse it, but we can not yet be too sure that the newcomer will take the position in our gardens so long held by the older plant. It is too soon to express an opinion in so far as our experience goes, but *B. lologensis* which, like the beautiful *stenophylla*, owes much of its magnificence to Darwin's, has a vigour which will back up its garden career.

Just as *B. Darwinii* asserts its individuality among its kind, so does *Rosa Moyesii* proclaim its supremacy in its own great genus. We grow a large number of the wild roses but I know of none so generously endowed as this. It is not less unique in the wonderful colour and texture of its sumptuous blossoms than it is in their form and poise. Its contributions to the autumn garden are equally striking and the entire plant has such 'tone' that I have seen people of the dullest perception arrested by the magic of its unearthly beauty. That this aristocrat may vary a good deal from seed in the colour of its flowers must be admitted, but I have not seen one unworthy of a place, and the variety *Fargesii* is among the most desirable pinks in the world of wild roses. But *R. + highdownensis* and *R. holodonta* are also so good in flower and fruit that they both can be associated with *Moyesii* and be not ashamed.

Two yellows of medium height which I do not hesitate to place in this brief mention of wild roses are the early *R. Hugonis*, which everyone knows, and *R. xanthina*. The former is said to be excelled by its hybrid daughter, *cantabrigiensis* in some gardens, but if we find little difference in the respective graces of the two shrubs, the latter is rather later and looks like being longer-lived. *R. xanthina*, not to be confused with *Ecae*, a burnet-like bush with flowers suggesting those of Farrer's potentilla, has won our esteem with its erect shapely habit, its determination to thrive unattended in a meagre soil, and the arching branches are unbelievably beautiful in June when wreathed with canary-yellow blooms, not too densely borne among the small coolly glaucous leaves. And these yellows, to which I must add *R. hispida*, both for its large ivory-yellow blooms and magnificent autumn leaf tints, are so independent and easy-going that, like the Moyesii group, they never ask anything in the way of cultural aid, bless their dear hearts!

Brooms we grow in quantity along the open woodland slopes, and grouped in the sunnier new garden, but it would be no easier with these than it is with the roses to name even a dozen of the 'best'. In hybrids I believe *Cytisus Burkwoodii* to be the finest ever raised, for it has such vigour and wealth of deep green foliage in addition to those amazing blooms, aflame with a subtle blending of crimson, scarlet and vermilion-red pranked with gold, which it bears in such profusion and which have completely eclipsed Dorothy Walpole's brightest efforts. Even

EUCRYPHIA
CORDIFOLIA

*Ranks high among
the most beautiful
of autumn flowering
shrubs*

HOHERIA
(PLAGIANTHUS)
LYALLII

*Brings paper-white
cherry blossom to the
late summer garden*

CERCIS SILIQUASTRUM

*The rosy cloud of the Judas Tree's pea-flowers is one of the loveliest
gifts of Spring*

so, Dorothy mated with the old white broom has given us the supremely elegant Mrs. Henry Norman and Geoffrey Skipwith, the earliest of all the tall ones to flower here. Crimson-scarlet, carmine and gold are united with rare artistry in G. S., while the sister hybrid is, in effect, a deliciously soft rosy-lilac. For these and several other fascinating things all growers of good shrubs owe much to Messrs. Burkwood and Skipwith, as much perhaps as they owe those successful hybridists for their introductions in ceanothus—and that is saying a great deal.

In broom species one must not pass by our own beloved *C. scoparius*, the very robust and handsome late-summer forms raised at Daisy Hill being specially valuable. *C. s.* Moonlight is also in high favour with us, for there is a unique fascination in its large and glossy ivory-yellow blooms which are 'just right' for going with the soft misty blues of ceanothus. We run these in double harness on a bank hard by an old Judas Tree (*Cercis Siliquastrum*)—another shrub of superlative merit which, though we have had 300 years to make up our minds about it, is still almost unknown. Bring into this grouping of blue and tender yellow the rosy cloud of the cercis, let *Genista virgata* be gilding its silvery billows hard by, and, within eyeshot, visualise the estimable *Rhododendron fastuosum fl. pl.* tumbling in a twenty foot cascade of blue-lavender down the slope, and you will get a glimpse of a scene which gives us as keen a pleasure as anything in the year's round.

Brooms of the *Andreanus* class, in a word, those which give a spotty or dappled impression, do not enjoy our hospitality to any extent. The Lady of the Garden endures some of them with fortitude, and it is true they are very apt to strike rather a noisy note when amid more or less natural surroundings. But with the hybrids mentioned and several others we escape that, for individually they give, in the mass, the effect of self-colours and that in harmonies of ineffable grace.

Genista cinerea follows the excellent *virgata* about mid-June, and even among the *élite* of the brooms this shrub must take high rank. More silvery in twig than *virgata*, more slender and longer in its weeping growths, and larger and more brilliant in flower, *G. cinerea* is in every way an admirable shrub. Yet in how many gardens will you see its streaming shower of silver and gold? It is a species which had been consistently neglected and our gardens are the poorer thereby, whereas it might be as indispensable to the shrub plantation as *Daphne Cneorum* is to the rock-garden—or, shall I add, as those delightful miniatures of the berberises mentioned which, raised at Daisy Hill many years ago, one hardly ever sees these days.

Spartium junceum must always be accorded a place above the salt, even among the choicest of shrubs, and its honest virtues need no eulogiums from me. But its relation of Teneriffe, *C. supranubius*, which is rare in gardens, has given us such satisfaction that I must put in a word for it. Its supposed tenderness has, one assumes, stood between this shrub and general garden use, but when I say that our old specimen has endured very severe frosts—even 25-30 degrees on a few occasions—without the slightest injury, I think one may dispose of that allegation. Up to a point, perhaps, no brooms are really hardy in the sense that a Lapland willow is hardy. But I am convinced that, given a poor, dry, stony soil with full exposure, this species is reliable enough for almost any locality.

C. supranubius is an almost leafless, rush-leaved broom which in this garden gets up to some eight feet. Its white flowers may not be as showy as those of many, but they are yielded in great quantity and a touch of pink gives the bush a pleasant rosy flush. It is, however, the exquisite scent of this bush which so appeals to us, the blossoms which throng the rather stiff twigs pouring upon the garden air that sweetest of all scents, the smell of an English beanfield. The late flowering *G. aetnensis* is another very fragrant broom which we hold in high repute, a most precious shrub when, perhaps from a height of a dozen feet, its slender tresses fall in a fountain of delicate emerald within whose mazy wisps a thousand little golden butterflies are caught as in a net.

Ceanothus enjoy our drier slopes no less than do the brooms, and while we are 'all out' for the evergreens, the others, which are rather 'beddy' and not too hardy, are represented by way of politeness. About thirty feet of a wall have been enveloped for years by those two well-tried old kinds, *C. Veitchianus* and *papillosus*, while other spaces are occupied by the rare *C. floribundus* Hooker, a slender very small-leaved plant with flowers of a peculiarly clear and pungent blue, and *rigidus* whose violet-purple clusters are always the first to greet the spring. Having given *rigidus* a severe test in the open we find it as hardy as most others, and with no little satisfaction have we thus far proved the large-leaved *C. r. grandifolius*, with bluer flowers, equally trustworthy.

As to the rest of these delightful shrubs, I need not repeat our indebtedness to Messrs. Burkwood and Skipwith who have been so successful in hybridising ceanothus that we now have a range of front-line evergreen varieties which will yield the bluest of blue trusses in luxuriant abundance from May to November. Delight and Dignity, Autumnal Blue, my own namesake—which, happily, does not disgrace the family reputation—and the entrancing *Burkwoodii*, which took the Cory Cup for the best hybrid of its year (1930)—all these are shrubs of superlative merit which give us blues of many exquisite shades and unimpeachable purity, in succession, the season through. There are many others, of course, in this beautiful family over which we lost our hearts and jeopardised our precious lives in the happy days of Californian trails, but with the mention of one more, *C. Russellianus*, which is in every way admirable in colour, habit and hardiness, I must to other things.

Embothriums are only just at the beginning of their flowering career here, but of *Tricuspidaria lanceolata* we have one specimen of ripe middle age, and few evergreens can rival the splendour of this magnificent Chilean when lit with its glowing crimson-cerise lanterns. We have this fellow on a north side, which means that it gets a share of the sun at that magic hour which intensifies most colours with such inspiring effect. Enjoying the same aspect is that queer twining shrub, *Berberidopsis corallina*, which adorns its horny leafage with clusters of blood-red waxen globes in late summer, what time another Chilean, *Mitraria coccinea*, enlivens its glossy foliage with flagon-shaped blooms of purest scarlet. This charming oddity does not seem to have made up its mind whether to be a climber or a creeper. It performs as both with equal skill, a long-established plant here rooting into the soil as well as into the wall behind it, while anon it thrusts six-foot shoots through a convenient *Pieris formosa*, to dangle aloft its strangely beautiful blooms in much the same engaging way adopted by *Trop-aeolum speciosum* and *Phygelius capensis*.

Eucryphia pinnatifolia (now *glutinosa*) so pre-eminent even among the *crême de la crême* of shrub society, with its perfection of balance and poise, its bowls of pearl-white lustre, red-peppered within and sweetly fragrant, its superb autumn colour and easy-going disposition in our lime-free soil, is one of the few that even in our restricted space justifies repetition if not grouping. No panegyrics of praise would be undeserved where this paragon is concerned, and the late flowering *E. cordifolia* is close up in ornamental value, for if it does not give us autumn colour it is, as an evergreen, singularly beautiful in winter. If the hybrid raised from these two eucryphias, and known as *E. nymansay*, is no better than its parents, it is such a robust grower that three or four of our plants have shot up at the rate of nearly two feet a year, and it seems that some who have not succeeded with the other two have been able to satisfy nymansay.

In blossom nymansay gives us the broader, more substantial, petal of cordifolia, this resulting in a firm, well-rounded bloom as wide as the more starry corolla of pinnatifolia. *E. lucida* we have also flowered, and there is nothing in the year's shrubs more elegant and dainty than this Tasmanian, whose snow-white saucers, filled with a freckling of gold which ripens to brown, nod singly on long and slender stalks in early July.

With the exception of *Magnolia stellata* and one or two more of the smaller ones, an early ambition to grow these noble trees had to be sternly suppressed. But having acquired the glade with its deep alluvial soil and more spacious elbow-room, we lost no time in planting as many representatives of this exalted genus as we could reasonably accommodate and still keep off the dole. Then came the new garden, with still more scope for indulgence, and results to date could not have been more satisfactory, for the plants put in went away with such vigour, some of them making a yard of new wood in a season, that most of them are now in the prime of youth. Which is to say, they are big enough to flower freely, to express their beauty of line and foliage to the full, and yet are not so tall that their blooms are

MAGNOLIA WILSONII

Whose bell-like, bone-white corollas embrace a wreath of crimson stamens

MAGNOLIA WATSONII
Salvers of waxen whiteness centred with ruby-red and maroon and richly scented

MAGNOLIA SOULANGIANA var. CONSPICUA ALBA SUPERBA

MAGNOLIA LENNEI
(*M. Soulangiana* var. *Lennei*)

skied. Moreover, they are just now, and will be for some years, nicely proportioned in size to the dimensions of the places they occupy, a point, by the way, of paramount importance in features of such assertive distinction as these.

In touching upon a few of these magnolias, all those of the *salicifolia* class, including the trusty *Kobus* and *stellata*, are invaluable species, and we are still faithful to a couple of early loves of the *Soulangiana* group, the pure white *conspicua alba superba* and the crimson-purple *Lennei* whose huge goblets appear not only just before the leaves in May but continue more or less the season through. I am not sure that the origin of this Melchizedek of the tribe, *Lennei*, has ever been traced, but it is obviously an affinity of *Soulangiana* with all the excellent qualities of that good all-round hybrid, which not only gives blossom in many colours from deepest violet-purple to pure white but gives them from babyhood onwards with ever-increasing generosity.

The adorable *M. parviflora* is only just beginning to flower here, the youngsters making such inordinate growth, but its allies *Watsonii* and *Wilsonii* took the stage some years earlier. *M. parviflora* is everything that a really choice shrub should be. It has a compact and pleasing habit and an ample foliage of moderate size in a lovely green. The four-inch, marble-white, red-centred cups it bears nearly all summer are endowed with that delicious fragrance which graces magnolias in general and it may be quickly raised from seed. *M. Watsonii*, which flowered here before it was six feet high, might be described as a much enlarged edition of *parviflora*. Its big leaves are singularly handsome and the blooms, which become salver shaped when mature, are five or six inches wide, marble-white with a bold wreath of crimson, and so richly scented that we have caught the sultry sweetness at a distance of fifty yards.

With the lovely *M. sinensis* our progress has not been according to plan. Several guineas have gone the way of most guineas in pursuit of the seducer, of which, it seems, it is still difficult to acquire a decent specimen. But we carry on, and meanwhile the excellent *M. Wilsonii* is doing its best—and a very good best it is—to fill the place of the tarrying *sinensis*. Yet, that is not putting it quite truthfully, for were the latter to prosper

like the wicked we should still have an honoured place for that
other discovery of Wilson's which bears his name. This species
may not be more beautiful than many of the others named here
—comparisons are distinctly odious where magnolias are concerned—but it has a peculiar elegance of foliage, the soft green
of which is mellowed, like the twigs, by an undercoating of
silvery-fawn, and the blossoms have a charm which, if not
entirely their own, is strikingly unique. That is to say, the
bowl-shaped corollas are bent over so that they hang like bells
at the tips of the twigs, covering with a milk-white canopy of
that wonderful waxen texture common to most magnolias the
rosette of brilliant red stamens. And again one has that per-
suasive perfume, rich and fruity and outpoured with lavish
prodigality.

M. glauca, which dandles globes of snow-white among its
refreshing green all summer, we have had going for a long
while, an admirable shrub for a smallish garden for it is leisurely
in growth. Its supposed hybrid daughter, *Thompsoniana*, a
later comer here, is only just beginning its career, and to its
very fragrant white balls it adds a foliage that is remarkably
handsome, this, as in *glauca*, being semi-evergreen. But a finer
hybrid in flower, leaf, symmetry and general tone is *Veitchii*
which, said to be a product of *M. Campbellii + denudata*, inherits
much of the rare charm of the one and the garden reliability of
the other. Our twelve foot *Veitchii* has quite settled down to
flowering and it is a magnolia of singular beauty, the magnificent blossoms cresting the leafless branches in April or May.
These erect blooms, narrowly vase shaped and finely-drawn,
are fully six inches in height, their colour is a glistening white
flushed with wild-rose pink, and their fragrance suggests a
blend of honey and lilac.

When these magnolias are a-bloom on the flat a sunny spot
on the wooded slope presents a conflagration in colour which
the most brilliant rhododendron can not equal. For there
Pieris Forrestii is adorning its sombre green with those astounding leafy shoots which fire the entire bush with flambeaux of
the intensest carmine-scarlet it is possible to conceive. Beautiful as all these 'andromedas' are in blossom—and we have long
grown all we can get of the genus—the gay cockades which

PIERIS FORRESTII

One of the many forms of a very beautiful species

PIERIS TAIWANENSIS

Clustered panicles of pure white carried erect adorn this delightful shrub in April

**TRICUSPIDARIA
LANCEOLATA**

'. . . *with its glowing
crimson-cerise lanterns*'

**CLEMATIS
FLORIDA BICOLOR**

*Its ivory-white sepals
centred by a wreath of
burnished violet-blue*

follow the flowers, and which touch their highest colour note
in *P. Forrestii*, would alone earn for these delightful plants a
place among the best of shrubs. There is not one unworthy—
the little *Mariana, ovalifolia,* the excellent *taiwanensis* and
formosa—even the old *P. floribunda* deserving a better fate
than is commonly afforded it. Indeed, if one may judge by a
surprising form of this species which Mr. Marchant has lately
acquired, and which has drooping ropes of large blossom,
longer than those of *P. japonica* at its best, this familiar
Cinderella may yet prove to be the princess of the party.

To *Zenobia* and *Kalmia*, to *Gaylussaccia* and *Arctostaphylos*,
notably *A. Manzanita* which has flowered in August for several
seasons, we are no less loyal, especially perhaps to *Z. pulverulenta* which is in every way so much better than what we have
always called *Z. speciosa*—that is provided you get a selected
form. As for the kalmias, *K. latifolia* in a good medium rose,
rather than a washy blush, is easily one of the most beautiful
shrubs in our garden. Nor can I pass by the dainty *glauca*, so
much earlier than any of the others with its silver-pink blossoms, and *K. angustifolia rubra* which never omits to repeat its
spring show of vivid ruby-cerise in autumn.

The clethras are exceedingly happy along the raised watersides of the glade, those which give us the fullest pleasure being
C. barbinervis, Fargesii and *Delavayi*. The last of these, now
some ten feet high, is very striking in the later summer, the
milk-white flowers in a six-inch raceme being half-an-inch wide
and set off with black anthers. *Fargesii* follows this with larger
but more slender racemes, and then comes *barbinervis* in
autumn—the trio giving a succession of nearly four months.
C. Delavayi is easily the pick o' the basket and a shrub to rank
with the most elect, a plant that stands out among its kind as
the charming *Rubus deliciosus* does among its relations. We
find Delavay's clethra a little tender at the tips when young,
but once it is well away it is not injured by 25 degrees of frost.

So might I ramble on among other ericaceous shrubs, dwell-
ing here upon the chaste loveliness of *Cassiope*, the adored of the
gods, there upon the charms of *Leucothöe*, the king's daughter
whom Apollo loved. The rosy stars of *Loiseleuria* might divert
our attention from the hummocks of the leiophyllums, whose

glossy green is reddening for their eruption of rosy crystal foam. And I could tell you—but could I?—how the Lady of the Garden has invoked the smiles of *Phyllodoce cœrulea*, of *Rhododendron Chamaecistus*, of that cherishable mite, *Arcterica nana*; how *Menziesia* and *Loisleuria* have responded to her coaxing, the rock primulas to an intimacy and patience which puts my share of these virtues to shame.

I could tell you also of her shingle bed which abuts on the green sweep of the glade and, forgetful of the shrubs I set out to describe, relate how upon that pseudo-scree she discusses the merits of worms with her attendant robin, the while she is performing mysterious incantations over gentians, androsaces and pentstemons. This, with the faithful Prometheus at call in the offing, with all her tools and half of mine, and with a collection of pails and moulds, grits and flower pots, labels, bits of glass, tin cans and other gear in so great multitude and confusion that a dustman's nightmare would pale beside it.

Yet, if all I know of these doings is that order and beauty rise out of chaos like the goddess of beauty from the foam, that there upon that heap of stones impossible things perform impossible feats, to explain how all this comes about is far from me. It is as far from me, indeed, as would be an attempt to reveal the secret of *Menziesia's* fascination, to undo the meaning of that mute appeal which emanates with such bewitching subtlety from those modest bells of silky rose which droop beneath the dove tinted green of their unfolding leaves, chiming those unheard melodies which do 'tease us out of thought as doth eternity'.

And it were easy to drift from these into the enchanted regions of the daphnes, to add to what has been already written something of our triumphs and disappointments with other of these wanton beauties who have beguiled us with their fragrance and elusive smiles. Easy, too, it might have been to linger awhile in the pleasant company of the roses—those roses of long years ago, dear old things which hold for us in such precious keeping time-sweetened memories of a more tranquil England than ours—to extol the virtues of *Philadelphus*, of *P. burfordiensis* in particular, and the gracious loveliness of the hoherias whose crystalline whiteness floats delicately as a

CLETHRA DELAVAYI

Earliest and best of the family, its dead-white cups set off by anthers of jet

CLETHRA FARGESII
A mid-season bloomer with long and slender racemes of striking elegance

PHYLLODOCE COERULEA
Rarest and most difficult of all native heaths

ARCTERICA NANA
A vanilla-scented shrublet from the Far North

summer cloud over the vehement blaze of a desfontainea's trumpets.

But these chapters must come to an end, even though from my window I can see more than enough to remind me of the many good and worthy plants which have been omitted—a cherry reaching whitened arms across the amber waters of the singing river, an exochorda waving its snowy flags over the irises' rising verdure. I can perceive that change of green which has crept over the cistus groups, token of coming blossom; and the strewn confetti of *Clematis Armandii*'s fragrant bridal hour tells me that a woodland *montana* is breaking into colour, that the even more beautiful *Spooneri rosea* is toppling bouquets of softest pink over a wall to meet the violet and orange of a solanum rising from below, that the exquisite *C. florida bicolor* is tossing forth its salvers of ivory and blue.

But all these and a multitude of others have to be passed over this time. Nor is there any need to apologise for absentees, for I set out, not to write an inventory of this garden, but to record, as much for our pleasure and satisfaction as for any interest it may be to others, some little of our doings since *A Garden in Wales* chronicled our earlier efforts.

The making of this book has, in truth, been something more than the achievement of a purpose. It has given us all along what old Bacon would have called a refreshment of spirit, re-calling brave and happy days of the past which might other-wise have slipped into the forgotten, inspiring, we hope, even braver and probably impossible projects for the future.

Still more, this narrative with all its imperfections, has done for us what the garden itself has done, if in a lesser degree. It has given us a panacea for the stress of life, a refuge kindly and unfailing from the knocks of an oftimes rude and noisy world. And the essence of that comforting respite is that touch with the fundamental things of the common earth, the eternal yet simple things of beauty and peace whose 'fostering star', it is our prayer, this garden may for all time keep.

INDEX OF PLANT NAMES

Page numbers in heavy type refer to Illustrations

PRINTED IN GREAT BRITAIN BY ROBERT MACLEHOSE AND CO. LTD.
THE UNIVERSITY PRESS, GLASGOW